Argument and evidence

How do we know whether or not an argument is valid? What counts as evidence? How does one make reliable estimates when the evidence is incomplete? *Argument and Evidence* offers an integrated treatment of these questions by bringing together the various approaches traditionally found in separate disciplines and literatures.

The ability to evaluate arguments in terms of their internal logic and to appraise the available evidence is critical in all fields of academic enquiry. Peter Phelan and Peter Reynolds present aspects of informal logic and statistical theory in an accessible way, enabling readers to acquire critical thinking skills without formal training in the more difficult aspects of those disciplines.

Throughout, the authors draw on examples from the human and social sciences, and relate the theoretical discussion to issues of current or recent media controversy. Each chapter ends with a summary of the main points discussed.

Argument and Evidence will enable students to develop a range of skills that can easily be transferred between academic disciplines and that will prove useful well beyond their undergraduate studies.

Peter Phelan is Lecturer in Business Ethics at Staffordshire University. **Peter Reynolds** is Head of the Economics Division at Staffordshire University.

Argument and evidence

Critical analysis for the social sciences

Peter Phelan and Peter Reynolds

London and New York

First published 1996
by Routledge
11 New Fetter Lane, London EC4P 4EE

Simultaneously published in the USA and Canada
by Routledge
29 West 35th Street, New York, NY 10001

© 1996 Peter Phelan and Peter Reynolds

Typeset in Times by Datix International, Bungay, Suffolk

Printed and bound in Great Britain by Clays Ltd, St Ives plc

British Library Cataloguing in Publication Data
A catalogue record for this book is available from the British Library.

Library of Congress Cataloging in Publication Data
A catalogue record for this book has been requested.

ISBN 0–415–11372–5 (hbk)
ISBN 0–415–11373–3 (pbk)

Contents

Illustrations

FIGURES

TABLES

Preface and acknowledgements

Argument and Evidence covers elementary principles of reasoning, various forms of evidence and important ideas and concepts underlying statistical techniques often used to draw wider inferences from available evidence. The book is aimed primarily at students who are beginning – or are about to begin – a course of serious study at undergraduate level. Although we wrote the book mainly for students of the social sciences, it should be of interest to other readers who seek seriously to consider the different ways in which both arguments and evidence can be used – and misused – in debate about serious issues of public concern.

We are grateful to Staffordshire University for a period of sabbatical leave in 1989–90 to work on this project. We also thank successive generations of students, colleagues and friends who in many ways helped us to develop the treatment of argument and evidence set out below. In particular, we wish to thank John Ramsey, David Marshall, Phil Gabriel, Alec Fisher and Jane Collier for comments on earlier drafts of the manuscript and Mike Fletcher, who generated the statistical tables reproduced in Appendix III. We are grateful to the following organisations for permission to reproduce extracts and figures: HMSO for extracts from Black (1984), Penguin Books for the extracts from Patterson (1986), the *Financial Times* for Box 10.1 and the *Independent on Sunday* for Box 7.1.

Peter Phelan and Peter Reynolds
Staffordshire University
August 1995

1   Introduction

This book considers and elucidates several ways in which argument and evidence can be used to reinforce or counter a particular stance.

But why is this necessary? After all, we have been subjected to arguments from the earliest of ages and surely, by now, we can distinguish between a 'good' argument and a 'bad' one. As for interpreting evidence, is it not a matter of common sense to see when a particular point of view is supported by the 'facts' and when it is not? Further reflection might suggest that there is no such thing as a right argument and no such thing as a wrong one. Yet, if the concepts of right and wrong are inapplicable, how do we choose which arguments to believe? Does it even make sense to refer to the notion of 'belief' when considering arguments? In the following chapters, unambiguous criteria are developed for formulating and evaluating arguments. But what about evidence? What counts as evidence? Can evidence be used to prove an argument? How does one evaluate the strength of a piece of evidence? The answers are by no means clear-cut. If they were, then there would be little scope for controversy to occur.

THE BURDEN OF PROOF

The elusiveness of conclusive evidence is something that students and researchers are familiar with and manifests itself in many ways. It provides one of the main reasons for the existence of most of the legal profession. It is the elusiveness of irrefutable proof that gives rise to the expression 'beyond reasonable doubt', which enters into the instructions given to jurors. An aspect of proceedings in British criminal courts is that a person is presumed innocent unless found guilty. The burden of proof falls squarely on the prosecution to present sufficient evidence that the accused person is guilty 'beyond reasonable doubt'.[1]

Yet even this apparently straightforward notion can lead to many difficulties, particularly if extended to applications beyond the confines of the criminal courts. This is illustrated by the following examples, drawn from various walks of life.

Early in 1991, in dawn raids on the homes of families living in the Orkney Islands, representatives of the welfare services snatched a number of children from their beds and took them away from their parents, placing them in the care of the local authorities. There were accusations that the children had been abused whilst under parental care. Rumours of strange rituals abounded and many parents faced court cases. The case against the parents was thrown out and the children were returned to their homes. Public attention then turned on the local officials.[2] The line of argument implicit in much press coverage was that if the parents were innocent then the officials must, at the very least, be guilty of over-zealously pursuing their public duty. Yet, this does not follow. If the local officials are to be given the same standards of justice accorded to the parents, then surely they too must be assumed innocent unless sufficient evidence is weighed against them. We appear to reach the paradoxical situation of being unable to find either party guilty. The reason is that a sufficient weight of evidence cannot be amassed in support of either case.

Not long ago, a young couple were arrested, following the death of their child. It seemed quite clear that at least one of the parents had a hand in the child's death. The mother was tried and found 'not guilty'. The father was tried and found 'not guilty'. Each was subsequently acquitted. Despite a wealth of evidence to the effect that at least one of the parents was guilty, taken individually it was not possible to amass sufficient evidence against either one.

One of the largest public health scares in recent years occurred in 1990. It was the alleged threat to human beings of contracting bovine spongiform encephalopathy (BSE), as a result of eating infected beef. The Government faced a most tricky dilemma. Should it ban the sale of beef, thereby condemning many farmers and other members of the meat trade to financial ruin or should it discount the threats to public health? A reasonable response would be to look at the evidence. Unfortunately, there was no conclusive evidence then to be found. The Government, through the appropriate Minister, issued public statements to the effect that there was insufficient evidence to establish that BSE could be passed on to human beings.[3] At the same time, various measures were taken to reduce the risk of humans eating contaminated meat and the public was reassured. It is a sobering thought that equally accurate statements could have been made to the effect that 'there was no evidence that BSE cannot be contracted by humans'![4] In considering this case – and many like it – a crucial consideration must be where to place the burden of proof. For whatever reason, the Government decided to place the burden on those who alleged that public health was threatened.

THE JUXTAPOSITION OF ARGUMENT AND EVIDENCE

The controversial nature of the cases mentioned above suggests that argument and evidence each have a part to play in settling disputes. It is appropriate to consider how argument and evidence combine in the presentation and evaluation of cases. Yet, to our knowledge, there is no single book which offers a unified treatment both of the structure of argument and of the use of evidence in the evaluation of positions adopted on controversial issues. Much of the academic discussion of the nature and appraisal of arguments occurs in logic texts while serious analytical treatment of evidence is the subject matter of books on statistical analysis. Many textbooks of both kinds are not accessible to the non-specialist. This book does draw on the literature from both disciplines. Equally importantly, it incorporates both a discussion of the requirement that sound arguments allow evidence to weigh in the balance and a consideration of how questions about what counts as evidence impact on the ways in which hypotheses are formulated. This approach aims to be sensitive to the interplay between argument and evidence and their bearing on methods of study and research design.

What follows is not a watered down version of material on formal logic. Our treatment of logical matters applies some of the ideas and approaches to *informal* logic, developed by philosophers in the USA and more recently in the UK.[5] Nevertheless, it is proper to respect what experts have to say and so we present the results of the formal logicians' endeavours so that the reader may acquire skills to recognise patterns of reasoning that can be trusted. In this way, some of the most important contributions in logic can be made available to a wider audience without the necessity for a formal training in some of the more difficult aspects of the discipline.

Similarly, our treatment of statistics should be considered in the context of the aims of this book. For example, most textbooks on statistics address the subject of 'hypothesis testing' from the starting point of having already formulated a hypothesis to be tested. From the previous discussion of 'the burden of proof', it should be apparent that the formulation of a hypothesis is by no means a straightforward matter. For the issue concerning BSE, should the hypothesis be that BSE does pose a threat to human beings or should it be that it does not? Although, to any reader not trained in elementary statistical analysis, this may seem a matter of simple semantics, the way in which a hypothesis is initially formulated can have a crucial bearing on the outcome of any subsequent test.

THE CONTEXT OF ARGUMENT AND EVIDENCE

In this section we use a topical controversy to explain and illustrate the importance of context to the interpretation of argument and evidence. An issue arose because of suspicions that emissions of radiation from the nuclear plant at Sellafield are causally linked with the incidence of childhood leukaemia in the surrounding area. This attracted much media coverage in the 1980s and continues to be controversial. Sellafield became operational in the 1950s and since then has contributed electricity generated by nuclear reactors to the national grid. It soon acquired a reputation for the reprocessing of nuclear fuel and the management of waste products. By the 1990s, having become a world leader, Sellafield was taking deliveries of radioactive materials for reprocessing from as far afield as Japan. Such a major project, with its inherent dangers for people and the environment, could not fail to raise serious questions about the safety of the undertaking. In 1977, Mr Justice Parker chaired what Stott and Taylor (1980: vii) have called 'the first major examination in public of the nuclear controversy', which according to Breach became 'the arena for fundamentally and intensely differing views of the way the modern industrial state should develop' (Breach 1978: 11). The public interest in this controversy grew so much that it was difficult to imagine that anyone, academic or otherwise, would not have a view on the matter.

On 1 November 1983, Yorkshire Television broadcast a 'First Tuesday' documentary entitled *Windscale – The Nuclear Laundry*. The programme was well publicised and over three million people watched it.[6] The general thrust of the programme was to draw attention to two apparent facts, namely, that the nuclear reprocessing plant at Windscale, Sellafield, has on various occasions been responsible for discharging substantial quantities of radioactive waste into the environment and that the incidence of childhood leukaemia in the surrounding area is apparently unusually high.[7] The viewer was steered towards the question, 'Is Sellafield responsible for these illnesses and deaths?' The impression conveyed was that the company which owned the plant, British Nuclear Fuels Ltd, was to some degree responsible.

The programme and the issue captured the attention of the press. Sufficient public interest and anxiety were generated that the British Government set up a public inquiry. A prominent scientist, Sir Douglas Black, chaired the deliberations and his report was published in 1984 (Black 1984). The inquiry had specific terms of reference, namely:

> To look at the recently published claims of an increased incidence of cancer in the vicinity of the Sellafield site:
> 1 examine the evidence concerning the alleged cluster of cancer cases in the village of Seascale,[8]
> 2 consider the need for further research,
> 3 and to make recommendations.
>
> (Black 1984: 7, para. 1.2)

For a public inquiry of the type being considered here, where should the burden of proof lie? The issues were complex. There was much at stake. Macgill points out that it is not possible to answer such a question without reference to the context of the particular inquiry under consideration:

> Its outward appearance is that of an authoritative scientific study, investigating the truth of the claim of suggested excess of leukaemia and other cancers in the vicinity of Sellafield, and investigating possible explanations of the cause of this phenomenon. To consider and elevate Black purely as a scientific study, however, is to have too narrow an appreciation of its character.
>
> (Macgill 1987: 141)

Macgill goes on to suggest that there are two other aspects of the inquiry, which she calls 'forensic' and 'policy' aspects, materially affecting the way in which the issues are to be understood and the evidence is to be interpreted. But consider first the context of the inquiry as a purely scientific one.

There is a well tried and generally accepted method available to the scientist to test hypotheses about the relationship between two phenomena. The method requires the scientist to specify a *null hypothesis* that there is no such relationship and then seek to amass sufficiently convincing evidence that the null hypothesis can be rejected with a high degree of confidence. Only then would the reputable scientist publicly claim that the evidence supported the belief that a relationship exists. Note the parallel with the British legal system.

From the purely scientific perspective, the burden of proof rests with those who claim that the relationship exists. If this approach is applied to the Sellafield cancer-link controversy then the burden of proof rests entirely with those who claim that the link exists. In other words, BNFL is presumed innocent of the cancer-link charge until evidence establishes otherwise. At this point other considerations come into play.

The forensic aspect of the inquiry, mentioned by Macgill, arose because if it were shown that BNFL was in any way responsible for any of the leukaemia cases, then the company or its employees might be liable for damages. In fact, if there were any finding of criminal negligence, then the implications for those concerned could be quite severe. This made the controversy an attractive media topic. The 'policy' aspect of the inquiry can be taken to refer to 'public health and safety'. But, from such a perspective, is it appropriate to assume that something is safe unless it can be shown, beyond reasonable doubt, to be dangerous? When a drug company seeks to market a new product it is required to undertake and document extensive testing to establish, with a high degree of confidence, that the new product is safe and that any side-effects are known. Should an unanticipated side-effect subsequently be identified then the drug company might expect costly litigation. Such was the case with the drug Thalidomide.

From the perspective of public health and safety, if society places the burden of proof with drug companies to demonstrate beyond reasonable doubt that any new product is safe, should it not place an equivalent burden on BNFL to demonstrate that its process for the treatment of nuclear waste does not have any harmful side-effects? Yet Black states that:

> We have found no evidence of any general risk to health for children or adults living near Sellafield when compared to the rest of Cumbria, and we can give a qualified assurance to the people who are concerned about a possible health hazard in the neighbour-hood of Sellafield.

> (Black 1984: para. 6.13)

To 'have found no evidence of a general risk to health' is not to establish that such evidence actually does not exist. The possibility of crucial evidence being overlooked or undervalued could not be ruled out no matter how thorough the conduct of the inquiry.[9]

However, it is clear that the Committee themselves were aware of the public health and safety aspect of their inquiry. Since the Committee's task was to make recommendations for public policy, a rather different and more balanced approach than that actually taken would seem appropriate. With such a 'balanced' treatment of argument and evidence there is no necessary presumption of a particular outcome. In these circumstances, the notion of 'burden of proof' is perhaps more appropriately replaced with a 'balance of probabilities', more akin to the procedures adopted in UK civil courts rather than those adopted in the criminal courts. This 'policy' aspect of the inquiry demonstrates that context has a bearing on the formulation of a hypothesis, on the kind of evidence required and on the ways in which evidence is to be treated and interpreted.

When context affects so much and especially when political considerations and vested interests are not entirely irrelevant, it is not surprising that the inquiry into the Sellafield cancer-link controversy should be chaired by an expert in argument and evidence. In matters of such import, great care is required to preserve neutrality. As authors, our prime concern is to present some ways in which the reader can realistically approach such controversies with some hope of arriving at a conclusion with confidence. Various aspects of the cancer-link debate are used throughout the book, where we subject both the arguments and the evidence to scrutiny.

TO WHOM THIS BOOK IS ADDRESSED

The authors' intention is that this book should be useful for anyone who encounters serious attempts to evaluate arguments either intrinsically or by recourse to empirical evidence. Also, in conveying one's own ideas, it is important to present the best case which is defensible in terms of argument and evidence.

In the normal course of events, most of us encounter serious attempts to evaluate lines of reasoning. The controversies mentioned above are typical examples. Media documentaries frequently evaluate arguments on specific issues by reference to what is intrinsically rational or what can be observed. Even at parties, there is always someone who is serious-minded. Of course, we are all entitled to enjoy the party but the very act of engagement in critical appraisal puts us into a context where skills in the evaluation of argument and the testing of hypotheses are both required and highly regarded. Typical of such contexts are those occurring and defined within the boundaries of the academic subjects studied in universities and colleges of higher education, where success is proportionate, in part, to the level of competence in conceptual and empirical analysis.

The material is presented at a level appropriate for first year undergraduates. The book will continue to be useful to students throughout their studies and postgraduate students should also find things of value in it. We provide an introduction to issues required for an appreciation of the interplay between argument and evidence and of the importance of context to interpretation. These considerations aim at the development of an integrated approach to critical appraisal, fundamental to effective study and research. Critical thinking skills are to a considerable degree transferable, having application over a range of different subject areas. In no sense are we proposing an inter-disciplinary methodology or panacea for all academic subjects. Our combined experience in higher education persuades us that skills in critical thinking can be identified and that they have to do with making the best use of ideas and facts at our disposal. Current trends in curriculum presentation make it possible to offer courses in transfer-able study skills alongside or in anticipation of methods modules, which are more appropriately studied within respective disciplines. The kinds of concern which might motivate interest amongst students in a variety of academic subjects are illustrated in the following remarks.

Social scientists have a tendency to build models, of which some of the most well known often form the backbone of the introductory courses in those disciplines. Economics students are likely to be introduced to models of supply and demand and to Keynesian and monetarist models of the economy. Geographers may encounter vari-ous models of settlement, urban planning and rural land use.[10] Sociologists consider several models of social interaction and political scientists model decision-making structures in both domestic and international contexts.

In model building, initial assumptions are made and a process of reasoning is used to deduce what follows logically from those assump-tions. The very act of reasoning with models involves a process of *deductive* logic. For some applications of models, the realism of assumptions is of secondary importance. In other circumstances, particularly when evaluating an argument for soundness, the accept-ability of assumptions is of paramount importance. Appreciating when the verifiability of assumptions matters is a crucial aspect of social scientific inquiry. Understanding the status of assumptions in different contexts is an issue on which many students and researchers flounder. The different roles played by empirical data in the testing of models and in the verifiability of assumptions is given careful treat-ment in the context of some of the different uses to which models may be put.

Students of the humanities are also required to make the best use of ideas and facts, and skills in the study of argument and evidence are appropriate in these subject areas. History, for example, is sometimes thought to help in understanding society, either in the past or in the present. If so, then it would be surprising if historians did not make use of at least some of the methods of the social scientist. They face many of the same problems, particularly when it comes to using evidence. It is not easy to generalise the attitude of historians to the use of statistical analysis; however, there are some who do adopt various approaches of the social scientist.[11] Furthermore, there is a branch of economic history sometimes called 'econometric history', whose methodology is very close to that of modern economics. Habakkuk refers specifically to what we take to be transferable study skills:

> The econometric historian starts by framing a hypothesis and then considers those facts that are relevant to the question of its validity. In the past most historians proceeded in a quite different way. They absorbed a large number of miscellaneous facts relating to the period in which they were interested or to problems very loosely defined.
>
> (Habakkuk 1971: 318)

But what of the student of literature? It is certainly possible to study literature with no knowledge of statistical analysis. In fact, it is probably the case that very few people would see any connection at all between what might appear to be two academic disciplines as far apart from each other as one could imagine. But let us, for a moment, consider some aspects of one or two great literary masterpieces. Tolstoy's *War and Peace* contains long sections of what appear to be Tolstoy's interpretation of history. Are we to take this seriously? If so, then should we not subject Tolstoy to the same careful scrutiny that we would apply to any other social commentator? Should his assertions and arguments not be subjected to the same critical analysis as those of any other social scientist and should his use of evidence not comply with whatever criteria might be set for a historian, sociologist or other serious student of human affairs? Similar issues might be raised in connection with the novels of D. H. Lawrence. Should we interpret his writing only as a comment on Lawrence himself or should we make inferences about social conditions and social relationships in nineteenth century Britain? To answer these questions effectively, we must develop some understanding of what is involved in the process of reasoning from the specific to the general. This is described as *inductive* reasoning.

It is our conviction that a grasp of the material presented in this book will help any serious student of any academic discipline to adopt a careful and rigorous approach to their studies and thereby obtain a deeper understanding of the very nature of academic enquiry.

The book contains a variety of examples to illustrate individual points and these are drawn from various issues, frequently controversial, which illuminate the concerns of a range of academic disciplines. They also remind us that, although our own interests may lie in one particular discipline, there are very few issues to which the methods of a wide variety of disciplines cannot each have something to offer. Hence, economic, historical, sociological, environmental, political, statistical and philosophical considerations all come in to play. This is not to mention contributions from the nuclear industry, environmental groups, public inquiries and others who have a direct or vested interest in the activities of these industries.

OUTLINE AND SUMMARY OF THE BOOK

Chapter 2 examines the nature of argument and evidence with reference to their context and explores aspects of the relationship between them at a basic level. The treatment signals a range of issues that arise in using argument and evidence to reinforce or to counter a particular stance. Where possible, we try to avoid the use of technical language, although words which have a range and variety of meanings in everyday use sometimes need to be defined in very precise terms. Key concepts and symbols, principles and methods are summarised at the end of each chapter.

Chapter 3 deals with context and convention as providing important clues for the clear and accurate interpretation of 'ideas' and 'facts' in the interests of communication.

One objective of Chapters 4 to 6 is to present an approach to understanding the logical aspects of deductive argument without the need to grasp the theoretical basis in detail. However, we take seriously what experts have to say about reliable lines of reasoning and present strategies for recognising valid moves. Throughout, a serious attempt is made to discuss arguments as they actually occur in ordinary discourse, even though a degree of simplification is sometimes required for reasons of clarity. Some examples are taken from media issues and others from matters of academic concern. Chapter 6 specifically raises questions about recognising values and the role that normative claims play in reasoning in the social sciences.

Critical appraisal in practice is discussed in Chapter 7, including consideration of the limitations of valid inference, the detection of fallacies and the making of cases. Chapter 8 deals with the role of assumptions and model building in the social sciences. These discussions naturally invite consideration of the role of evidence in argument.

The focus of the next three chapters is evidence. Its role in argument is considered in Chapter 9 which examines several types of 'ground for belief' and some associated problems of interpretation. Chapter 10 addresses the question 'What counts as evidence?' in the context of practical considerations for the collecting of information. Answers to this important question are often taken for granted but the serious investigator must address explicitly this kind of issue. Chapter 11 deals with some of the ways in which information is conveyed.

The subtleties and difficulties in the interaction between argument and evidence in the context of furthering knowledge are considered in Chapter 12. Facts are rarely uncontentious. Rationality is to some degree socially determined. We address questions about the ways in which conclusions may be drawn from limited evidence and about how adopting a theory may colour our perception of the facts. These concerns and the way in which concepts come to be defined and events explained are considered throughout the book. This discussion prepares for Chapters 13 to 16, which explore some approaches to the assigning of probabilities to as yet unknown events, to strategies for making reliable estimates when evidence is less than complete and to the testing of hypotheses about the world. Such skills in critical analysis, integrated into a unified approach to argument and evidence in context, can facilitate a rigorous appraisal of controversial issues.

2 Argument and evidence

The term 'argument' denotes several different things.[1] Sometimes argument amounts to quarrelling where rules and conventions for the management of ideas and facts are abandoned. Most people prefer the friendliness of discussions even when in practice they frequently amount to little more than polite exchanges of views. Such exchanges, though informative and interesting, often fall short of serious debate where arguments are advanced and evaluated in the light of evidence. Cases are presented for various reasons. Investigating hunches in the light of evidence or defending arguments as rational are two fundamental concerns of critical analysis. Competence in presenting and evaluating cases is an asset for career development whether academic or otherwise. Though technical, the skill involved need not be beyond the reach of most people.

BASIC GROUND RULES

One method for making a case is to persuade others that its claim is rational because it is sound. A *claim* is a challengeable assertion; for instance, that 'nuclear power stations are dangerous'. An *argument* is a set of at least two claims which are connected in a precise way. It is not a mere list of assertions. The connection, called an *inference*, involves a movement from one or more claims presented as reasons, R, to the claim argued for and designated the conclusion, C. For example, it is said that 'nuclear power stations are dangerous because they discharge radiation into the environment'. Two different claims are made in this assertion. First, that 'nuclear power stations are dangerous' and second, that 'nuclear power stations discharge radiation into the environment'. Since the second is offered as a reason for the first, the dual claim is an argument.

Appreciation of arguments is facilitated by some recognised

procedures. Inferences can be signified by using a symbol, ⇒, and the argument can be set out thus:

R ⇒ C

More precisely, with logical words to depict the role of each claim, the argument reads as follows:

Example 2.1

> Because,
> R   Nuclear power stations discharge radiation into the environment.
> ⇒   Therefore,
> C   Nuclear power stations are dangerous.

The persuasive power of this argument depends on two conditions that are basic criteria for the evaluation of arguments. First, the reasons must be accepted. Second, the conclusion must be adequately supported by the reasons. Provided that both conditions are satisfied, an argument is *sound*.

There are several types of ground available for accepting claims designated as reasons. Argument and evidence are but two. Equally, if one were to trust whoever made a claim, one could, on that basis, accept it. This is not uncommon with the use of expert witnesses in legal cases. Ultimately, anyone may prefer to adopt a claim or even suppose it for the purposes of an argument. Such matters are discussed in Chapters 8 and 9. At this stage, it is sufficient to note that the first condition for soundness is one of *acceptance* and that the grounds are of secondary importance.

The extent to which reasons support a conclusion depends on how arguments are evaluated. Methods are needed to measure the strength of the connection between reasons and a conclusion. At one extreme, reasons *entail* a conclusion. This is a definitive standard. Either the conclusion is entailed by the reasons given or it is not. In Example 2.2, the reasons, with subscripts '1' and '2', conjoined by the symbol '&', guarantee the conclusion:

Example 2.2

> Because
> R_1 All intelligent young women are generous.
> &   and because
> R_2 Isla is an intelligent young woman.
> ⇒   Therefore,
> C   Isla is generous.

Where reasons entail a conclusion, the inference is *deductively valid*.

At the other extreme, arguments are worthless when no support is offered for a conclusion because, for instance, the reasons are irrelevant. Consider this argument:

Example 2.3

     Because
R_1 All drug-takers have problems.
&   and because
R_2 Andrew is a drug-taker.
⇒   Therefore,
C   Andrew is a graduate chemist.

In this case, if the reasons have been advanced as an argument then the presenter has missed the point. The legitimate conclusion is that 'Andrew has problems'.

Between these two extremes, there is a range of arguments where the reasons render a conclusion more or less probable, which means that the inference is either *inductively strong* or *inductively weak*. Consider two examples which oversimplify the issues but, nevertheless, illustrate some basic points about arguing from evidence. Final year undergraduates who are anxious about examinations are often encouraged by tutors to keep working regularly in order to pass. This is good advice since it is helpful to offer this sort of encouragement but some tutors might attempt to justify it on the basis of evidence. A possible case for such counsel might be:

Example 2.4

     Because
R_1 Helen is a final year undergraduate, reading business studies.
&   and because
R_2 More than 90 per cent of business studies finalists pass their examinations.
⇒   Therefore,
C   Helen will pass.

The phrase more than '90 per cent' summarises large amounts of information collected over many years from many institutions awarding degrees in business studies. However, the impressive evidence cannot guarantee that Helen will pass the examinations because the projected event is outside the scope of the evidence. Furthermore, no cited reason rules out the possibility that she could be one of the failed candidates. Nevertheless, in the context of the advice to work regularly and assuming Helen to be a typical student, there appears to be strong inductive support for a successful outcome. Her tutors might even bet on it.

The second example concerns the issue of wearing seat belts in the interests of driving safely. Most people consider this practice sensible and might argue that not wearing seat belts contributes to the death of drivers in road traffic accidents. Let's suppose that 37 per cent of drivers failing to wear seat belts die in road traffic accidents. This argument is based on such a claim:

Example 2.5

> Because,
> R   37 per cent of drivers who die in road traffic accidents did not wear seat belts.
> ⇒   Therefore,
> C   It is dangerous to drive not wearing a seat belt.

The reason offered would summarise some aspects of the data about fatal road traffic accidents in, say, the UK during a specific time period. Whether this evidence is strong support for the conclusion that 'it is dangerous to drive without wearing a seat belt' depends on the proportion of all drivers who do not wear seat belts. To take an extreme case, if 97 per cent of all drivers do not wear seat belts when driving then a case can be made for the claim that it is relatively safe to drive without wearing seat belts. Example 2.5 offers inductively weak support for its conclusion. Clearly, care is required when making inferences from evidence.

Arguments may be listed according to the power of the inference and the strength of the evidence, as follows:

1 Deductively valid inferences entail conclusions.
2 Inductively strong inferences render claims probable.
3 Inductively weak inferences are merely suggestive.
4 Worthless and deductively invalid inferences establish nothing.

Evaluating arguments raises a fundamental question about the strength of the support given by reasons to a conclusion, namely, *could a rational person accept the reasons and deny the conclusion?*[2] Various ways of responding to this question are introduced throughout the book but a brief discussion of Examples 2.2 to 2.5 would be helpful now. A person who accepts the reasons cannot rationally deny the conclusion of an argument which has a deductively *valid* inference. In Example 2.2, to think of Isla as not generous would be irrational, if the reasons were accepted. However, it is permissible to accept the reasons and deny the conclusion of a deductively *invalid* argument. In

Example 2.3, it is consistent to think that Andrew is not a graduate chemist and yet accept that he is a drug-taker and that all drug-takers have problems. The analysis is not so clear-cut with inductively strong and inductively weak inferences. One difficulty is drawing the line between strength and weakness. If it is arbitrary, it is possible to establish almost anything but, if the line is fixed, who decides where it should be? These issues are considered in Chapters 15 and 16. For now, it is sufficient to appreciate that, having specified the level at which the strength of evidence is adequate, the fundamental question can be transformed into a test for evaluating the evidence. There is far more to this procedure than this preliminary discussion suggests but, for purposes of argument, suppose that support is strong when more than 60 per cent of actual or estimated cases corroborate the conclusion and weak when fewer than 40 per cent do. This unsophisticated test establishes strong inductive support for the claim that 'Helen will pass' the final examinations. By the same token, it establishes inductively weak support for the claim that 'it is dangerous to drive not wearing a seat belt'. Even so, other inductively strong or deductively valid grounds are not ruled out.

Premise is a standard word for a reason from which a conclusion is drawn in an argument. In this context, the terms 'premise' and 'reason' can be used interchangeably. The premises of deductively valid and inductively strong arguments offer adequate support to their conclusions. When this happens, the soundness of an argument depends on the acceptability of the reasons given. The main points may be summarised as follows:

1 Arguments offer reasons in support of conclusions: R ⇒ C.
2 Arguments are sound, provided that:
   a) the reasons are accepted and
   b) the conclusion is adequately supported by the reasons.
3 Reasons are acceptable when available grounds hold.
4 Valid deductive support entails a conclusion.
5 Strong inductive support renders a conclusion probable.

Recognising these features of arguments in text or speech facilitates critical appraisal.

HIDDEN ASSUMPTIONS

Evaluating arguments is easier when hidden assumptions are made explicit. The earlier argument in Example 2.1 from the nuclear controversy is set out again to be considered in detail:

Because,

R   Nuclear power stations discharge radiation into the environment.

⇒   Therefore,

C   Nuclear power stations are dangerous.

Anyone seriously advancing this argument would naturally assume that there is a link between danger and the discharge of radiation, probably taking for granted that the existence of such a link is generally accepted. This implicit assumption, required to legitimately infer the conclusion, is a new assertion, namely, that 'all radiation discharged into the environment is dangerous'. The undeclared assumption can be incorporated into the argument by using subscript 'a' to mean *assumed* and undeclared and subscript 's' to mean specifically *stated*:

$$R_{1a} \text{ \& } R_{2s} \Rightarrow C$$

The entire argument is presented as follows:

Example 2.6

Because, as assumed,

R_{1a} All radiation discharged into the environment is dangerous.

&   and because, as stated,

R_{2s} Nuclear power stations discharge radiation into the environment.

⇒   Therefore,

C   Nuclear power stations are dangerous.

This complete version more clearly indicates that the two reasons taken together, R_{1a} & R_{2s}, entail the conclusion. The validity of the argument can be assessed by asking the question, 'Could a rational person accept the reasons and deny the conclusion?' If it is accepted that the discharge of radiation is dangerous then it follows that everything discharging radiation must be dangerous. The implication that there are no exceptions is crucial. It would be inconsistent and irrational to accept the two premises and deny the conclusion. In other words, the premises deductively entail the conclusion. Deductive arguments of this kind are very powerful. The conclusion asserts explicitly a claim implicit or already contained in the premises. The missing assumption, when declared, helps make the case effectively. Consequently, the argument's soundness depends on whether or not the premises are accepted. It is here that evidence can become essential to establish the soundness of deductive arguments.

The stated premise, R_{2s}, is uncontroversial. Those in control concede that nuclear power stations discharge some radiation into the environment. But there is a difficulty concerning the undeclared assumption, R_{1a}, that all radiation is dangerous. If there were an exception such that some kind of radiation is safe – or that radiation up to a certain level is safe – then it could be argued that nuclear power stations both discharge radiation and are not dangerous. Alternatively, some radiation could be safe and it could still be the case that nuclear power stations are, as a matter of fact, dangerous. The issue depends on whether the acknowledged radiation is dangerous, either by virtue of its type or the level of exposure. This may be established by further argument, by recourse to evidence or by a combination of both.

Many who object to the generation of nuclear power because of the radiation discharged into the environment take for granted and fail to defend the assumption that radiation is dangerous. It is essential to expose undeclared, undefended assumptions when appraising arguments, especially when the assumption can be challenged. In this case, the National Radiological Protection Board's figures for 1986 reproduced in Figure 2.1 show that radon and thoron in our homes comprise 37 per cent of all radiation and a further 17 per cent occurs inside our bodies. If radiation can be lived with, perhaps all radiation is not genuinely dangerous. Thus challenged, the argument is rendered unsound and the conclusion can be resisted, despite the

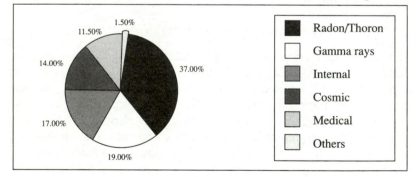

Figure 2.1 Source of radiation exposure of the UK population

Source: NRPB, 1986

Notes: a) By percentage of the total radiation exposure
    b) 'Others' includes 0.1 per cent from nuclear discharges

validity of the deductive inference which remains a feature of the argument. This means that anti-nuclear groups are not entitled to use this argument alone to defend the claim that nuclear power stations are dangerous. Other arguments are needed if this conclusion is to be established.

INTERPLAY BETWEEN ARGUMENT AND EVIDENCE

In the explicit argument about nuclear power stations, a deductive inference is made such that the premises taken together entail the conclusion. Such arguments are valid. Notice that the level of generality in the conclusion is less than that of the premises from which it is deduced. Nuclear power stations are not the only entities which discharge radiation into the environment and many things other than radiation are dangerous. The drawing of a relatively specific conclusion from relatively more general premises is characteristic of many forms of deductive argument. An argument's validity ensures that its soundness depends ultimately on matters of fact. This may invite inferences drawn from evidence. Such reasoning is inductive and does not entail a conclusion. At best, it is a question of how strong the supporting evidence happens to be. We now examine this interplay between argument and evidence.

Directly or indirectly, evidence will have alerted people to possible dangers associated with nuclear power stations. There are pressure groups whose aim is to prevent the construction of more nuclear installations and decommission those presently operating. As the argument stands, it is important to establish that nuclear power stations do discharge radiation into the environment. If this did not happen, there would be no case for decommissioning old plant and objecting to new installations, based on the ground of danger from radiation. Crucially, the claim that nuclear power stations discharge radiation into the environment would hardly be made in the absence of evidence. Supporters of the anti-nuclear case would collect evidence, possibly including that cited in the Black Report (1984) and presented in Table 2.1. The man Sv.[3] figures are the collective dose commitment resulting from the airborne discharges of radioactive substances from nuclear installations in the UK during 1978. This evidence can be summarised and expressed as a reason for the required conclusion in a simple argument as follows:

Table 2.1 Airborne radioactive discharges from UK nuclear installations, 1978

Installation	ARD	Installation	ARD	Installation	ARD
Berkeley	0.79	Bradwell	0.57	Dungeness A	0.42
Amersham	0.56	Hinkley Pt A	0.73	Hinkley Pt B	1.40
Hunterston	0.61	Oldbury	0.73	Sizewell	0.52
Trawsfynydd	0.61	Wylfa	0.45	Dounreay	0.0052
Harwell	0.47	Winfrith	0.25	Capenhurst	0.0015
Chapelcross	0.16	Springfields	0.46	Windscale	3.70

Source: Black (1984)
Note: Figures are man Sv.

Example 2.7

Because,
R   Nuclear power stations, namely those in the UK in 1978, discharged radiation into the environment.
⇒   Therefore,
C   All nuclear power stations discharge radiation into the environment.

The general conclusion is not warranted. However, the cited evidence justifies the more restricted claim that 'in the UK during 1978, nuclear power stations discharged radiation into the environment'. This statement is a description of the then available information. Yet, the actual conclusion is a much more general assertion about all nuclear power stations anywhere in the world, including those as yet unbuilt. Citing and describing the observed cases is clearly insufficient. Nuclear installations about which little is known do exist, for example, those in countries where information of this kind is not published. More seriously, there never can be evidence about future installations. Consequently, the argument attempts to generalise from a known sample of nuclear installations to a wider population, including some for which information is not available. Arguing from evidence in this way constitutes an inductive inference from a claim about every member of an observed but restricted set of installations to all possible instances. Thus the conclusion asserts a claim beyond the available evidence. When arguing from evidence in this way, it is important to compensate for the insufficiency of available evidence.

It is helpful to think of evidence cited in inductive arguments as a series of observations. They can be recorded in a list of assertions. Using subscripts to indicate individual observations, inductive arguments display the following pattern:

$R_1, R_2, R_3, \ldots, R_n \Rightarrow C$

Example 2.7, with logical words depicting the role of each claim, can be rewritten thus:

Example 2.8

	Because, as observed,
R_1	The Berkeley installation discharges radiation into the environment.
&	and because, as observed,
R_2	The Bradwell installation discharges radiation into the environment.
&	and because, as observed,
R_3	The Harwell installation discharges radiation into the environment.
...	and there is an unspecified number of similar observations.
&	and because, as observed,
R_n	The nth nuclear installation discharges radiation into the environment.
$\Rightarrow$	Therefore,
C	All nuclear power stations discharge radiation into the environment.

There is always a chance that inductive inferences could be mistaken. Only one exception is required to refute the conclusion that all nuclear power stations discharge radiation into the environment. Unavailable information about installations past, present and future may well do this and certainly no-one knows the answer. Confidence in the conclusion is therefore shaken. There are serious implications for acquiring, sharing and critically appraising knowledge because most academic disciplines use unrestricted general claims that are based on a restricted set of observations. For example, 'metal expands when heated' is asserted by physicists and 'less money keeps inflation down' is seriously claimed by at least one school of economists. The limited evidence behind such claims materially affects the confidence with which we are able to accept them. The same holds for the conclusion about nuclear power stations discharging radiation – to say nothing about which type and how much is dangerous. But confidence in relatively general conclusions about the world drawn from limited evidence is measurable when the chances of being mistaken can be assessed. That this should be done with care is fundamental to critically appraising argument and evidence.

STYLES OF REASONING

Arguing deductively is different from arguing inductively. Deductive arguments are sound by virtue of *entailment*. This means that, provided that the premises are accepted, it is impossible to rationally resist the conclusion. Inductive arguments might be considered *reliable* when, given that the factual premises are accepted, there is a low probability of mistakenly asserting that something is the case when it is not. The probability of this kind of error is sometimes believed to be known and in other instances it might be estimated. These issues are taken up in Chapter 13. However, it is inappropriate to distinguish too sharply between deductive and inductive reasoning. Many claims can be defended in both ways. More importantly, the two styles of reasoning are interdependent. When premises are challenged, assumptions often require grounding in evidence, the quality of which can vary. In practice, particular arguments are but part of a complex web of thought and experience. The difference between deductive and inductive reasoning is useful for purposes of analysis but arguments may involve inferences of both kinds. When revealed in detail, they usually do. The task is to spot the relevant implication at each stage.

The interaction and interdependence between argument and evidence are seen in reasoning with deductive and inductive inferences employed at different stages. The two arguments about nuclear power stations are a case in point. They are stages of a complex argument in which inferences of both kinds are used. The claim that 'nuclear power stations discharge radiation into the environment' plays a different role in each of the two stages. It is the conclusion of the inductive stage, Example 2.8, and the second reason, R_{2s}, in the deductive stage, Example 2.6. Our notation signifies the two roles respectively 'C' and 'R'. Using subscripts 'i' and 'm' to distinguish the *intermediate* conclusion from the *main* conclusion, the two stages can be expressed formally as follows:

$$R_1, R_2, R_3 \ldots R_n \Rightarrow \{C_i \Rightarrow R_{2s}\} \,\&\, R_{1a} \Rightarrow C_m$$

Other combinations are possible and many arguments are complex in these ways. Critically appraising argument and evidence is made easier by setting out arguments plainly and identifying the kind of inference made at each stage.

Box 2.1 Albania after the European experience of 1989

In January 1990, political commentators in the media were persuaded that the Albanian Government would succumb to people power in a matter of months. The revolutions during 1989 in Poland, Czechoslovakia, Hungary and Romania were cited as grounds for believing that soon there would be a similar breakdown of government in Albania. Yet it was more than two years before the revolution broke in that country. It began in 1992. The journalists were, in principle, correct but over-optimistic.

Consider the situation described in Box 2.1. It cites evidence from which we might inductively infer that revolution in Albania would set its people on the road to democracy. This case is interesting because a relatively specific, rather than a more general, conclusion is drawn from the available evidence. Yet the inference involved is inductive. It is clearly a projection forward in time based on limited evidence. It assumes that perceived patterns and trends persist and may be projected into unknown or future situations. One way to express this assumption is to say that 'nature is uniform'. A deductive argument, expressing the assumption R_{1a} and summarising the available evidence R_{2s}, can be presented as follows:

Example 2.9

	Because, as assumed,
R_{1a}	Nature is uniform.
&	and because, as we observed in 1989,
R_{2s}	Revolutions in four European countries set the peoples on the road to democracy.
⇒	Therefore,
C	Revolution in Albania will set its people on the road to democracy.

Whether or not the assumed uniformity of nature is justified is a complex issue. It is a matter of argument and evidence. If there are grounds for not accepting the claim that nature is uniform then, to that extent, the conclusion is also unacceptable, despite the deductively valid inference. Human experience broadly confirms that attempts to predict outcomes, even with privileged knowledge, frequently fail. Crucially, evidence might lead one to believe that 'nature is uniform'. If it did then the soundness of the revised deductive argument would be dependent on an inductive inference. Ironically, this defeats the object of adding the claim that 'nature is uniform' to make the case secure. Whatever the final verdict on this use of reasoning, it is clear that argument and evidence need to be handled carefully.

Another aspect of interdependence between deductive and inductive inferences concerns the testing of hypotheses. This can be illustrated by reference to a classic study of suicide by the sociologist, Durkheim (1952). He supposed that belonging to a socially cohesive group helps to improve a person's resistance to stress. From the additional assumption that Catholic Christians tend to be more socially cohesive than Protestants, he concluded that Protestants are prone to exhibit the effects of stress more than Catholics. This conclusion is a rational expectation based on the assumptions about stress and religious groups. Provided that some reliable, observable indicator of stress is available, it is possible to formulate precisely the conclusion as a prediction or testable hypothesis. Durkheim stipulated suicide rates for this purpose. The resultant hypothesis claimed that 'suicide rates amongst Protestants are higher than amongst Catholics'. Information about the incidence of suicide can be used to test the hypothesis and, if the evidence provides reliable empirical support, then the claim can be confidently asserted. Procedures used in the testing of hypotheses are considered in Chapter 16.

In Durkheim's study, the hypothesis is deductively concluded from assumptions. Then after tests, it may be established as reliable by evidence. However, nothing can be concluded about the acceptability of the prior assumptions. Some people would maintain that assumptions must be well grounded. Others consider this to be of little consequence. These contrasting positions are often associated with different views about the purpose of academic inquiry, a topic which is discussed in Chapter 12.

SUMMARY

1 Arguments offer reasons, called premises, in support of conclusions:

R ⇒ C

2 Successful premises either entail a conclusion or establish a claim as reliable.

3 Support which entails a conclusion does so by deductive inference.

4 Deductive inferences usually deliver relatively less general conclusions from relatively more general premises.

5 Arguments are deductively valid when the reasons entail the conclusion:

$$R_{1a} \& R_{2s} \Rightarrow C$$

6 Entailment occurs when a deductively inferred conclusion explicitly states a claim already implicit in the reasons, such that no rational person could deny it.
7 Support establishing a claim as probable does so by inductive inference.
8 Strong inductive inferences characteristically establish claims beyond the evidence enlisted in support.
9 Arguments are inductively strong by virtue of adequately compensating for the incompleteness of the evidence:

$$R_1, R_2, R_3 \ldots, R_n \Rightarrow C$$

10 Arguments used in serious discourse frequently combine deductive and inductive inferences, leaving assumptions, often important, unsaid.
11 Arguments are sound provided that, at each stage, the inference is valid or probable and the reasons are accepted.

3　Context, convention and communication

Context and convention provide clues which are helpful and sometimes essential when interpreting argument and evidence. The perspective from which a situation is observed influences the selection of words used to describe it. For example, the military groups in Nicaragua, known as the 'Contras', are described by some as terrorists and by others as freedom fighters. The different impressions arise because the words have a contrasting emotive content; the one of disapproval and the other of approval. The acknowledgement of conventions helps one to interpret verbal expressions as they are intended. Students of people and society pay attention to body language for this reason. Conventions also set the protocol for critical appraisal by influencing the ways in which discourse is conducted. Context and convention have an important bearing on how argument and evidence are to be understood and on the effectiveness of communication.

CONTEXT

Context is relatively straightforward. The setting in which discourse takes place suggests what might be going on. What appears in a book of poems is different from the contents of a motor vehicle manual. A law court is a place in which disputes are settled by the presentation of argument and evidence. Understanding the context helps observers to follow the proceedings. This is also required at cricket matches. Priests chanting proofs and wielding cricket bats in churches is strange precisely because the behaviour is incongruous in these surroundings. This could not be appreciated without a sense of context. Reading a situation correctly is frequently a matter of familiarity with a setting. Those who fail to acknowledge the context are often the ones who do not understand a joke.

Academic subjects are contexts which affect how terms are understood. What counts as a psychological 'crisis' is different from a crisis in history. The term 'class' similarly means different things in mathematics as compared with sociology. Even within a subject area the same word can be interpreted differently. For example, the meaning of 'class' as used in sociology depends on whether Marxist assumptions are accepted. If so, then the social structure of Britain would comprise two broad groups, with membership determined by whether one owns capital. The *have-nots* would be the much larger class whilst the *haves* would be the smaller class. Alternatively, if non-Marxist criteria were used then the word 'class' would mean something different. Take, for instance, the Registrar-General's classification of social groups in terms of occupation. This criterion alone generates many classes, each having subsets. With additional categories, including education and accommodation, the social structure of Britain would appear to have many levels in a pyramidal structure. In such ways, the definition of key words in the context of academic disciplines materially affects how the social world is to be described and interpreted. This is considered in Chapter 9.

CONVENTION

Conventions can be subtle and sophisticated. They include cultural rituals inherited through families or groups along with agreed patterns of thought, investigation and analysis which are developed in academic disciplines. Linguistic conventions are difficult to detect in everyday discourse but making conventions clear is part of the teaching and learning process in academic disciplines. This is best done within each discipline but there are some general points worth making. Being an expert, whether economist, political scientist or sociologist, involves thinking and talking like such experts. Experts acknowledge conventions. Different experts use different conventions. However, the point about being an expert is that accepted practice has to be learned. When learned, it provides a basis for creative independence of thought.

Two basic conventions give meaning to words. Semantic conventions assign meanings to individual words so that, for example, *'chat'* and 'dog' stand for groups of domesticated creatures, loved by the French and English. Semantic conventions define and are located in the fabric of a culture. To that extent, they are relative if not arbitrary. Syntactical conventions stipulate rules for generating strings of words in meaningful combinations. Linguistics offers a technical study of such rules, including the debate about whether they are

innate or acquired.[1] Those conventions constituting acceptable practice in the presentation and critical appraisal of argument and evidence
can be identified less formally. We attempt this after reflection on
what people do with words.

LANGUAGE USAGE

Words are used for many purposes: for example, reporting, joking,
inviting, promising, ordering, questioning, persuading, describing, classifying, moralising, arguing and many more. There are conventional
ways of signalling their functions. Because we acknowledge the signals,
transgressions are noticed as amusing or worthy of censure. Deliberate
miscategorisation can be a source of amusement, as when people talk
to plants or encourage cars to start on cold mornings by uttering
terms of endearment. Speaking out of turn breaks a convention and is
a ground for censure. A complete study of all such conventions might
be interesting but is hardly necessary. However, *conversational implication*, a key concept discussed by Fogelin (1978: 23), is fundamental to
understanding what counts as acceptable practice in serious discourse.

Grammarians classify sentences in terms of mood. For instance,
indicative sentences state facts, *interrogatives* ask questions, *imperatives*
issue orders and *expressive sentences* reveal feelings. In an indicative
sentence, the stated fact is either the case or it is not. For instance,
'some kinds of radiation are dangerous' and 'pigs can fly'. Questions
and orders are non-assertions and whether or not things are the case
is irrelevant. For example, it makes no sense to ask if 'What time is
it?' is the case. It is equally silly to try and establish that 'Be quiet!' is
not the case. Yet words not indicative in mood may be communicative.
The rhetorical question is a device for making a point interrogatively.
But indicative expressions are not necessarily communicative. Sometimes they may constitute a performance.

Expressive sentences are less clear and more difficult to get right.
Consider the lyric, 'Oh, what a beautiful morning; oh, what a beautiful
day!' If it expresses a feeling then, without confusion, it cannot be a
statement that the morning and day are beautiful. Equally it is not
categorically stating that the singer has those feelings – after all, he
may be acting. The next line of the song from *Oklahoma*, namely,
'I've got a wonderful feeling, everything's going my way', is a statement by the character that the character has those feelings. In this
context, it does not follow that the actor playing the part has those
feelings. So what is the status of expressions of feeling? There is good
reason to suppose that they are neither facts about the world nor facts

about the psychological state of those who utter them.[2] Consequently, expressions of feeling are not indicative in mood. This kind of consideration also has implications for the analysis of aesthetic and moral judgements. Acceptable practice in serious discourse requires that expressions of feeling, interrogatives and imperatives cannot be treated as though they were statements of fact. To do so is inappropriate and a source of confusion. A satisfactory response might be to recognise them by saying 'I hear what you say' and, what's more, 'Bravo!'

Expressions of feeling are awkward in another sense. If they do not state facts then how could they be communicating anything? Seeing *Oklahoma* to hear the facts suggests that there is little point in going again unless one's memory is defective or something else were involved, for example, enjoying the performance. The latter reason accounts for people going to see shows many times. Enjoying the performance is what matters. Communication in this context is not a major concern. It is a common mistake to regard all language usage as primarily communicative. Expressive sentences are first and foremost performances.[3]

Making a promise is a *performative* speech act. When I make an appointment and promise to keep it, I thereby promise to arrive at a specific time and place. The *thereby test* is a useful method of discovering whether statements have a performative function. When a judge says, 'I find you guilty as charged', she thereby finds you guilty. She is not saying that you are guilty; there may have been a miscarriage of justice. She simply finds you guilty, just as a football referee declares a goal scored, when as sometimes happens a goal is not scored. Performatives signal that certain conventions are in force. The promise makes sense only if the promisee is entitled to expect fulfilment and the promisor makes every effort to comply. The verdict 'guilty as charged' holds only if the judge has been properly installed and there has been no malpractice. These conventions give speech acts their meaning and are conversationally implied when promises are made or verdicts announced. Similarly, when evaluating argument and evidence, language usage signals inferences. Several conventions are implied in the act of critical appraisal. These conventions improve the likelihood of effective communication in serious discourse.

CO-OPERATION AND EFFECTIVE COMMUNICATION

If participants in serious discourse fail to co-operate then they could not present argument and evidence in critical dialogue. Co-operation is implicit in following a line of reasoning and explicit in acknowledging the conventions. Before examining what is implied by engaging in serious discourse, it is worth commenting on the *charity principle*. Much discussion is befuddled by the rejection of arguments either because some obvious blunder has been made or because prejudice dictates that certain contributors always blunder. Celibate clergy engaged as marriage advisory counsellors are frequently the subject of prejudice. The charity principle requires that the best possible construction be put on any contribution to any debate. This strategy ensures that if the best version of an argument is deficient then, because technically less secure accounts are more deficient, the case is made effectively. In any case, it is rude to be less than polite.

Language usage in discursive contexts implies acceptance of at least four rules. Grice (1975, in Fogelin 1978: 333) describes them as the rules of quantity, quality, relation and manner. *Quantity* has to do with the amount of information presented. It recommends the avoidance of over-informing and under-informing. Offering too much information is an unacceptable practice, which signals that the abilities to generalise and to judge what really matters are minimal. This typically occurs when giving travel directions and is commonly described in other contexts as twaddle or waffle. Under-informing is simply unhelpful and sometimes impolite. *Quality* is the requirement that what is said should be the case, as far as one can tell. More explicitly, one should neither say what is believed not to be the case nor assert anything for which there is a lack of adequate evidence. The point is that anyone is entitled to challenge anything. In co-operative activities, no-one is expected to mislead, still less tell lies. To disregard the rule of quality is to leave oneself open to severe penalties, including serious censure or loss of reputation. *Relation* is the relevance requirement, dependent on circumstances and the concerns of either the case or the contributor. Arguments cannot be followed and disputes cannot be settled if participants keep changing the subject. This is an instance of irrelevance and is typically the result of interruptions. *Manner* is a matter of being clear. It amounts to avoiding ambiguity and obscurity of expression, and being brief and orderly.

Breaking the rules of language usage in discursive contexts often gives rise to bewilderment. For example, lies may be difficult to recognise in the absence of argument and evidence. Ultimately reputations are at stake but unacceptable practices undermine confidence in the results of serious attempts to critically appraise argument and evidence.

APPLICATIONS

Serious discourse is a co-operative venture. In practice, this means that some basic requirements for discussion must be shared. They include agreements about key concepts and ways of thinking about experience, methods of investigation and criteria for interpreting the significance of findings. Whether academic or otherwise, the acknowledgement of conventions is basic to study skills. To the extent that the various spoken and written media for serious discourse are conventional, their character is worthy of comment.[4]

Lectures are given by those entitled to be called experts by having acquired knowledge that is worth sharing. Comprehending the content of a lecture requires listening skills. One such skill is to distinguish opinions from facts. Another is the ability to distinguish the reasons supporting an argument from the conclusion to be established. Yet another is competence in separating what is claimed from the implicit ways of thinking about the issues. For instance, a feminist perspective may influence the formulation and presentation of claims made about gender issues such as sexual harassment at work. A lecturer's failure to alert the audience to such matters during delivery may result in an impressive performance but it would hardly be liberating in an educational sense. At best, lectures are less than efficient in sharing knowledge because learning processes are inhibited by the lack of opportunity for adequate feedback from the audience. However, engaging positively with the lecture affords opportunities for discovery. This can be achieved to some extent by acknowledging conventions both in the delivery and in the discipline.

Group seminars and individual tutorials offer better prospects for furthering knowledge and sharing understanding. Such discursive encounters will not be successful unless contributors, both speakers and listeners, genuinely try to identify and to follow arguments, acknowledging the conventions in doing so. People are experts not simply because they know something but also because they know how to think about it. There is no guarantee that because someone shares their knowledge with you that they will share their understanding, based on how that knowledge is acquired and how the evidence is understood. Seminars are more likely to be successful when contributors are challenged to explain their assumptions about method as well as content. Suppose that you were discussing whether the electoral process in the UK is more democratic than that in the USA. Progress in understanding a position depends on the clarity with which a presenter indicates the basis for it. Consider Box 3.1 which gives opposing points of view. Both views rest on evidence about the average turn-out but each case employs a different criterion for democracy. One case relies on the *general election* turn-out and the other on turn-out in the *pre-electoral nomination* procedures. The opposing conclusions arise because of the different assumptions about a reliable indicator of 'democracy'.

Box 3.1 Democracy and electoral processes

The electoral process in the UK is more democratic than that in the USA because more than two-thirds of UK electors vote in a general election compared with just over one-half in the USA. Alternatively, the USA electoral process is more democratic because more than two-thirds of American electors participate in the nomination procedures compared with less than one-fifth of the UK electors.

It is the responsibility of students and enquirers to challenge experts to define their terms and methods as well as to inform.

What counts as acceptable practice for lecturers and disputants in discussion usually applies also to writers and readers, whether of books, articles, papers or examination scripts. If an attempt at any of these were to present an argument appropriately supported by evidence then it would have conventional features. Suppose an attack is launched on the nuclear power industry in order to justify a cut in expenditure to finance some preferred project. This in itself is context that informs the argument, cultivates suspicions about possible undeclared assumptions and generally helps in the preparation of a thorough critical appraisal. Awareness of a writer's motive can be helpful to the critic in so far as it accounts for the author's assumptions about the burden of proof. The writer's position is not always evident but this need not be a problem. It is always possible to develop an analysis based on an assumption about the motive and contrast it with alternative assumptions. This approach both challenges the position and demonstrates the writer's power of analysis. Such methods are considered in Chapter 8.

An essay justifying the suggested attack on the nuclear power industry could be planned as follows. A case might be based on the claims that 'dangerous practices are unacceptable' and that 'unacceptable practices should be abolished'. Each point is open to challenge but relatively easily defended. Thus, on this view, 'anything dangerous must be abolished'. A defence of the premises presumes that 'funds are released when a practice is abolished'. This assumption is not well grounded because, in the case of nuclear power stations, decommissioning is very expensive indeed. The defence also assumes that 'the nuclear power industry is dangerous'. This claim is at best contentious. The case is complex. The essayist needs to state and to set out clearly all the relevant claims. Attention would inevitably focus on defending the weakest part of the case. The resulting imbalance may not adversely affect the quality of the essay. To consider carefully the weakness of a case is wise, since any critic would attack it.

The nature of argument and evidence clearly has implications for acceptable practice in presentation and analysis. It is clear also that acknowledging the conventions of serious discourse makes communication effective and fruitful dialogue possible. A systematic pursuit of acceptable practices in reasoning is likely to improve the quality of discourse over the range of activities in which people seriously engage.

SUMMARY

1 Context influences how words are to be understood and how the social world is to be described and interpreted.
2 Conventions are prevalent in the social world and academic disciplines.
3 Language is used for many purposes. Each usage has its own conventions and is signalled by a context.
4 Conventions are implied in the act of critical analysis.
5 The following practice facilitates critical appraisal:

 a) Identify and follow patterns of reasoning.
 b) Acknowledge linguistic conventions and conversational implications.
 c) Make clear all material assumptions.
 d) Be alert to the limits of evidence.
 e) Presume the best case from opponents.
 f) Make contributions as informative as the purposes of discourse require.
 g) Assert nothing believed not to be the case.
 h) Assert nothing for which adequate evidence is lacking.
 i) Be relevant and keep to the point.
 j) Be clear.

4   An informal analysis of arguments

It is frequently difficult to perceive the arguments contained in written
or spoken words. The problem arises because we do many things with
words. We use them to signal conventions, to provide context and to
report evidence besides making claims and presenting arguments.
Consequently, a general method of argument analysis is required to
identify the main features in a piece of reasoning. An approach, based
on the R $\Rightarrow$ C notation with subscripts, is developed in this chapter as
a method for eliciting argument from text and setting out the reasoning
in a clear and intelligible way.

BASIC ARGUMENTS

Arguments, even of the simplest kind, are rarely presented in a clear
and straightforward fashion. The whole case often is not presented
either because the conclusion is thought to be obvious or because
some premise has been assumed. For instance:

Example 4.1

In an interview (*Going Live*, BBC1, 14 October 1989), a sixteen year old
London girl said, 'I want to get on a Youth Training Scheme but I'm
homeless so I can't.'

The case made here is contained in one sentence. There are several
components, all of which contribute to the presentation of the point
being made but not all of them are part of the reasoning. By using the
definitions and notation introduced in Chapter 2, it is possible to
identify the argument.

The definition of 'argument' as a set of at least two claims makes
Example 4.1 a possible argument. The claims must be connected in a
precise and relevant way. When the assertions have been identified,
our notation differentiates reasons, R, from the conclusion, C.

The first two phrases about the interview give the context and assist our interpretation of the point made. They are important words but they do not form part of the reasoning. Since the passage reports what the teenager said, the argument is contained in the words attributed to her. The quotation comprises three clauses as follows:

1 I want to get on a Youth Training Scheme.
2 I'm homeless.
3 I can't . . . (presumably, get on a YTS).

If two of these claims are connected in a relevant way then there is an argument. The first clause expresses the girl's desire to work. It offers context in terms of her psychological background. This expression of feeling is a piece of stage-setting which communicates the force of the point being made but is not an assertion – see pp. 26–7, 28–9. The argument lies in the last five words, 'I'm homeless so I can't'. Understood in context, being homeless is offered as a reason for not getting a place on a YTS. With the help of logical words, the precise connection is shown as follows:

Example 4.2

	Because,
R	I'm homeless.
⇒	Therefore,
C	I can't (get on a YTS).

Unfortunately, this is not the whole story. The conclusion follows only if homelessness prohibits individuals from placement on a YTS. The complete argument was not made by the disadvantaged teenager, probably because the missing premise was taken for granted. The entire case, explicitly presented, using subscripts to distinguish between the two reasons, reads:

Example 4.3

	Because, as assumed,
R_{1a}	Homelessness prohibits placement on Youth Training Schemes.
&	and because, as stated,
R_{2s}	I'm homeless.
⇒	Therefore,
C	I can't (get on a YTS).

The undeclared assumption accurately described the relevant legislation in 1989, which can be confirmed by appropriate documentary evidence. The importance of this evidence to the argument is that if it shows the assumption to be mistaken then there may be a remedy for the homeless teenager. She could get onto a YTS and, being employed, qualify for housing. Sadly, this was not the case at the time. Displaying the complete argument illustrates how evidence interacts with the reasoning. Furthermore, it reveals that the teenager's point was not just to explain her predicament but also to imply a criticism of the legislation responsible for her predicament. Spelling out an argument to the fullest possible extent, giving appropriate consideration to context, convention and evidence, is a valuable aid to critical analysis. Eliciting an argument from text involves the following steps:

1 Disregard context and text where claims are not made. Nevertheless, such words may facilitate an accurate interpretation of claims which form part of the reasoning process.
2 Label each claim either as a reason, 'R', or as a conclusion, 'C'. Logical words, for example 'because' and 'therefore', distinguish reasons from conclusions.
3 Identify each claim using subscripts, for example, R_{2s} for the second reason which also is stated in the text.
4 Specify undeclared claims. One's intuitions are a good guide when expressing missing claims, whether reasons or conclusions. Further useful hints are given in Chapters 5 and 8.

REASON INDICATORS AND INFERENCE INDICATORS

A disciplined application of the methods for spotting reasoning in text enables us to identify arguments but, because they are seldom presented clearly, further skills are needed. An argument, typical of the controversy which led to the Black Report (Black 1984) is set out plainly in Example 4.4:

Example 4.4

      Because, as known,
R_1 Radiation causes leukaemia in children.
&   and because, as established,
R_2 The plant at Sellafield discharges radiation into the environment.
$\Rightarrow$ Therefore,
C   The plant at Sellafield causes leukaemia in children.

Displaying an argument's content in this way makes an evaluation of it much easier. In this case, it would be irrational to deny the conclusion that 'the plant at Sellafield causes leukaemia in children', while accepting the premises. Paragraph 5.17 in the Black Report (see p. 40) is difficult to appraise critically because it is not obvious which claims are premises and which are conclusions. The problem is worse when arguments are inadequately and badly presented. In the examples so far examined, the logical words 'because' and 'therefore' were used respectively to identify premises and conclusions. The English language contains many such words and equivalent phrases which occur in arguments. One convention is to mark them on a copy of the text. Fisher (1988) recommends that a circle or box is drawn around logical words . By the same convention, one brackets [premises] and underlines conclusions. Revising Example 4.4 in these ways gives the following result:

Example 4.5

	Because , as known,
R₁	[Radiation causes leukaemia in children.]
&	and because , as established,
R₂	[The plant at Sellafield discharges radiation into the environment.]
⇒	Therefore ,
C	The plant at Sellafield causes leukaemia in children.

One obvious point about this convention is that the conclusion is placed last since it is said to *follow from* the premises. However, conclusions are often mentioned first and in some texts they may be pages away from the supporting claims. Consequently, skill in spotting textual indicators of the role claims play in an argument facilitates critical analysis. Reasons or premises are signalled by such words and phrases as the following:

because . . .	follows from the fact that . . .
for . . .	may be inferred from . . .
on account of . . .	seeing that . . .
since . . .	the reason being . . .

These words and phrases are called *reason indicators*. It is not an exhaustive list nor should one be needed. What counts is that reasons are offered *in support of a conclusion*. This feature is the indicator, whichever words are used. The absence of role-depicting words and phrases sometimes makes it necessary to gauge the role of a claim from sense and context. Conversely, the words listed above do not always signal a reason or premise in an argument. For example, 'for' may indicate use or purpose as in 'Boots are made *for* walking'.

Inference indicators, signifying implication, indicate conclusions. They include the following words and phrases:

all things considered . . .	consequently . . .
. . . demonstrates that . . .	. . . establishes the fact that . . .
I conclude that . . .	it can be argued that . . .
it follows that . . .	. . . justifies the belief that . . .
logically . . .	rationally . . .
so . . .	therefore . . .
thus . . .	ultimately . . .
. . . which implies that . . .	. . . which proves that . . .

Again the list is not complete. What matters is that the words and phrases identify what *purports to be established*, irrespective of the words used. Furthermore, it is not always the case that such words signal conclusions. For example, 'thus' can indicate manner or style as in 'One plays a violin *thus*'. Because valid deductive arguments successfully establish their conclusions, forcing words such as 'must', 'cannot', 'impossible' and 'necessarily' sometimes indicate inferences. For instance, 'The look on his face means he *must* be guilty' is a piece of reasoning – however poor.

Sometimes, a word or phrase may indicate reasons or inferences less than clearly. When this happens, substituting one indicator for another or using them in combination can help to confirm whether an assertion is a reason or conclusion. For example, in some contexts, the word 'whence' could signal a conclusion. This might be confirmed by substituting 'whence it follows that . . .' in the original text and checking that its sense remains unchanged. This approach has to be used with care because there is a danger of reading too much into a text. Nevertheless, with care, inserting inference indicators and checking against a change in sense can be used successfully.

The logical words 'and' and 'but' deserve mention in the context of identifying reasons and conclusions. They are both conjunctions and both may be symbolised by '&', even though 'but' indicates that what follows is somehow different, usually negative in some sense. Conjunctions are sometimes used in ways that have nothing to do with reasoning, as when items on a shopping list are conjoined by 'and' and those items not required or to be obtained elsewhere are signalled by 'but'. However, when it is clear that an argument is being presented, each word may connect two claims in support of a third, thereby indicating both an inference and that the conjoined claims are reasons or premises. For example, 'Democracy is promoted by revolution but Albania has not yet experienced revolution'. Notice the negative claim following the conjunction 'but'. The text of this argument is conventionally marked thus:

Example 4.6

[Democracy is promoted by revolution] but [Albania has not yet experienced revolution].

Apparently, there is no conclusion since no claim is underlined. Either the conclusion is suppressed or there is no argument. In Europe during 1989–90, the conclusion was generally appreciated. The media understood that Albania is still not democratic. Having identified the reasoning and made the undeclared conclusion explicit, Example 4.7 sets out the entire argument. Subscript 's' indicates that the reasons were stated and subscript 'u' indicates that the conclusion was *undeclared* in the text:

Example 4.7

    Because , as stated,
R_{1s} [Democracy is promoted by revolution.]
&   and because , as stated,
R_{2s} [Albania has not yet experienced revolution.]
$\Rightarrow$ Therefore , though unstated,
C_u Albania is still not democratic.

As news reporters confirmed at the time, the Albanian system of government was not democratic but their evidence is not the reason for accepting the conclusion. It is accepted by force of argument. Appropriate grounds for the premises, including evidence, would render the argument sound. However, an informal analysis which sets out the argument plainly also facilitates an evaluation of it in these terms.

In Example 4.6, the conjunction 'but' indicates two reasons, from which there follows an unstated conclusion. The negation suggested by 'but', when conjoining R_{2s}, appears in the conclusion. The complete argument is presented as follows:

$$R_{1s} \,\&\, R_{2s} \Rightarrow C_u$$

This pattern is not the only one which may occur when 'and' and 'but' are used as *reason indicators*. It may not be the case that the conclusion follows from the reasons taken together. Sometimes, two reasons offered in support of a conclusion may support it independently. Thus, there are two arguments as follows:

$$R_{1s} \Rightarrow C \;\boxed{\text{and}}\; R_{2s} \Rightarrow C$$

When an undeclared assumption is needed to complete one of the arguments, they might be expressed thus:

$R_{1s} \Rightarrow C$ [and] R_{2s} & $R_{3a} \Rightarrow C$

The informal analysis of arguments presented above is summarised thus:

1 Circle or box logical words indicating inferences.
2 Underline <u>conclusions</u>.
3 Bracket [premises].
4 Specify undeclared premises or conclusions.
5 Set out the argument in the 'R $\Rightarrow$ C' notation.

These conventions help facilitate critical appraisal.

IDENTIFYING A COMPLICATED ARGUMENT

Consider the following passage:

> ... the incidence of leukaemia in Seascale is unusual, but not unique; and we acknowledge that those who have drawn attention to it may have performed something of a public service. However, the suggestion that in the neighbourhood of Sellafield there is a causal relationship between an increased level of radioactivity and an above-average experience of leukaemia, while it is possible, is by no means proven. The causes of leukaemia are not fully established, even though radiation is one acknowledged factor; and ... the doses received by the population are insufficient to account for the additional cases of leukaemia in the area. On the other hand, the proposition cannot be completely discounted, and it is difficult to see what scientific evidence would suffice to do so.
>
> (Black Report 1984: 89, para. 5.17)

The text is not straightforward. Remarkably, it contains none of the listed inference indicators. Although this makes the argument difficult to find, it helps to remember that the committee was chaired by a reputable scientist and therefore its conclusions need interpretation consistent with good scientific practice. Furthermore, the context of the media attention given to the Sellafield cancer-link controversy in the 1980s which led to a public inquiry guides analysis of the report. Using our conventions, a marked copy of the text appears as follows:

> ... the incidence of leukaemia in Seascale is unusual, but not unique; and we acknowledge that those who have drawn attention to it may have performed something of a public service. However, the

suggestion that in the neighbourhood of Sellafield there is a causal relationship between an increased level of radioactivity and an above-average experience of leukaemia, while it is possible, is by no means proven. [The causes of leukaemia are not fully established, even though radiation is one acknowledged factor]; and ... [the doses received by the population are insufficient to account for the additional cases of leukaemia in the area]. On the other hand, the proposition cannot be completely discounted, and it is difficult to see what scientific evidence would suffice to do so.

Now that the conclusion has been underlined, the point of the text is clear. It is interesting to reflect that British Nuclear Fuels, the company under scrutiny, have a reputation to defend. Even so, radiation-induced cancer in human beings is a serious matter and the analysis needs to be conducted systematically and with care.

The main reasoning is contained in the second and third sentences, the second stating the conclusion and the third specifying two supporting reasons or premises. As noted earlier, because these reasons independently support the main conclusion there are two separate arguments. Example 4.8 plainly sets out the first:

Example 4.8

R_{1s} Because , as stated,
[The causes of leukaemia are not fully established.]

$\Rightarrow$ Therefore ,

C The suggestion that in the neighbourhood of Sellafield there is a causal relationship between an increased level of radioactivity and an above-average experience of leukaemia, while it is possible, is by no means proven.

In R_{1s}, the words 'even though radiation is one acknowledged factor' have been excluded because the phrase 'even though' discounts the point that radiation is a factor. The Report apparently justifies this by placing the burden of proof on those who make the cancer-link claim. However, the conclusion is a special case of the premise and requires no further support.

The second argument does require further support for the conclusion to follow legitimately. There is an assumed, undeclared premise which, when made explicit, establishes the case. To see more clearly what it might be, it is helpful to restate the given premise in clearer but equivalent terms. Example 4.9 gives the completed second argument:

Example 4.9

	Because , as stated,
R$_{2s}$	[The doses received by the population around Sellafield, which allegedly account for the additional cases of leukaemia in the area, are causally insufficient.]
&	and because , as assumed,
R$_{3a}$	[Causal insufficiency implies 'by no means proven'.]
⇒	Therefore ,
C	The suggestion that in the neighbourhood of Sellafield there is a causal relationship between an increased level of radioactivity and an above-average experience of leukaemia, while it is possible, is by no means proven.

Identifying the two main arguments was tricky. It is worth re-emphasising that the difficulties arise as much from what motivates the case as from the arguments themselves. Political and commercial objectives, for example, that Sellafield should have a clean bill of health, are sometimes in conflict with scientific ideals.

ASPECTS OF COMPLEXITY

No matter how skilful and entertaining the presentation of an argument may be, the reasoning is comprised of assertions or denials. Groups of words which do not make claims often help to confirm interpretations of the claims made. Some genuine assertions may not be essential to an argument because their role is a matter of stage-setting. This is one aspect of complex reasoning but arguments become complex also by virtue of the reasoning itself. Putting Examples 4.8 and 4.9 together displays the argument's complex structure:

$$R_{1s} \Rightarrow C \boxed{\text{and}} R_{2s} \,\&\, R_{3a} \Rightarrow C$$

This is a list of arguments which are connected only by the fact that they share the same conclusion.

The extract from the Black Report is interesting for, although some conclusions are not drawn, there are no superfluous words. Other forms of reasoning are complex because there are several inferences. This can be compounded by the inclusion of superfluous words. Multi-staged arguments are difficult to disentangle, especially when there are missing claims. Consider Box 4.1, which presents a passage conventionally marked. Here, the argument occurs in a different context from that in which it was originally presented. Happily, immediate remedy is possible. The quotation can be found in *Practical*

Ethics by the philosopher, Peter Singer (1979: 78), in a chapter entitled 'What's wrong with killing?'. It is part of a longer argument comprising seven inferences, not all of which are actually made, but which most people could follow in context. Knowing that it appears in a debate about the sanctity of life helps in drawing out any undeclared conclusion. Having marked the premises, conclusions and their indicators, it is useful to strike out ~~superfluous words~~. This has been done for the text in Box 4.1. We invite the reader to clarify the argument's structure, using informal methods of analysis. Those who need encouragement may consult Appendix I to see our version. If you are tempted, work out the relationship between the marked text and the plain version of the argument, including the hidden assumptions.

Box 4.1 The sanctity of life

Is there special value in the life of a rational and self-conscious being as distinct from a being that is merely sentient?
One line of argument for answering this question affirmatively runs as follows. [A self-conscious being is aware of itself as a distinct entity, with a past and a future.] (~~This, remember, was Locke's criterion for being a person.~~) [A being aware of itself in this way will be capable of having desires about its own future.] ~~For example, a professor of philosophy may hope to write a book demonstrating the objective nature of ethics; a student may look forward to graduating; a child may want to go for a ride in an aeroplane~~.

(Singer 1979: 78)

Many forms of reasoning are complex but the same benefits accrue from using an informal analysis of arguments. When, for instance, the presenter of an argument suspects that an audience is alert to a case's weakness, so many words may be devoted to defending a premise as an intermediate conclusion that focus is diverted from the main case. In the sanctity of life example, Singer did not even state the intermediate conclusion, perhaps because he presumed that his readers were able to infer the obvious in that context. The remedy, when faced with such aspects of complexity, is the same. Set out the argument in detail but plainly and evaluate each stage separately.

SUMMARY

Informal argument analysis elicits arguments embedded in text. The following methods set out reasoning plainly and make it clear and intelligible:

1 Mark a copy of the text thus:
   a) Circle or box $\boxed{\text{logical words}}$ indicating inferences.
   b) Underline <u>conclusions</u>.
   c) Bracket [premises].
   d) Strike through ~~contextual claims~~ and words making ~~no claim at all~~.
2 Set out the argument again using the 'R $\Rightarrow$ C' notation.
3 Specify the role each claim plays in the argument by:
   a) Inserting logical words, for example, 'because' and 'therefore'.
   b) Using role depicting phrases, for example, 'as assumed'.
   c) Using appropriate subscripts, for example, R_{2s}.
4 Specify undeclared reasons or conclusions.
5 For complex arguments with several inferences:
   a) Deal with each stage separately.
   b) Set out each stage of the complex argument as above.

5   Patterns of reasoning

A high proportion of arguments exhibit one of two common patterns of reasoning.[1] Recognising these patterns, called *argument form*, helps to clarify an argument and to identify its strengths and weaknesses. Two styles of deductive argument are described below. For each, we examine the logical form of individual claims as a preliminary to making explicit the respective patterns of reasoning.

STYLES OF DEDUCTIVE ARGUMENT

Arguments sometimes concern whether and to what extent members of one group are members of another. Example 5.1 is such a case:

Example 5.1

	Because ,
R_1	[Twenty-two year old councillors are rare politicians.]
&	and because ,
R_2	[Christopher Leslie was a councillor at twenty-two.]
⇒	Therefore
C	Christopher Leslie was a rare politician.[2]

The argument contains three sentences. Each sentence has a subject term which defines one *group* and a predicate term which defines another, though it should be noted that a group might comprise only one member. The groups specified in Example 5.1 are 'twenty-two year old councillors', 'rare politicians' and 'Christopher Leslie'. Since the claims *predicate* that all or some of one group's members are members of the other, the method of analysing this style of argument is called *predicate logic*.

Now consider Example 5.2, which illustrates a different style of argument:

Example 5.2

	Because ,
R₁	[If [Christopher Leslie worked for national politicians] then [he would be elected councillor when very young].]
&	and because ,
R₂	[He worked for national politicians in the UK and the USA.]
⇒	Therefore
C	Christopher Leslie was elected councillor when very young.

The first reason, R_1, contains two claims combined in one sentence by the logical words, 'If . . . then . . .' . The argument hinges on how the two claims are joined together. On this occasion, they are combined such that the second is conditional upon the first. Logical words, such as 'If . . . then . . .', are called *connectives* and the claims connected by them are called *propositions*. Hence, *propositional logic* is the method of analysing deductive arguments of this kind.

Individual claims which comprise predicate and propositional styles of reasoning can be expressed in explicitly formal ways. When several claims are presented as an argument, each pattern of reasoning has a corresponding style of argument form, respectively, *predicate form* or *propositional form*.

STATEMENTS IN PREDICATE FORM

This section offers strategies for making explicit the logical form of individual statements which claim or predicate that all, some or none of one group's members are members of another. Consider the first reason from Example 5.1:

R₁   [Twenty-two year old councillors are rare politicians.]

This statement has the following features:

1 Two groups are mentioned, namely, 'twenty-two year old council-lors' and 'rare politicians'.
2 The claim is that all members of the first group are members of the second.
3 Both groups are comprised of people.

These features provide a basis for identifying the claim's predicate form. With a standard notation, predicate form can be made transparent but some definitions are needed.

A sentence contains subject and predicate terms. The *subject term* defines the group about which a sentence is predicated. The *predicate term* defines the group, which is claimed to contain all, some or none of the individuals defined by the subject term. The subject term in R_1 of Example 5.1 is 'twenty-two year old councillors' and by convention is represented by the symbol, 'S'. Similarly, the predicate term, 'rare politicians', is represented by the symbol, 'P'. Substituting symbols for the corresponding ordinary language terms, the formal statement that 'S are P' is obtained. Neither this nor the ordinary language version is explicit about the precise relationship between the two groups. However, context normally confirms the implication that *all* members of group 'S' are *included* in group 'P'. On this point, there is a rule of thumb for interpreting text. It states that: 'Whenever *part* of a subject term is not specified by the word "some" or an equivalent phrase, it is normal to suppose that the claim is predicated of *all* members.' Therefore, the proposition is accurately expressed as follows:

All twenty-two year old councillors *are* rare politicians.

This can be expressed in notation as follows:

All S are P.

Though accurate, this abstract version takes no account of the claim's third feature, namely, that 'both groups are comprised of people'. This stipulates a *universe of discourse* that defines what the groups have in common and indicates the context within which the point is being made. By inserting the relevant term in the ordinary language expression, a revised version of the sentence reads:

All people who are 'twenty-two year old councillors' *are* people who are 'rare politicians'.

Though far removed from normal prose and speech, this makes the assertion clear by revealing its predicate form. Making the universe of discourse explicit is helpful especially when text is obscure. Difficulty in deciding what the universe of discourse might be is frequently removed by using a very general term. Perhaps the most general, all-embracing term is 'thing'. There is no objection to using such a broad term because the description of each group *rules in* what sorts of 'thing' a claim is about. By the same token, it *rules out* every 'thing' else. The object of specifying a universe of discourse is to distinguish the subject group from the predicate group. Thus, the relationship between them – a matter of the extent to which membership is shared – can be accurately described.

One characteristic of expressions such as R_1 in Example 5.1 makes them unique, namely, that one group falls entirely within the other.

Whatever their content, these claims are described as *positive, universal* propositions. They are 'positive' by virtue of *including* the members of one group in the other and 'universal' because *every* individual is involved. Claims with different content can have the same predicate form. For instance, the statement that 'radiation is dangerous' may be expressed formally as 'All S are P'.

The terms 'universal' and 'positive' each have their opposites. The opposite of 'positive' is *negative*, where the members of one group are *excluded* from the other. The opposite of 'universal' is *particular*, where only *some* members of one group are included or excluded from the other. Conventionally, 'some' is taken to mean 'not all and possibly one'. The criteria for inclusion or exclusion and all or some, taken together, define the four logical forms that predicating claims may take. The first has been considered already, namely, 'All S are P' is a positive, universal proposition.

Taking the remainder in turn, the *negative, universal* proposition is a claim which excludes all the members of one group from the other. With negative claims, it helps to define the groups positively, especially the predicate term. Consider the example 'radiation-induced cancer is no laughing matter'. Taking the universe of discourse to be 'things', the subject term is 'things which are instances of radiation-induced cancer'. The predicate term is 'things which are laughing matters'. Thus the proposition asserts that:

No things which are instances of 'radiation-induced cancer' *are* things which are 'laughing matters'.

Using our notation, the claim can be expressed formally as follows:

No S are P.

This version states that '*no* members of S are *included* in P' and is equivalent to saying that '*all* members of S are *excluded* from being members of P'.

'Some students are clever' is a *positive, particular* proposition. The universe of discourse is 'people', comprising 'student' people and 'clever' people. The relationship between the groups is positive because members of the first group are *included* in the second. Since only *some* students are included, the claim is particular. The proposition asserts that:

Some people who are 'students' *are* people who are 'clever'.

This can be expressed formally thus:

Some S are P.

The claim that 'Christopher Leslie was a councillor at twenty-two', can also be construed as a positive, particular proposition.[3] Christopher Leslie is clearly *included* amongst 'twenty-two year old councillors' but the kind of inclusion needs more attention. Defining 'some' as including 'possibly one' covers cases where a group contains only one member. Thus, it is appropriate to interpret 'Christopher Leslie' as 'some person, namely, Christopher Leslie'. With the universe of discourse specified, the proposition asserts that:

> *Some* person, namely 'Christopher Leslie', happens to be a person who *was* a 'twenty-two year old councillor'.

Again, using our notation, the claim can be expressed formally as follows:

> Some S is P.

The fourth type of proposition is *negative* and *particular*. Consider, for example, the claim that 'some Eastern European countries did not have a people's revolution during 1989'. Here the universe of discourse is 'countries'. The claim asserts that:

> *Some* countries which are 'Eastern European' *are not* countries which 'had a people's revolution during 1989'.

The formal expression of this statement is that:

> Some S are not P.

The logical form taken by each of the four basic propositions is as follows:

All S are P . . .	a positive universal proposition
No S are P . . .	a negative universal proposition
Some S is/are P . . .	a positive particular proposition
Some S are not P . . .	a negative particular proposition

Claims as they occur in text and speech may be difficult to analyse because the subject and predicate terms may be complicated and the context may be less than clear. The techniques for setting out propositions formally often help to make their predicate form transparent. They are summarised as follows:

1 Specify the universe of discourse, possibly *things*.
2 Identify and define the subject term, 'S'.
3 Identify and define the predicate term, 'P'.
4 Express the claim in notation to make explicit its predicate form.

USING DIAGRAMS TO FORMULATE CLAIMS

Claims which have a predicate form can be represented in Venn diagrams. In order to standardise methods for analysing arguments, it is necessary to use clear conventions, applying to all cases.[4] Each basic proposition can be expressed in a drawing of two interlocking circles, one for each group specified, as in Figure 5.1.

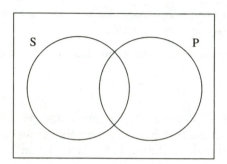

Figure 5.1   Simple Venn diagram

Conventionally, a box delimiting the universe of discourse is drawn around the circles. It includes those outside both circles, though the claim is about individuals inside the circles. The interlocking circles depict three segments. By convention, universal propositions are indicated by shading and particular propositions by an asterisk.[5]

Any claim of the form, 'Some S are P', asserts that *some* S are *included* in P. Consequently, the asterisk is placed in the overlapping segment. This is exactly where Ss that are Ps would be found – see Figure 5.2. When there exist *some* Ss which are *excluded* from P, the asterisk must be placed in the segment of S which is outside the P circle – see Figure 5.3. The shading convention is used to shade *out* those segments known to contain no members. For instance, the expression, 'No S are P', has a predicate form which *excludes all* Ss from the P circle. It is natural, therefore, to shade *out* the overlapping segment. This leaves open the possibility that there might be Ss that are not Ps and Ps that are not Ss. Notice that the diagram in Figure 5.4 contains no asterisk.

Alternatively, 'All S are P' effectively rules *out* the possibility of an S occurring outside the P circle. Thus, the segment of the S circle

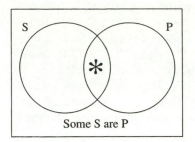

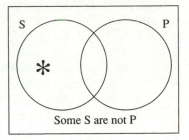

Figure 5.2 Positive particular proposition

Figure 5.3 Negative particular proposition

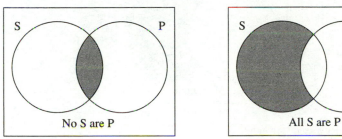

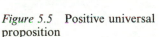

Figure 5.4 Negative universal proposition

Figure 5.5 Positive universal proposition

which lies outside the P circle is shaded *out*. It seems odd that this picture leaves open only a *possibility* that there may be Ss, all of which are Ps. 'All S are P' appears to make a strong, positive claim. There is a very good reason for this peculiarity. Modern logicians broadly hold that expressions which are positive and universal do not have *existential import*. This means that 'All S are P' does not imply that any Ss exist. For example, the claim that 'all leprechauns are small people' does not imply that there ever have been, are or ever will be any leprechauns. One implication of the shade-out convention is that the lack of existential import implies that positive, universal assertions are definitions rather than empirical claims. However, those claims describing *all* the members of a *finite set* do have existential import. For example, the assertion that 'all the vats of whisky in store on Islay are single malts', is a claim about a wonderful state of affairs in a beautiful part of the world and, what is more, there is a definite implication that the vats of whisky exist.

Positive, universal propositions are peculiar in another way deserving attention. To take a simple but awkward example, 'Only silly people take drugs'. The problem is to work out precisely what is being claimed. Many people might suppose it means that 'all silly people take drugs', but this is incorrect. The original claim rules out the possibility of a drug-taker who is *not* silly. It would be more accurate to shade out what the claim rules out, namely, the segment of the P circle lying outside S. Figure 5.6 presents a Venn diagram shaded in this way.

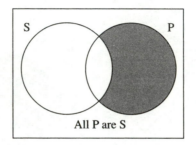

Figure 5.6   Reversed universal

The terms 'S' and 'P' are reversed in the expression of Figure 5.6, as compared with Figure 5.5. 'P' is now the subject term and 'S' is the predicate term. This means that 'Only S are P' has the same predicate form as the expression 'All P are S'. The fact that both expressions can be represented by identical Venn diagrams demonstrates that the two are logically equivalent. The point can be made formally as follows:

'Only S are P' = 'All P are S'.

This use of Venn diagrams shows how valuable they can be as a device for confirming the predicate form of difficult expressions.

ARGUMENTS IN PREDICATE FORM

The first step towards identifying argument form is to set out the reasoning plainly as in Example 5.1. This argument contains three claims – two premises and a conclusion. They specify three groups in the universe of discourse. Consequently, the key for allocating symbols to groups needs modification. It is conventional to assign 'S' to the *subject term in the conclusion* and 'P' to the *predicate term in the conclusion*. In Example 5.1, these two terms occur only once in the premises and each in a different premise. The subject term, 'Christopher Leslie' occurs in R_2 and the predicate term, 'rare politician', occurs in R_1. The third term, 'twenty-two year old councillors' or an equivalent phrase does not feature in the conclusion but is present in both premises. Not surprisingly, it is called the *middle term* and is denoted by the letter 'M'. By elaborating each claim as described on pp. 46–9, the reasoning is as follows:

Example 5.3

R₁   Because ,
[All people who are 'twenty-two year old councillors' are people who are 'rare politicians'.]

&   and because ,
R₂   [Some person, namely, 'Christopher Leslie' happens to be a person who was 'a councillor at twenty-two'.]

⇒   Therefore
C   Some person, namely, 'Christopher Leslie' happens to be a person who was 'a rare politician'.

This rather cumbersome version has the merit of being clear about two aspects of the reasoning.[6] The groups are clearly specified and the relationship between them is also clear. Thus, by substituting the newly defined symbols for the revised claims in Example 5.3, the argument is formally expressed as follows:

All M are P.
Some S is M.
Thus Some S is P.

This approach to recognising argument form is useful when confronting difficult text. You are invited to confirm that the main argument about ethnic cleansing in Box 5.1 is formally expressed in the same way as Example 5.3. The text contains several lines of reasoning, some of which are incomplete and require assumptions to be made explicit. The main argument is conventionally marked in accordance with the first part of the step by step approach summarised below:

Box 5.1 Ethnic cleansing in the former Yugoslavia

Fighting in the former Yugoslavia during the early 1990s has been atrocious. Emotions must have been pent up for so long that violence would be inevitable. Not all aspects of the war were indefensible but some Serbian atrocities on the Muslims were wholly unacceptable. They were called 'ethnic cleansing' as if they were different from the nationalist-cum-racist atrocities perpetrated by the Nazis on the Jews during the Second World War. Call it what you like, [ethnic cleansing is always wholly unacceptable], as it was then in Germany and currently in Rwanda. There is no doubt that [some of the Serbian atrocities against the Muslims amounted to ethnic cleansing] of the same kind. It raises serious questions about what the rest of the world should do.

1 Identify the conclusion and premises by marking a copy of the text.
2 Set out the argument in the 'R ⇒ C' notation.
3 Establish a key for 'S', 'P' and 'M'.
4 For each claim, decide which Venn diagram is appropriate.
5 Make explicit the argument form by substituting symbols for text when setting out the premises and conclusion.

ARGUMENTS IN PROPOSITIONAL FORM

Sometimes, logical words indicate precise connections between propositions. Such words, known as connectives, include 'not', 'and', 'or' and 'if . . . then . . .'. Each of these basic connectives has its own role, governing what follows in arguments. When they appear in the text of an argument, recognising propositional form is relatively easy, provided that each component proposition is expressed simply. This can be done using appropriate notation. Although it is often difficult to translate ordinary language into a standard formal language, with discernment and due regard to context and convention, adequate approximations can be made.

Example 5.2 was introduced as a deductive argument whose validity depends on the logical words connecting the elemental propositions in R_1. It is represented as:

Example 5.4

R_1 Because ,
     [If] [Christopher Leslie worked for national politicians]
     then [he would be elected councillor very young].]
&   and because ,

R₂   [He worked for national politicians in the UK and the USA.]

⇒   ┌──────────┐
     │ Therefore │
     └──────────┘

C   Christopher Leslie was elected councillor very young.

R₁ is the focus of interest. The elemental propositions are connected by logical words, expressing a conditional relationship between them. The overall claim asserts that 'working for national politicians' is a *material condition* for Christopher Leslie being 'elected councillor very young'. The use of double brackets clarifies that this is a *composite claim*, and that the style of argument is about propositional relationships, having a corresponding propositional form. Because it is conventional to use the letters 'p', 'q', 'r', etc. to stand for individual propositions, the logical form of this premise is:

If p then q.

R₂ claims that 'he worked for national politicians in the UK and the USA'. This second premise amounts to an affirmation of the first proposition in R₁, namely, 'p'. The two claims taken together entail the second proposition in R₁, namely, q, the conclusion. The reasoning can be expressed in notation which makes explicit the argument's propositional form:

[[If p then q] & [p]] thus , q.

Normally, basic arguments with propositional form have two premises, one of which is a composite proposition, and a conclusion. There are two other common logical connectives, namely 'and' and 'or'. All three composite propositions are formally expressed as follows:

p and q	conjunction
p or q	disjunction
if p, then q	material conditional

Logicians also think of negation as a logical connective. One consequence of this is that asserting the double negation, not [not p], is equivalent to asserting that p. Furthermore, using the curly symbol, ~, to stand for 'not', [p & [~p]] is a contradiction whereas [p & [~q]] is not.

Problems in recognising propositional form arise for a number of reasons. One is that, in practice, presenters of arguments string several inferences together, sometimes omitting crucial steps. The solution is to fill in the gaps systematically and conduct an analysis one stage at a time. Another reason is that language is so rich that each propositional connective has an indefinitely large number of equivalent, alternative versions. Listing them all would be a fearsome task and probably very boring, unless one were a dedicated logician or a student of language usage. Clearly, judgement needs to be exercised when approximating the sense of a composite ordinary language claim to an appropriate formal expression. Awareness of propositional forms helps because the patterns provide simple models which guide the making of such judgements.

SUMMARY

1 Propositions about the extent to which members of one group are members of another can be expressed in notation as follows:

All S are P	a positive universal proposition
No S are P	a negative universal proposition
Some S is/are P	a positive particular proposition
Some S are not P	a negative particular proposition

2 A technique for setting out propositions in predicate form involves:
   a) Specifying the universe of discourse, possibly *things*.
   b) Identifying and defining the subject term, 'S'.
   c) Identifying and defining the predicate term, 'P'.
   d) Expressing the claim in notation to make explicit its predicate form.
3 Each basic proposition in predicate form has a corresponding Venn diagram.

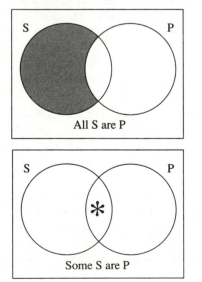

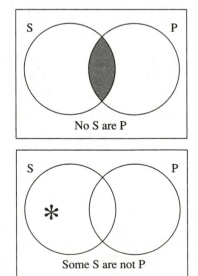

4 Reference to Venn diagrams helps to confirm the predicate form of ordinary language expressions, especially in difficult text.

5 The word 'only' reverses the subject and predicate terms in a proposition. 'Only S are P' means the same as 'All P are S'.

6 Presenting an argument in notation to make explicit its predicate form involves:

   a) Identifying the conclusion and premises by marking a copy of the text.

   b) Setting out the argument in the 'R ⇒ C' notation.

   c) Establishing a key for 'S', 'P' and 'M'.

   d) For each claim, deciding which Venn diagram is appropriate.

   e) Making explicit the argument form by substituting symbols for text when setting out the premises and conclusion.

7 The symbols 'p', 'q', 'r', etc. stand for individual propositions.

8 The basic set of logical connectives can be expressed in notation to make their respective propositional forms explicit:

negation	not p
conjunction	p and q
disjunction	p or q
material conditional	if p then q

9 Basic arguments having propositional form normally have two premises, one of which is a composite claim comprising two propositions logically connected and a conclusion.

6 Establishing validity

When arguments are valid, conclusions must follow from the premises. One way to establish whether a conclusion follows from its premises is to check its consistency by asking, 'Could a rational person accept the reasons and deny the conclusion?' More exact approaches to establish the validity of arguments are also available. For arguments in propositional form, the patterns of reasoning are compared with those argument forms which logicians have shown to be valid. Venn diagrams are used to establish the validity of arguments in predicate form.[1] We conclude with a discussion of the role of value judgements in the context of valid reasoning.

BEING CONSISTENT

The notion of what a rational person would think is a curious one. It suggests that absolute standards are available by which to judge whether reasoning is consistent. Probably, such people and standards do not exist. Nevertheless, inconsistency is generally thought to be irrational. Contradiction is one kind of inconsistency. Asserting the contradiction 'p and not-p' is inconsistent. But asserting a claim at one time and its opposite at another time is permissible because a change of mind or circumstances might explain the difference. Economists sometimes refer to a *rational person* who behaves consistently sensibly. Model people embody prevalent views about rational thought and behaviour. Yet, some academics, including the anthropologist, Lévy-Bruhl (1923), have attempted to establish that some primitive societies both permit contradictions and are rational in ordinary discourse.[2] Whatever the outcome of that debate, critical thinking is characterised by the fact that consistency is upheld. To deny the conclusion of a valid argument, whilst accepting the reasons, is to be inconsistent.

The concept of *entailment* means that the conclusion is contained in its premises and makes explicit what is already implicit. Thus, denying a valid conclusion is inconsistent because the denial rejects what is claimed by the reasons taken together. Equally, accepting the premises implies acceptance of all that is entailed by them. Rejecting a valid conclusion amounts to not accepting at least one premise.

Look again at the earlier argument about nuclear power stations:

Example 6.1

R_{1a} $\boxed{\text{Because}}$, as assumed,
       [All radiation discharged into the environment is dangerous.]
& $\boxed{\text{and}}$$\boxed{\text{because}}$, as stated,
R_{2s} [Nuclear power stations discharge radiation into the environment.]
$\Rightarrow$ $\boxed{\text{Therefore}}$,
C <u>Nuclear power stations are dangerous.</u>

Consider the question, 'Could a rational person accept the reasons and deny the conclusion?'. Its purpose is to establish whether the reasons entail the conclusion. If so, the conclusion cannot be denied.

There are problems in spotting entailment. A strategy is required for detecting this feature of valid reasoning. Reading the argument carefully sometimes works, and probably does with Example 6.1, but this strategy presupposes that one's rational instincts are in tune with those of the mythical rational person. One difficulty is that the question requires a negative answer to positively establish that an inference is valid. Furthermore, the reliance on rational instincts makes the outcome relative to conventional wisdom about what rationality means. Despite the difficulties, two considerations make attempts to answer the question worthwhile. First, human beings are by nature rational and instincts are often trustworthy. Second, some features of valid reasoning offer strategies which improve the chances of spotting entailment. These are now considered.

Consistency rules out the denial of a conclusion which is validly deduced from its premises. This is the power of a valid inference and suggests that valid conclusions are *forced*. It is possible therefore to reformulate the question in these terms, 'Does the acceptance of premises force acceptance of the conclusion?'. This version has the advantage that a positive answer means that the inference is valid. Accepting the reasons demands acceptance of the conclusion. For example, a moment's thought makes it clear that, in Example 6.1, accepting the reasons does force acceptance of the conclusion that 'nuclear power stations are dangerous'. This approach may be more helpful but the technique still depends on instinct and is relative to conventional wisdom about what counts as rational.

Though the above approach is tentative, with practice it can produce satisfactory critical appraisals. Reconsider the argument from paragraph 5.17 of the Black Report, now presented in Example 6.2:

Example 6.2

	Because , as stated,
R_{2s}	[The doses received by the population around Sellafield, which allegedly account for the additional cases of leukaemia in the area, are causally insufficient.]
&	and because , as assumed,
R_{3a}	[Causal insufficiency does not mean proven.]
⇒	Therefore ,
C_m	The suggestion that in the neighbourhood of Sellafield there is a causal relationship between an increased level of radioactivity and an above-average experience of leukaemia, while it is possible, is by no means proven.

Using the methods outlined above, we present an analysis in these terms. First, the conclusion that 'the suggestion . . . is by no means proven' is *forced* by the considerations that [causal insufficiency does not mean proven] and that [the doses received . . . are causally insufficient]. The point is reinforced because to deny that 'the suggestion . . . is by no means proven' would be *inconsistent*. We cannot resist the conclusion that 'the suggestion . . . is by no means proven'. The power of this case is impressive and it is not surprising that many were reassured by the Black Report.

MODEL PROPOSITIONAL FORMS

Logical theory provides models of valid reasoning that can be used as aids to critical appraisal.[3] The models are set out in propositional form and the text of any reasoning, amenable to presentation in this form, may be compared with them for purposes of analysis.

Reaffirming the given

Reaffirming a given claim is to make an *immediate* inference, moving directly from one proposition to another. Such reasoning states the obvious. For example, '"Nuclear installations are dangerous" implies that "Nuclear installations are dangerous"'. This sentence has the propositional form, 'p ⇒ p'. Entailment is painfully evident but consider the following claim:

People's lives are seriously threatened by the existence of devices designed to capture energy released from the disintegration of the positively charged central portion of atoms.

This version contains over six times as many words as the claim that 'nuclear power stations are dangerous'. Only the word 'are' is common to both. Even the order of ideas is reversed in so far as 'dangerous' comes at the end of the first sentence but an equivalent phrase begins the second. In different ways, each asserts the same proposition. They mean the same thing and the same state of affairs would render both assertions acceptable. Thus, the two versions, taken together, are a less obvious example of 'p ⇒ p'.

The *conjunction* of two claims is formally 'p & q', where conventionally the letters 'p' and 'q' stand for different propositions and '&' is the logical connective. It is possible to draw an immediate inference from a conjunction. The conclusion, 'p', is entirely consistent with the premise, 'p & q', because it reaffirms part of what is stated in the premise. Example 6.3 is typical:

Example 6.3

R   [p [Political change is imminent.]
&   and ,
      q [The Liberal Democrats won a seat in the European parliament.]]
⇒   Therefore ,
C   p Political change is imminent.

Again, it states the obvious and is expressed formally as:

[p & q] ⇒ p

The conclusion of a *case-in-point* argument reaffirms the given premise in respect of a specific instance and requires no further support. Example 4.8 is typical, though wordy. It is represented as Example 6.4:

Example 6.4

     Because , as stated,
R_{ls} [The causes of leukaemia are not fully established.]
⇒   Therefore ,

C_m   The suggestion that in the neighbourhood of Sellafield there is a causal relationship between an increased level of radioactivity and an above-average experience of leukaemia, while it is possible, is by no means proven.

Another kind of immediate inference may occur when the disjunction 'or' is used. Such claims are formally expressed as '$p \lor q$', where '$\lor$' stands for 'or' which can mean 'one or the other and possibly both'. The phrase 'possibly both' gives 'or' its *inclusive* sense. For instance, saying that '[[it will rain] or [the sun will shine]]', is consistent with the experience of both happening at the same time. When they do, it is a spectacle to behold. The *exclusive* interpretation of 'or', namely, 'one or the other and not both', plays a different role in reasoning. Reference to sense and context is required to tell the difference. In the rain or sun example, experience suggests the inclusive interpretation. Stating that a student will pass or fail an examination suggests the exclusive interpretation.

Affirming or denying an option

The exclusive interpretation of the expression [$p \lor q$] does not permit immediate inferences. It requires a second premise before a valid conclusion may be drawn. The first premise offers two options, 'p' or 'q', and the second premise either affirms or denies one of them. The four possibilities are distinguished from each other by the role of the respective second premise. *Affirming* one option *rules out* the other, giving a negative conclusion. *Denying* one option *rules in* the other, giving a positive conclusion. Using the symbol $\sim$ for not, the four valid propositional argument forms are as follows:

1	$[[p \lor q] \& p] \Rightarrow \sim q$	affirming an option
2	$[[p \lor q] \& q] \Rightarrow \sim p$	affirming an option
3	$[[p \lor q] \& \sim p] \Rightarrow q$	denying an option
4	$[[p \lor q] \& \sim q] \Rightarrow p$	denying an option

Consider an example of 'or' in its exclusive sense. When a footballer, available for transfer, can sign a contract to play for Arsenal or Liverpool but it turns out that he cannot sign for Liverpool, it follows that he can sign for Arsenal. Context suggests the exclusive 'or' and the reasoning is formally expressed as $[[p \lor q] \& \sim q] \Rightarrow p$. By ringing the changes, examples of the other versions of affirming and denying an option can be constructed. Any propositional argument in each of these forms is valid, no matter how complicated. Now suppose that one disjoined option were negative, having the form [p v ~q]. A second premise, [~q], would then affirm an option and the valid reasoning would be expressed as [[p v ~q] & [~q]] ⇒ ~p. Negation can be tricky but with care it can be accurately expressed.

Affirming the antecedent

Example 5.4, the argument about 'Christopher Leslie being elected when very young', is formally expressed as follows:

[[If p then q] & [p]] thus , q.

A conditional relationship between 'p' and 'q' is asserted in the first premise. The word 'if' signals that the specified claim, 'p', is sufficient to justify asserting 'q'. The sufficient condition is called the *antecedent* and the resulting claim is called the *consequent*. There is a relationship of implication between the two propositions. Therefore, the first premise can be read as 'p implies q', which in notation is [p ⇒ q]. In text, 'if p then q' sometimes appears as 'q if p'. These two expressions are logically equivalent, having the propositional form [p ⇒ q]. The second premise asserts 'p', which is *affirming the antecedent*. Together with the conclusion, 'q', the argument in propositional form reads:

[[p ⇒ q] & p] ⇒ q

Jean McSorley presents the story of 'the people of Sellafield', citing Professor Body, who 'believes radiation from Sellafield has to be considered in relation to other sources of radiation' (McSorley 1990: 149–52). Example 6.5 is the text of his statement about the cancer-link controversy, conventionally marked to reveal its conditional form:

Example 6.5

[If [people insist on saying that radiation must be the sole cause and other things are not looked at] then [we're missing a vital opportunity to find out what might be the cause of any additional childhood leukaemias].]

This extract is a single assertion, formally expressed as [p ⇒ q]. It is not an argument. Body does not explicitly affirm the antecedent nor does he draw the consequent as the conclusion. McSorley's contextualisation of Body's argument leads the reader to believe that [people do insist on saying those things] and thereby conclude the consequent that we are missing vital opportunities.

Denying the consequent

Starting with a conditional premise, if the consequent is subsequently denied then to deny the antecedent is a valid inference. Example 6.6 is a caricature of Body's argument which might have been made, had the consequent been denied:

Example 6.6

	Because ,
R₁	[If p, [people were to insist on saying what Body claims],
	then q, [vital opportunities would be missed].]
&	and because ,
R₂	[∼q, vital opportunities are not being missed.]
⇒	Therefore ,
C	∼p, people have not insisted on saying such things.

The propositional form is expressed as:

$$[[p \Rightarrow q] \text{ \& } \sim q] \Rightarrow \sim p$$

Without help from context, it is impossible to say which of the two valid arguments is being presented. If Body does not complete his argument, as he did not, then consistency would permit either conclusion. In this instance, McSorley's contextualisation leads the reader to affirm the antecedent.

NECESSARY OR SUFFICIENT CONDITIONS

The standard and explicit conditional connective is the one mostly used, namely, 'if . . . then . . .'. Others include the following:

. . . on the condition that . . .	. . . provided that . . .
. . . subject to . . .	suppose . . . then . . .
whenever . . . then . . .	

Normally, it is not difficult to tell whether propositions are connected conditionally but the words 'only' and 'unless' require further scrutiny because they often cause confusion.

Only

Consider the impact of the word 'only' on the meaning of the conditional claim in Example 6.7:

Example 6.7

Only if [they gain seats in the south],
[will the Labour Party win the general election].

What follows from this claim depends on how it is to be understood. Commonly, it is incorrectly taken to mean that gaining southern seats is *sufficient* to guarantee a Labour victory but this interpretation seems to ignore the word 'only'. Taking a different view, 'only' plausibly suggests that gaining southern seats is *necessary* for Labour's victory. Under this interpretation, the claim can be formally expressed as 'only if p then q'. This is closer to what is meant but it implies that 'winning the general election' is the antecedent. This reverses the direction of the implication.[4] The result is that 'only if p then q' is correctly expressed as [q $\Rightarrow$ p].

The addition of the word 'only' completely changes the nature of a conditional claim. 'If p then q' implies that an occurrence of p is *sufficient* for an occurrence of q. 'Only if p then q' implies that p is *necessary* for the occurrence of q. Failure to understand the difference between a necessary and a sufficient condition can be the cause of much confusion. For example, in the 1970s, the doctrine of monetarism gained ascendancy in economics. This led to heated debates about the relationship between increases in the money supply and inflation. Many agreed that the two phenomena are related but should increases in the money supply be understood as a necessary or as a sufficient condition for inflation? The answer has implications for the design of monetary policy.

The use of the word 'only' has another consequence. It is possible to articulate formidable claims by the conjunction of the standard implication, [p $\Rightarrow$ q], and the reversed implication, [q $\Rightarrow$ p]. The result is a complex claim where 'p' implies 'q' and 'q' implies 'p'. In these circumstances, p is both a sufficient and a necessary condition for q. The two-way implication makes the claim *bi-conditional*, indicated in ordinary language by the words 'if and only if . . . then . . .'. This is sometimes formally expressed as 'iff . . . then . . .'. Example 6.8 is a bi-conditional claim:

Example 6.8

[The Soviet Union will make real progress towards democracy]
if and only if [every Russian has a genuine conversion].

Again, the text does not contain the helpful consequence indicator, 'then', but there is no doubt that the conditional antecedent is '[every Russian has a genuine conversion]'. The correct propositional form of this claim is $[[p \Rightarrow q] \& [q \Rightarrow p]]$. But each proposition can be either antecedent or consequent with the result that there are four valid argument forms containing a bi-conditional premise. From $[[p \Rightarrow q] \& [q \Rightarrow p]]$, it follows that:

1 affirming p	justifies concluding q
2 denying q	justifies not concluding p
3 affirming q	justifies concluding p
4 denying p	justifies not concluding q

Bi-conditional claims present a logically secure basis for all these arguments.

At this stage, it is worth commenting on what Fogelin (1978: 140) describes as 'the conversational force' of conditional reasoning. He states that the bi-conditional claim, [if and only if] p [then] q], with the propositional form $[[p \Rightarrow q] \& [q \Rightarrow p]]$, 'is more often conversationally implied than explicitly stated in everyday discourse'. This means that the subtleties of ordinary language must be taken seriously by following conventions and noting sense and context, as we discussed in Chapter 3. There can be no method which guarantees one interpretation against others because language has a living dynamic which changes with time, place and circumstances. Spotting clues of any kind is crucial in detecting whether [if] p [then] q] has the conversational force of a bi-conditional claim. It is more likely to be conversationally implied by [only if] p [then] q] but it depends on the point of the argument.

Unless

'Unless' is another tricky word that features in conditional reasoning and requires care to interpret its use correctly. Consider a revised version of Example 6.8, about the Labour Party, presented as Example 6.9:

Example 6.9

[Unless] [they gain seats in the south], [then]
[the Labour Party will [not] win the general election].

The conversational force of this revision seems stronger than the original, Example 6.8, and suggests that the claim is bi-conditional. The word 'unless', in combination with the negated consequent, tends to confirm this interpretation. However, it would be inaccurate to regard this example as a bi-conditional claim. The logical words 'unless ... then ... not ...' mirror the words 'only if ... then ...'. In this case, the antecedent, 'p', namely, to 'gain seats in the south' is regarded as a necessary condition for the consequent, 'q', namely, 'winning the general election'. Thus, Example 6.9 has the propositional form, [q $\Rightarrow$ p]. In practice, 'unless . . . not . . .' has the same impact on conditional claims as the word 'only'. Both reverse the implication. Whatever the *implications*, affirming the antecedent and denying the consequent are valid argument forms. The basic features of conditional reasoning are as follows:

1 Affirming the antecedent is valid:

$$[[p \Rightarrow q] \& p] \Rightarrow q$$

2 Denying the consequent is valid:

$$[[p \Rightarrow q] \& \sim q] \Rightarrow \sim p$$

3 'Only' and 'unless . . . not . . .' reverse implication. Thus the following are valid forms of reasoning:

$[[q \Rightarrow p] \& q] \Rightarrow p$, affirming the antecedent
$[[q \Rightarrow p] \& \sim p] \Rightarrow \sim q$, denying the consequent

4 Bi-conditional claims have the propositional form, $[[p \Rightarrow q]$ $\& [q \Rightarrow p]]$. In such cases, p and q are both necessary and sufficient conditions for each other.
5 What is meant or *conversationally implied* is often different from what is stated.

The models of entailment outlined above guide the search for valid propositional reasoning.

VENN DIAGRAMS

Simple arguments in predicate form contain three claims. Venn diagrams present them all visually in the same picture. There are several ways in which this might be done but the method used by Fogelin (1978) is preferred. Figure 6.1 displays a diagram, comprising three interlocking circles, one for each group in the universe of discourse. Venn diagram analysis requires first, that each reason is coded into the diagram and second, that the diagram is interpreted. Conventions for coding claims into the diagram were introduced in Chapter 5. Interpretation is a matter of reading the coded diagram accurately. There are seven segments inside the circles and one outside them but inside the box. The box contains the universe of discourse, which stipulates what the argument is about.

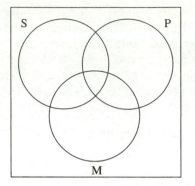

Figure 6.1   Universe of discourse

Reconsider Example 5.1, set out as Example 6.10:

Example 6.10

|Because|,
R₁   [Twenty-two year old councillors are rare politicians.]
& |and||because|,
R₂   [Christopher Leslie was a councillor at twenty-two.]
⇒ |Therefore|
C   Christopher Leslie is a rare politician.

Using methods described in Chapter 5, the argument is formally expressed as:

All M are P.
Some S is M.
|Thus| Some S is P.

Figure 6.2 presents the Venn diagram, using the conventions described earlier. Two pieces of information are specified in the diagram, one for each of the reasons. Both segments of 'M' outside 'P' are shaded out to signify that 'all M are P'. An asterisk is placed in the only available segment of 'S' that is inside 'M', which shows that 'some S is M'. It is wise to code universal premises first because this simplifies the locating of an asterisk. Notice that the conclusion has not been entered into the figure. Understanding why only the reasons are coded is to grasp the concept of entailment. Valid arguments entail their conclusions. This means that a conclusion is contained in the supporting premises. In other words, conclusions make explicit

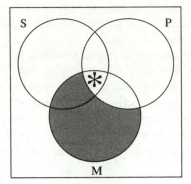

Figure 6.2 Venn diagram for Example 6.10

what is implied by them. The Venn diagram is then examined to see whether the conclusion is displayed, without the need for further amendment. Given the conclusion 'some S is P', there should be an asterisk in a segment of 'S' that is inside 'P'. The asterisk in Figure 6.2 is located precisely there. Consequently, the conclusion is entailed by the reasons and the inference is valid.

This interpretation can be checked by drawing a separate two-circle diagram for the conclusion and comparing it with the larger one. Figure 6.3 gives a simple diagram for the conclusion 'some S is P'.

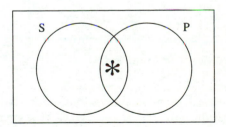

Figure 6.3 Conclusion of Example 6.10

Notice that the asterisk may lie anywhere within the segment of 'S' that is inside 'P'. In Figure 6.2, this overlapping area comprises two segments because the third circle for 'M' bisects it. All that is required to establish entailment is that an asterisk appears in a part of 'S' that lies inside 'P'. Provided that only the premises have been coded, the appropriate appearance of the asterisk visually demonstrates the argument's validity. It does in this case.

Example 4.9, the cancer-link argument from the Black Report, is a more difficult case. Problems in identifying the argument arose because an important premise was not explicit in the text. Provided that the argument has been correctly identified and expressed in predicate form, demonstrating whether it is valid by using Venn diagram analysis is just as easy as with less difficult ones. It is unnecessary to set out the cancer-link argument again. Its predicate form is as follows:

> Some S is M.
> No M are P.
> Thus, Some S is not P.

Again, using the conventions described earlier, Figure 6.4 presents the Venn diagram.

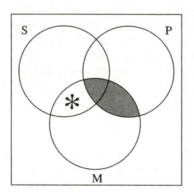

Figure 6.4   Venn diagram for Example 4.9

Coding the universal premise shades out both parts of the M–P segment. As a result, only one of the two S–M segments is available for the asterisk. This happens to be a part of 'S' outside 'P' and is exactly what the conclusion requires. Consequently, the conclusion is entailed by the supporting reasons. The cancer-link argument presented by Black is demonstrably valid.

There are 256 predicate argument forms but only fifteen are valid. All fifteen can be displayed in eight Venn diagrams. The valid predicate forms set out in Appendix II can be used to check the validity of such arguments. The stages of a Venn diagram analysis are listed as follows:

1 Identify the conclusion and premises from the text.
2 Set out the argument in 'R $\Rightarrow$ C' notation.
3 Establish a key for 'S', 'P' and 'M'.
4 Set out the argument formally by substituting letters for text.
5 Display the premises by coding a Venn diagram.
6 Interpret the figure – note that the argument is valid if the conclusion is displayed in the diagram without amendment, otherwise it is invalid.

Many arguments in predicate form comprise several stages. Provided that each stage is identified and evaluated in turn, the Venn diagram method can be used to establish the validity of complex arguments encountered in the social sciences. When used together with the fallacy indicators presented in Chapter 7 (see pp. 76–9) the technique is a powerful aid to critical thinking.

RECOGNISING VALUES

Normative claims are statements of *what ought to be* rather than statements of *fact*. For example, asserting that 'fox hunting should be outlawed' is a statement presupposing particular *values* concerning such activities.[5] Alternatively, the claim that 'fox hunting is a blood sport' is a statement about the *world*. This type of statement is called an *empirical claim*. Reference to the facts normally settles disputes about empirical claims. However, normative claims are not settled by appealing to the facts alone. They are based on the value judgements we make about what is good and bad. Different people have different opinions about what is right and wrong and ultimately they may have to agree to differ.

There are words which may indicate that normative issues are at stake. Such words include 'right', 'wrong', 'good', 'bad', 'fair', 'unjust', 'should' and 'ought'. In these circumstances, values normally underpin any reasoning involved. However, the use of such words does not guarantee that a claim is normative. For instance, in some situations *a good economic policy* may be one which as *a matter of fact* satisfies specific fiscal requirements. In this case the word 'good' is shorthand for a factual description of the policy. It is said to possess recognisable features. In other situations, 'a good economic policy' may be one that squares with a value judgement, for example, that low inflation is better than low unemployment, assuming that both cannot occur at the same time. Reference to context often clarifies whether a claim is normative or empirical. Students and researchers are naturally inclined to take a normative stance on various issues in which social scientists have an interest, for example, child abuse, nuclear power and health care. Recognising values and the role that normative claims play in reasoning are fundamental to critical thinking about the issues. Consider Example 6.11:

Example 6.11

	Because ,
R₁	[Blood sports should be outlawed.]
&	and because ,
R₂	[Fox hunting is a blood sport.]
⇒	Therefore ,
C	Fox hunting should be outlawed.

This argument is formally expressed as follows:

All M should be P.
Some S is M.
Thus, Some S should be P.

Notice that 'fox hunting' is 'some sport, namely, fox hunting'. Hence, the claim has the positive, particular, predicate form which implies that the sport goes on in the world. The reasoning is valid, as shown in Figure 6.5.

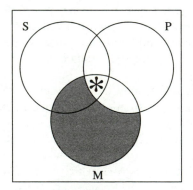

Figure 6.5   Venn diagram for Example 6.11

The normative force of the conclusion can be traced back to R₁ which is a normative claim containing the word 'should'. Since valid conclusions make explicit what is contained in the premises, had R_1 claimed *as a matter of fact* that 'blood sports *are* outlawed', then the lack of normative import in the premises would logically preclude its occurrence in the conclusion. Provided that at least one of the premises is a normative claim then it is in principle possible to legitimately conclude a normative statement from a valid line of reasoning. With this proviso, reasoning which includes normative claims is possible and the social scientist can include values in critical thinking about social issues.

SUMMARY

1 Consistency rules out the denial of a validly deduced conclusion.
2 Informal approaches to establishing consistency include:
   a) Asking the question, 'Does the acceptance of the premises force acceptance of the conclusion?' Note that an affirmative answer indicates validity.
   b) Spelling out the argument more carefully.
3 Valid propositional argument forms include:
   a) Reaffirming the given.
   b) Affirming an option.
   c) Denying an option.
   d) Affirming the antecedent.
   e) Denying the consequent.
4 The logical words 'only' and 'unless . . . not' reverse the implication and give the following alternative valid propositional argument forms:
   a) Affirming the antecedent:

$$[[q \Rightarrow p] \& q] \Rightarrow p$$

   b) Denying the consequent:

$$[[q \Rightarrow p] \& \sim p] \Rightarrow \sim q$$

5 The logical words 'if and only if . . .' signal bi-conditional premises having the propositional form, $[p \Rightarrow q] \& [q \Rightarrow p]$. Such powerful reasons generate four basic versions of valid propositional argument form, for example:

$$[[[p \Rightarrow q] \& [q \Rightarrow p]] \& p] \Rightarrow q$$

In such cases, p and q are both necessary and sufficient conditions for each other.

6 Venn diagram analysis can be used to establish the validity of arguments with predicate form. The procedure is as follows:
   a) Identify the conclusion and premises from the text.
   b) Set out the argument in 'R ⇒ C' notation.
   c) Establish a key for 'S', 'P' and 'M'.
   d) Set out the argument formally by substituting letters for text.
   e) Display the premises by coding a Venn diagram.
   f) Interpret the figure – note that the argument is valid if the conclusion is displayed in the diagram without amendment, otherwise it is invalid.
7 A normative claim is a statement about what ought to be and presupposes particular *values* concerning the activities involved.
8 Conclusions which are normative claims require at least one normative premise.

7 Critical analysis in practice

Any argument whose premises do not entail the conclusion can be rejected as illogical. However, valid inference alone does not ensure that an argument is sound. Detecting a fallacy or other inconsistency is normally sufficient to discredit a line of reasoning without further examination. Identifying an undeclared claim clarifies an argument to facilitate critical appraisal. Deductive analysis also works positively to make a logical case which presents a sharpened focus on the role of evidence.

THE LIMITATIONS OF VALID INFERENCE

A valid argument might have the predicate form and Venn diagram of Figure 7.1.

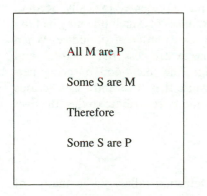
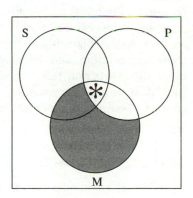

Figure 7.1   A valid argument form

Some curious arguments fit this pattern of reasoning. Example 7.1

illustrates that valid arguments can be constructed from obvious falsehoods:

Example 7.1

	Because ,	
R₁	[Everyone over twelve years old is a teenager.]	
&	and because ,	
R₂	[Some babies are over twelve years old.]	
⇒	Therefore ,	
C	Some babies are teenagers.	

Example 7.2 is more worrying because its conclusion is plausible:

Example 7.2

	Because ,	
R₁	[All single-parent mothers claim social security benefits.]	
&	and because ,	
R₂	[Louise is a single-parent mother.]	
⇒	Therefore ,	
C	Louise claims social security benefits.	

Though this argument is valid, R_1 is a premise that is false even though it might appeal to a prejudice that some people hold. Consequently, the reasoning is unsound.

An argument's validity sometimes misleads us into believing that unsound reasoning is to be taken seriously. The failure to satisfy the acceptability requirement for premises takes many subtle forms. Our somewhat contrived examples illustrate what can go wrong with reasoning. First, blatant falsehoods can be presented logically. Second, plausible claims can be entailed by premises of which one may be false and yet appear plausible or be held as a matter of prejudice. When style, presentation and language usage are less than helpful and especially when one lacks knowledge, the likelihood of being persuaded by unsound arguments – because they are valid – is a serious concern. Considerations other than validity contribute to the effectiveness of reasoning.

DETECTING FALLACIES

A *fallacy* is an invalid inference. Detecting fallacies is a matter of spotting that a pattern of valid reasoning has been broken. In Chapter 6, several common patterns were presented in ways that help to define errors of argument in both propositional and predicate styles of reasoning.

In propositional form

Although affirming the antecedent is a valid propositional argument form, making an inference on the basis of *denying the antecedent* is a fallacy. Consider the motion tabled by the National Association of Probation Officers at the Trades Union Congress in September 1990 at Blackpool. It sought to change TUC policy which recommended that individuals should pay the poll tax. One argument which captures some aspects of NAPO's case is set out in Example 7.3:

Example 7.3

R₁   Because ,
     [If p, [We agree with the poll tax legislation],
     then q, [we should pay the poll tax].]
&   but because .
R₂   [~ p, We do not agree with the poll tax legislation.]
⇒   Therefore ,
C   ~ q, We should not pay the poll tax.

R₂ denies the antecedent and renders the inference invalid because the conditional premise fails to rule out other possible reasons sufficient to justify paying the poll tax. For instance, the primacy of the rule of law may be considered paramount. This is typical of how long and sometimes difficult debates begin. It is worth remembering that NAPO's case is not completely flawed by the fallacy. It simply means that this line of reasoning is not available to those wanting to justify civil disobedience. Different arguments, satisfying both criteria for soundness, would be required to defend that position.

Three common fallacy indicators in propositional reasoning are listed as follows:

1 Denying the given.
2 Denying the antecedent.
3 Affirming the consequent.

In predicate form

One fallacy indicator in predicate form is that *all premises are negative*. Consider Example 7.4:

Example 7.4

	Because ,
R₁	[Some politicians do not take bribes to ask questions in the House.]
&	and because ,
R₂	[No-one who is trustworthy takes bribes.]
⇒	Therefore ,
C	<u>Some politicians are not trustworthy</u>.

Both premises are formally presented as negative in Figure 7.2. The invalidity of such arguments is corroborated by Venn diagram analysis. First, indicate the universal, negative premise, 'no P are M', by shading the two segments where the P and M circles overlap. Second, an asterisk is required to show the Ss that are not Ms. Since there are two unshaded segments of the S circle which lie outside M it is not clear where the asterisk should be placed. This is because one of the two possible locations is not ruled out by the shading for the universal premise. Thus, by convention, the asterisk is placed on the boundary as in Figure 7.2. It should now be clear that the conclusion does not *necessarily* follow from the two premises. For the argument to be valid, the asterisk would have to be unambiguously in the segment of S outside M and P and this is not the case.

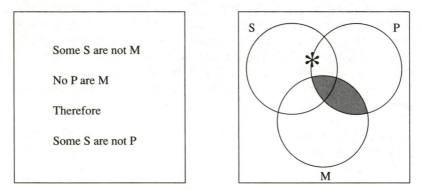

Some S are not M	
No P are M	
Therefore	
Some S are not P	

Figure 7.2   The 'all negative premises' fallacy

A 'worst case' assumption is required when interpreting Venn diagrams. In this case, not knowing the location of the asterisk is taken to mean that the reasons do not entail the conclusion. Nothing follows from two negative premises.

Example 7.4 illustrates what is involved in detecting a fallacy in predicate form. Five conditions when reasoning in predicate form inevitably lead to fallacy:

1 All premises are particular.
2 All premises are negative.
3 There is at least one negative premise and a positive conclusion.
4 All premises are universal and there is a particular conclusion.
5 A term is illicitly distributed.

Confirmation by Venn diagram analysis that each of the above types of syllogism is invalid would reveal that the first two have asterisks on boundaries. The third has an asterisk in the wrong place and the fourth has no asterisk, despite having a particular conclusion. The first four fallacy indicators can be spotted in their respective formal expressions and Venn diagram analysis is not required, though it provides an additional check. Illicit distribution is a technical matter that requires more attention. When none of the first four conditions apply but the Venn diagram shows that the reasoning is invalid then illicit distribution must be the reason. Were a fallacy indicator present in the formal expression of the argument then it would be difficult, without reference to logic books, to say that the argument was invalid by virtue of illicit distribution. This is not a problem because only one fallacy is sufficient to invalidate an argument and further analysis to discover other fallacies is unnecessary for most purposes of critical appraisal. Critical thinking requires only that fallacy indicators are known and an ability to detect them.

NON-FALLACIOUS INCONSISTENCIES

Some inconsistencies in reasoning do not amount to fallacies even though they are frequently called 'fallacies' in ordinary language. One typical example occurs when definitions are changed. For instance, governments may change what counts as being 'unemployed'. This is sometimes called *massaging statistics* for political advantage. Though annoying, it is not a fallacy. Rather it is a matter of personal or corporate inconsistency, which changes the basis on which evidence is collected. Two other kinds of non-fallacious inconsistency are worth mentioning.

The pathetic fallacy

According to Flew, the pathetic fallacy 'refers to the mistake of believing that something, which is not a person at all, nevertheless has plans and purposes and feelings such as only a person could have' (Flew 1975: para. 1.49).

This *so-called fallacy* involves thinking and talking about one thing as though it were something quite different. For example, non-persons may be mistakenly categorised as persons. This kind of error is called a *category mistake*. It may be bewildering or silly – as in the assertion that 'Green ideas sleep furiously' – but the mistake is not a fallacy. In a broader discussion about meaningfulness, the treatment of category mistakes by Hospers mentions several thought-provoking examples, including:

The number 7 is blue.
Quadratic equations go to horse races.

(Hospers 1970: 89)

He explains the error in these terms:

If someone claimed that he had tasted a smell or smelled a taste, he would be guilty of a category mistake. Whatever you smell, whether it is acrid or pungent or stale, it is always a smell and not a taste. Smell words apply to smells and taste words apply to tastes.

(Hospers 1970: 89–91)

Although category mistakes make life difficult they are never fallacious.

Absurdity

Sometimes we say things which are not obviously inconsistent but which are nevertheless absurd. Take for instance the view that 'the British weather is always unpredictable'. By definition, a claim standing alone could not be a fallacy since an inference comprises several statements including premises and a conclusion. The inconsistency in the claim about the British weather is that if the weather is *always* unpredictable then there is one feature that is predictable, namely, its unpredictability. In other words, the *absurdity* of an assertion is that it implies a contradictory claim. Suppose that it were claimed that 'all claims are false'. This statement makes an assertion about claims in general. Consequently, the assertion of falsity must apply to the sentence which makes this claim. That is, the truth of the claim that 'all claims are false', implies its own falsity. This is formally expressed as $p \Rightarrow \sim p$ which is absurd. Because the absurdity of a claim can be established on purely logical grounds, futile discussion can be avoided and arguments containing such claims rejected.

IDENTIFYING UNDECLARED CLAIMS

Arguments are occasionally difficult to evaluate because one of the claims is not explicit. Identifying undeclared claims clarifies the detail of an argument prior to critical appraisal. Deductive analysis can be applied to identify the undeclared reasons which have been assumed or the undeclared conclusion implied by an incomplete line of reasoning.

Undeclared reasons

The task is to make explicit whatever must be asserted to force acceptance of the conclusion. Reconsider the incomplete argument in Example 2.1, represented as Example 7.5:

Example 7.5

	Because ,
R	[Nuclear power stations discharge radiation into the environment.]
⇒	Therefore ,
C	Nuclear power stations are dangerous.

The conclusion's subject term, 'S', is 'nuclear power stations' and its predicate term, 'P', is 'dangerous things'. The premise provides the middle term, 'M', as things which 'discharge radiation into the environment'. The incomplete argument is formally expressed with its Venn diagram in Figure 7.3.

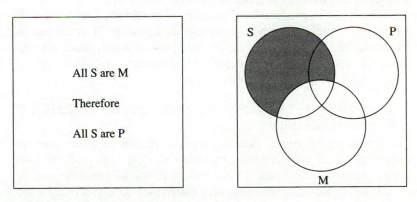

All S are M

Therefore

All S are P

Figure 7.3　Incomplete reasoning

To justify the conclusion 'All S are P', the undeclared premise must assert a relationship between M and P. Furthermore, validity requires that the unshaded segment of the S circle outside P must be ruled out. Consequently, the missing expression is the positive, universal claim, 'All M are P'. It literally claims that 'all discharges of radiation into the environment are dangerous'.[1] The completed predicate form and Venn diagram are shown in Figure 7.4.

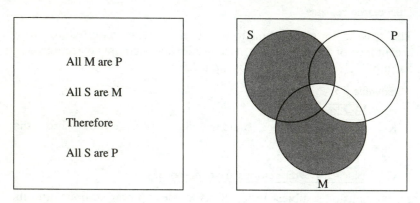

All M are P

All S are M

Therefore

All S are P

Figure 7.4   Completed argument

This deductive technique for clarifying what is assumed and unstated sharpens the focus for critical appraisal. In Chapter 2, we suggested that evidence might show that it was not the case that 'all discharges of radiation into the environment are dangerous' and, to that extent, although valid the argument's soundness is questioned.

Similarly, valid propositional patterns of reasoning help to identify a logically required but undeclared reason. Example 7.6 is the text of an incomplete argument, typical in newspapers, which presumes that the reader can work out and accept what is taken for granted:

Example 7.6

[Because] [they won the general election] the Labour Party [must] have gained seats in the south.

The boxed logical words indicate that the reason is, '[they won the general election]' and that the conclusion is, 'The Labour Party have gained seats in the south'. The reason is an affirmation and, in conditional arguments, *affirming the antecedent* is a valid move. Hence, the text presents a condensed version of the valid argument form, [[p ⇒ q] & p] ⇒ q. Inserting a conditional first premise, '[p ⇒ q]', into the text, the complete argument reads:

[If [the Labour Party win the general election] then [they will have gained seats in the south]] and [they did win the general election] so the Labour Party have gained seats in the south.

Having identified the undeclared reason, further analysis focuses on whether political scientists can produce evidence sufficient to accept the assumed conditional claim. In this sense, empirical inquiry rather than logical analysis ultimately settles the matter. The interplay between argument and evidence is manifest and structures the design of critical appraisal.

Undeclared conclusions

Sometimes, a conclusion may be undeclared because it is thought to be obvious. The task is to specify what the reasons together imply. Consider Example 7.7:

Example 7.7

It is not surprising that [[minority groups use violence] when [there are large scale public protests]], as [there were against the poll tax in Britain during 1990].

This comment was typical of the debate in the media at the time. The essentials of the case seem not to include a conclusion. The phrase 'not surprising ' is a forcing phrase which suggests that 'minority groups use violence' is the conclusion. But the word 'when ', which functions like 'if', gives the following premise: '[[if][there are large scale public protests] then [minority groups use violence]]'. An air of generality in both claims appropriately confirms that the composite assertion is conditional. Thus, [p ⇒ q] is the propositional form. That '[there were large scale public protests against the poll tax in Britain during 1990]' affirms the antecedent and hence the best case scenario is that the argument concludes validly that 'minority groups did use violence on those occasions'.

Failure to state the conclusion in Example 7.7 may cause confusion and sometimes suspicion. Attention may be drawn away from what might be considered an implausible, conditional premise. The assertion that '[[if][there are large scale public protests] then [minority groups use violence]]' needs the support of evidence. Whether the missing claim is a premise or a conclusion, an appropriate response is to identify the claim and clarify the case argued. A strategy for doing this involves:

1 Expressing the incomplete argument formally.
2 Making the best case presumption, that the inference is valid.
3 Specifying the assertion required to ensure a valid inference.
4 Setting out the completed argument.
5 Confirming its validity.

Since, for purposes of analysis, the completed argument is made valid, a *best case* strategy ensures that the focus of critical appraisal falls on whether the premises are acceptable. Sound cases need both a valid inference and acceptable premises.

MAKING A CASE

Professionals make cases. For instance, lawyers defend clients and academics present ideas. Good advocates and teachers appreciate the interplay between argument and evidence. Helping the audience or readership to follow an argument adds considerably to the success of any case made. Skills used for this purpose can also be employed in writing essays, contributing to discussions, delivering lectures or even political speeches. Competent performances in these activities are highly regarded.[2]

Consider the following response by an undergraduate student of literature to a question, which asked her to outline the structure of the case that she had argued in a first year essay.[3] She elected to present her case as an argument, stating that 'John Donne's poems are incomprehensible [because] [they are metaphysical] [and] [metaphysical

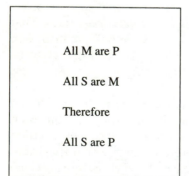

All M are P

All S are M

Therefore

All S are P

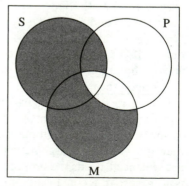

Figure 7.5 Metaphysical poetry

poems are always incomprehensible]'. The case is validly argued, as the predicate form and Venn diagram in Figure 7.5 demonstrate.

Additionally, she needs to convince the reader that she has a worthy point by establishing that the premises are acceptable. Her essay would deal almost exclusively with these tasks. First, she would try to show how the language of metaphysical poetry makes extraordinary demands on the reader, thereby making it difficult to comprehend. Second, she would demonstrate that John Donne is correctly described as a metaphysical poet. A high grade would be awarded – in so far as the premises were shown to be well grounded and entailed the conclusion – the point of her case.

Articles or lectures in the social sciences sometimes appear to be extensively detailed. Reporting facts might tell an interesting story but this is not to make a case. Control over one's material, comprising concepts and ways of thinking about the issues as well as the data, is fundamental to the presentation and critical appraisal of a case. Guidelines based on the material so far considered in this book include the following:

1 Make reference to context regarding research objectives and substantive issues. This guides the delivery or review.
2 Give clear criteria for the selection and rejection of data and methods of analysis. This keeps the work within relevant limits and facilitates appraisal by colleagues.
3 Connect the evidence logically to the point being made. This improves the likelihood that a case is effectively established.

These recommendations provide an overall strategy for critical analysis. When a sound case is made, comprising valid inferences and well grounded premises, the argument may constitute an explanation.[4] One objective of study and research in the social sciences is to produce satisfactory explanations of social events. Using these guidelines, you are invited to identify the reasoning in Box 7.1, evaluate the argument and evidence and consider what, if anything, has been explained.

Box 7.1 Crime study

Tories ignore crime study

By Terry Kirby and Glenda Cooper

Home Office ministers are ignoring the results of the most wide-ranging study yet on the links between unemployment and crime, according to a leading expert on working with young offenders.

Dr James Maguire, a clinical psychologist at Ashworth Special Hospital, Liverpool, said it was wrong to build more secure units when ministers had evidence that – contrary to claims by Michael Howard, the Home Secretary – prison does not work.

Mr Howard's Criminal Justice Bill, currently passing through Parliament, creates stiffer sentences for young offenders and new tough 'secure units' for repeat offenders. Mr Howard told the Conservative Party conference last year that 'prison works'.

Ministers' refusal to reconsider their commitment to prison for young and persistent offenders was highlighted last week when figures were released showing a fall in both unemployment and crime rates. In 1993, crime in England and Wales dropped for the first time since 1988, a fall of 1.1 per cent over the previous year. Figures show that unemployment also stopped increasing about a year ago – about the time that crime began to drop.

But at a Home Office news conference last Tuesday, David Maclean, the Home Office Minister of State, declined to make the link, and refused to comment on reports that his officials had advocated greater provision of employment as 'the single biggest intervention' likely to tackle persistent offending.

The internal briefing paper – leaked to the *Independent on Sunday* – on which senior officials based their proposal also suggests that the sense of 'relative deprivation' between rich and poor is a contributory factor to rising crime.

The *Independent on Sunday* has now established that the source of the principal message of the paper was an internal seminar on re-offending held at the Home Office in February.

During the seminar, entitled, despite the Home Secretary's public certainties, 'What works?', Dr Maguire outlined the results of the biggest-ever study on projects dealing with habitual young criminals. That 1990 study, by an American criminologist, Dr Mark Lipsey, surveyed 397 projects on working with young offenders from around the world.

Dr Maguire told the Home Office that Dr Lipsey had concluded that employment for offenders reduced repeat offending by more than one-third, but deterrence programmes, including prison sentences, increased offending, also by 30 per cent. Such research, he told the seminar, indicated 'what works'.

He said last week that it was apparent that Home Office officials were picking up the message, but politicians were ignoring it.

'It shows that it is not going to do any good to build any more secure units. Prison is counter-productive.'

The evidence of Dr Lipsey's research was that there were positive measures that could be taken to tackle juvenile crime, he said.

Research published over the past six months also confirms that unemployment and deprivation are linked to crime. Three studies – one by the Probation Service, the others at Cambridge University and the University of Middlesex – all indicate that, while no one factor causes crime, rising crime can be linked to social deprivation.

The Probation Service carried out research through its employment working group between July and December last year. Using 28,000 pre-sentence reports from around the country, it found that nearly 70 per cent of offenders were registered unemployed.

Professor Jock Young, of the University of Middlesex, said that free-market values had sown disillusionment for those trapped in poverty.

(*Independent on Sunday*, 24 April 1994)

SUMMARY

1 Valid inference alone does not ensure that an argument is sound.
2 A fallacy is an invalid inference.
3 Fallacy indicators in propositional form include:
   a) Denying the given.
   b) Denying the antecedent.
   c) Affirming the consequent.
4 Five conditions when reasoning in predicate form inevitably lead to fallacy:
   a) All premises are particular.
   b) All premises are negative.
   c) There is at least one negative premise and a positive conclusion.

    d) All premises are universal and there is a particular conclusion.

    e) A term is illicitly distributed.

When a fallacy indicator is not present in the formal expression of an argument but the Venn diagram indicates a fallacy, illicit distribution must be the reason.

5 Inconsistencies occur when:

    a) People change their definitions or their minds.

    b) Category mistakes are made.

    c) What is asserted implies a contradictory claim.

Nevertheless, these are not strictly fallacies.

6 Incomplete arguments lack at least one crucial claim:

    a) Undeclared reasons invite the question, 'What does the conclusion assume?'

    b) Undeclared conclusions invite the question, 'What do the reasons imply?'

7 Identifying undeclared claims involves:

    a) Expressing the incomplete argument formally.

    b) Making the best case presumption, that the inference is valid.

    c) Specifying the assertion required to ensure a valid inference.

    d) Setting out the completed argument.

    e) Confirming its validity.

8 When a sound case is made, comprising inferences that are valid and premises that are well grounded, the argument constitutes an explanation.

8 Assumptions

Validity alone does not ensure that arguments are sound. A sound argument must also be based on acceptable premises. However, in certain circumstances, it is legitimate and worthwhile to suspend the 'acceptability' requirement. Sometimes reasoning is based on claims for which no defence is offered. We refer to such claims as assumptions. Following Lemmon:

> By an *assumption*, we shall understand a proposition which is, in a given stretch of argumentation, the conclusion of *no* step of reasoning, but which is rather taken for granted at the outset of the total argument.
>
> (Lemmon 1971: 8)

By convention, assumptions characteristically do not need grounds to justify believing them. The focus of attention is to establish what they imply.

THE PROBLEM OF INFINITE REGRESS

Grounds for believing a premise may not be satisfactory. However, any statement made in defence of a premise also requires, in principle, a ground for belief. A series of unending challenges to reason after reason, called an *infinite regress*, makes it difficult to get an argument started. Geach offers a solution to this problem when he says that 'if we are to believe anything at all, there must be uninferred beliefs to start with' (Geach 1976: 23).

He suggests that any argument or explanation must contain some claims which are taken for granted, in the sense that they do not require the support of argument or evidence. All arguments, at some stage, must be based on *assumptions*.

ASSUMPTIONS AND MODELS IN THE SOCIAL SCIENCES

The status of assumptions in a particular piece of reasoning is often the source of confusion. This is at least in part because assumptions may fulfil different roles in different circumstances. There is a set of circumstances, pervasive in the social sciences, where assumptions are made as the starting points for analysis, but where there is no implication that these are well grounded. In some instances, it might be that the presenter is offering what philosophers sometimes call 'suppositional argument'. This takes the form, 'Let us suppose, for purposes of argument, that something is the case and let us investigate what would follow if such circumstances were to hold'. This is, in effect, a form of 'model building'. The presenter is building an artificial construction, based on premises for which no justification is offered. This commonly occurs, for a variety of reasons and in a variety of circumstances.

The presenter might believe that the assumptions are well grounded but choose not to justify them immediately. This could happen because she wishes to concentrate on other aspects of the argument, possibly intending to substantiate the assumptions later. Alternatively, the assumptions might be the subject of extensive discussion elsewhere so that further considerations are unwarranted. For example, many economists believe that individual people are motivated by a desire to 'maximise utility' and individual firms are motivated by a desire to 'maximise profits'. There is an extensive literature on the motivation of both individuals and firms and there are numerous models which are based on these assumptions as well as numerous models which are not. For individual students or researchers, systematically trying to come to terms with the voluminous subject matter of their discipline, there is much merit in addressing the logical structure of a piece of analysis separately from addressing whether or not the assumptions are justified.

Versions of models may at one extreme involve the inferences from a formal model containing hundreds of equations, whereas at the other extreme they might be very informal, consisting of an individual sentence. A technique, known as 'model simulation', used by economists is to use an economic model to simulate the change in an economic policy instrument. For example, H. M. Treasury, like many business schools and other econometric forecasting institutions, uses an econometric model, consisting of over 200 equations, which simulates the essential features of the UK economy. The model user can change one variable, for example the rate of income tax, and investigate how this influences other variables, such as the rate of unemployment. Implicitly, there is an argument which runs as follows: if the rate of income tax is reduced by (say) 1 per cent and if the UK economy behaves in the same way as the model being used, then the unemployment rate will change by x per cent. Both of the assumptions are being made for purposes of investigating the consequences. If the user had grounds for believing that the model performed well, perhaps based on the evidence from previous simulations, then he or she might be tempted to make policy recommendations based on the results. A more cautious researcher might be tempted to repeat the simulations with a wide variety of models before being so rash.

Model-building is used to a greater or lesser extent in all of the social sciences, as the following passage illustrates:

> Anyone who attempts to isolate the components of a geographical system will soon realise that most of the systems that interest geographers are enormously complex no matter what the scale of analysis. Therefore, the study of a geographical system inevitably requires a degree of abstraction or simplification to be made. Scientists . . . term this process *model-building*.
>
> (Thomas and Huggett 1980: 3; our emphasis)

For illustration, consider a stylised version of a model at the core of central place theory, developed by human geographers.[1] This is concerned with the way in which cities, towns, villages and hamlets are distributed and provide facilities such as shopping, entertainment and education. It is assumed that settlements are located on a limitless, featureless plain with population evenly distributed and inhabitants are assumed to obtain each service from the nearest settlement which provides it. This offers a framework for analysing the distribution of settlements of different sizes and the allocation of various services between them. There is no suggestion that the assumptions of the model accurately *describe* reality. Rather, they are made so as to help the geographer focus on those factors which are considered to be important for an understanding of reality.

Similar considerations apply to the study of almost any system of potential interest to social scientists. The work of geographers includes building models of cities, land use and settlement patterns. Sociologists model families, organisational structures and societies. Political scientists model bureaucracies, decision-making processes and power struggles and psychologists model different forms of human behaviour.

SIMPLIFYING AND CRITICAL ASSUMPTIONS

Sometimes assumptions are made to simplify an argument. Features which the presenter considers to be irrelevant to the case being made may be 'assumed away' for purposes of focusing attention on the main topic of interest. For example, economists often make the assumption *ceteris paribus*, loosely translated as 'other things remain the same'. This is for the purpose of analysing the effect of a change in one particular feature, without having to consider all of the other changes which may be occurring simultaneously. This does not mean that economists believe that other things do not change. Rather, they choose to analyse the effect of one thing at a time.

There is an approach to economics, discussed further in Chapter 12, which maintains that there is no necessity to justify the assumptions on which a particular model or theory is based. Proponents of this approach, which we refer to below as 'instrumentalism', maintain that a theory should be judged according to how well it predicts, irrespective of any considerations relating to the realism of its assumptions. Thus, 'monetarist' economists, seeking to understand how changes in the money supply affect the rate of inflation, frequently make recourse to what is known as the 'quantity theory of money'. In a simplified form, this states that under the assumptions that the volume of transactions in the economy and the velocity of circulation of money – loosely interpreted as the number of times an individual piece of currency changes hands in a given time period – both remain constant, then the price level varies in proportion to the money supply. Few if any economists believe that these assumptions hold. Nevertheless, the quantity theory of money focuses attention on the relationship between changes in the money supply and changes in the price level. Because many of its proponents appear to believe that changes in the price level can be predicted from information about the money supply, the quantity theory provides the basis for a policy recommendation that maintenance of a tight monetary policy should be the centrepiece of any anti-inflation strategy.

Further appreciation of the role of assumptions in reasoning in the social sciences may be fostered by considering an analogue from the world of manufacturing. Consider an aircraft manufacturer who has designed a new jet airliner. Before investing millions of pounds in building a prototype, the firm will probably build a small model. This will be tested in a wind tunnel where it will be subjected to different external forces to investigate its aerodynamic properties. In terms of external shape and weight distribution the model will resemble the real thing as closely as possible. Yet there will be no seats, no internal trimmings and not even an air hostess to serve drinks! Such unnecessary features are, in effect, 'assumed away' for the purpose of investigating aerodynamic behaviour. Yet the configuration of fuselage, wings, rudder and tailplane will be modelled to precise specifications. For the purpose at hand, nothing is lost by simplifying the model as far as the internal features are concerned but anything which affects its aerodynamic properties is critical. In fact, in the late twentieth century, an aircraft manufacturer may replicate or even replace the model with a set of equations on a computer. In many respects, this version of the aircraft builder's model may look very similar to a model built by a social scientist. For example, economists sometimes build models of individual markets or of the whole economy, so as to investigate how such things as national output or employment might be affected by changes in, say, the money supply, unemployment benefit, enlargement of the European Union or any other factor that the model-builder chooses to investigate.

Note how both the aeroplane builder and the social scientist make a series of assumptions so as to investigate what follows from them. In some cases the assumptions fulfil a simplifying role and are patently unrealistic. In other cases the assumptions are 'critical' in the sense that the important conclusions of the analysis may no longer follow if they are relaxed. Identifying whether an assumption really is a 'simplifying assumption' in the sense that it merely abstracts from unnecessary complications or whether it is a 'critical assumption' in the sense that it is an essential prerequisite for what follows is no easy task. Often it is a matter of experience and deep understanding of the discipline involved.

INFORMAL MODELLING

Academics often construct arguments based on premises which they do not attempt to substantiate. Such reasoning is a kind of thought experiment where the assumptions comprise a framework to explore what is implied by thinking in such terms. The reasoning, to be worthwhile, must be valid but the question of soundness does not arise. Language usage frequently indicates that informal modelling is taking place. Fisher (1988b: 86) mentions several indicative phrases, including:

consider the hypothesis/theory that . . .   imagine that . . .

let us assume, for the sake of argument,   let us postulate that . . .
that . . .
suppose that . . .

Context also suggests that arguments are presented to investigate the logical consequences of the assumptions. Analysis can begin by asking, 'What follows from the assumed premises?'

Against the background of *glasnost* and *perestroika* in the 1980s, President Gorbachev said at the beginning of the 1990s that he was committed to the USSR becoming a market economy. Some might not take the president seriously but *let us suppose* that his words accurately indicated his political and economic objectives for the then USSR. Making this assumption is not to accept that there are grounds available for doing so. There may not be. It merely sets out a scenario to be explored.

In a political context, it may be plausible further to assume that initiating changes of an appropriate kind would indicate that the proposer of a policy was serious. The suggestion might be expressed in the claim that '[[If] [it is Gorbachev's policy to make the USSR a market economy] [then] [he will have initiated changes to bring it into effect]]'. If, in addition, we observe that no such policies have been introduced then this observation, together with the conditional claim and the original assumption, comprise the premises of an argument that *denies the consequent*. The complete argument is set out in Example 8.1:

Example 8.1

|Because|

R₁   [|If| p, [it is Gorbachev's policy to make the USSR a market economy],

      |then| q, [he will have initiated changes to bring it into effect].]

& |and| |because|,

R₂   [∼q, Gorbachev has not initiated changes to bring it into effect.]

⇒ |Therefore|,

C   ∼p, Gorbachev has no policy to make the USSR a market economy.

This valid argument is formally expressed as:

$$[[p \Rightarrow q] \ \& \sim q] \Rightarrow \ \sim p$$

The argument is valid but because the acceptability requirement was suspended, the issue of soundness does not arise. However, by taking care of the logical considerations, the analysis has produced a coherent framework for empirical study. Provided that the indicators of 'change' are clearly defined, one can investigate whether Gorbachev should be taken seriously. It depends on the evidence. Logic cannot decide the issue but a deductive analysis of the assumption establishes a coherent framework of thought, within which to conduct an empirical investigation.[2]

USES AND LIMITATIONS OF MODELS

Whatever the context, critical appraisal of any argument, theory or piece of analysis requires that assumptions are made explicit. One of the assumptions, illustrated by the econometric simulation example referred to above, is that the behaviour of the model closely replicates the behaviour of whatever is being modelled. Although this may appear obvious, it can mislead even the most experienced scientists, as the following example illustrates.

In investigating the possibility of a link between the nuclear facility at Sellafield and the·incidence of childhood leukaemia in the surrounding area, the Black Report (1984) referred to both epidemiological and radiobiological studies. Radiobiological studies identify the composition and extent of radioactive discharges and the various 'pathways' by which cancer-inducing agents could get from the nuclear plant at Sellafield into human beings and the possible biological effects of the various substances, particularly their potential effect on the incidence of leukaemia in children. To identify the pathways it is necessary to identify all the different routes by which contamination might reach people, particularly children of the locality. The Black Committee adopted a particular model in which there are two main sets of 'pathways'. These are via discharges into the *atmosphere* and the *sea*. For example, airborne discharges may land on grass eaten by cattle or sheep and again enter the food-chain, as was feared following a serious fire in 1957.[3] Liquid waste may contaminate plankton, enter the food-chain and ultimately be ingested by those who eat contaminated fish. Also, when liquid waste enters the sea, some particles may become washed ashore and come into contact with children playing on the beach.

Black (1984) presents a diagram of these pathways, which is reproduced as Figure 8.1. The analysis is conducted on the basis of previous scientific medical research, based far more widely than just around Sellafield and drawing on information obtained from a variety of sources, including, for example, the effects of the bombs dropped

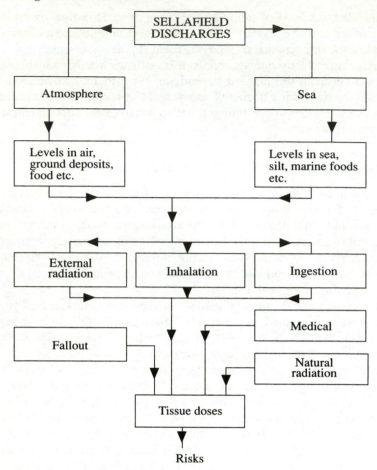

Figure 8.1   A model of 'pathways'
Source: Black 1984 (with amendments). Crown copyright is reproduced with the permission of the Controller of HMSO

on Hiroshima and Nagasaki. However, previous studies relating to the victims of the Hiroshima and Nagasaki bombs attached no importance to genetic transmission as a possible pathway.

The expected number of cancers occurring in the under twenty-five year old population of Seascale, resulting from the reported discharges from Sellafield, were consequently calculated. The model predicted 0.1 cases. There were four cases.

The question of whether to accept or reject this particular model was not addressed by Black. In fact, the tone of the Black Report is to take it for granted that the model used is 'correct'. It is as if the model is being taken as a *description* of reality.[4] Yet the model used in the Black Report may be deficient. This view is made more credible by the results of a case-control study of young people living near Sellafield subsequently published by Professor Gardner and others (Gardner *et al.* 1990). According to Gardner's study, there is at least a suggestion that a further 'pathway' exists. A potential father may be subjected to radiation doses before a child is conceived. Thus, a critical factor may be parental employment – particularly the dosage of radiation received whilst in that employment – during a certain period prior to conception, so that the apparent clustering of cases around the Sellafield complex reflects nothing other than the fact that people tend to live near to their work! At the time of writing, this issue has yet to be settled. What is highlighted by Gardner's work is that it was inappropriate to take for granted that the particular model used was the 'correct' one just because there was no reason to believe that other pathways existed.

The crucial point is that researchers must always be aware that their conclusions are predicated on their assumptions, including the assumption that their model is in some sense the 'correct' one.

SUMMARY

1 Assumptions are taken for granted at the outset of an argument or piece of analysis.
2 A series of unending challenges to reason after reason is called an *infinite regress*. Assumptions avoid this problem.
3 Assumptions may fulfil different roles.
4 Argument based on assumptions, where the latter are not necessarily well-grounded, is called suppositional argument.
5 Social scientists use models which are predicated on assumptions.
6 A common ploy is to assume that 'other things remain the same' for purposes of analysing the effect of a change in one particular feature.
7 An assumption may be a 'simplifying assumption' in the sense that it merely abstracts from unnecessary complications. However, it may be a 'critical assumption' in the sense that it is an essential prerequisite for what follows.
8 Modelling sometimes occurs in an informal way, indicated by such expressions as:

consider the hypothesis/theory that . . .   imagine that . . .

let us assume, for the sake of argument,   let us postulate that . . .
that . . .

suppose that . . .

9 The conclusions drawn from reasoning with a model are predicated
  on the model's assumptions. In making inferences about the world,
  this includes the assumption that the model is in some sense the
  'correct' one.

9 Evidence as ground for belief

The word 'evidence' is rich in meaning. *The Oxford English Dictionary* mentions eight uses. The first definition in the concise edition cites 'evidence' as: 'the available facts, circumstances, etc. supporting or otherwise a belief, proposition, etc., or indicating whether or not a thing is true or valid.'

Some people think that evidence is the 'available facts' but the complete definition presents a complex picture. The reference to 'circumstances' indicates the importance of context and the phrase 'whether or not a thing is true or valid', suggests that argument and evidence are interconnected. It is legitimate to draw conclusions from evidence besides using it directly to support premises. The voluminous edition of the dictionary defines the term 'evidence' as 'ground *for belief*' and 'testimony or facts tending to prove or disprove any conclusion'.

A NOTE ABOUT BELIEF

Belief generally is thought to be a personal matter because an apparent lack of grounds makes it difficult for the non-believer to share the belief. Suppose one believed in the paranormal. The credibility of reports about telepathy, poltergeists and out-of-body experiences would depend on what counts as evidence. In these circumstances, disputes would be settled only if definitions of basic terms were agreed. Alternatively, consider the statement that 'Queen Elizabeth II is married to Prince Philip'. Film and written documents are widely accepted grounds for accepting the claim. Such cases depend on the availability of objects that can be observed and double-checked. The role played by definitions and evidence in serious discourse has implications for approaches to study but how do we tell what matters?

A QUESTION OF DEFINITION OR EVIDENCE

In practice, it is frequently difficult to decide whether a belief stipulates the meaning of a word or describes a state of affairs. Consider two examples: 'Whales are mammals' and 'Radiation is the emission of energy particles'. Both read like descriptions of the world but may be definitions. There is a procedure for establishing whether a statement defines the meaning of a word or makes a claim about the world.

The negation test

First, negate the sentence 'Whales are mammals'. Substitute the meaning of 'whale' for that word in the negated sentence. This is a legitimate move since a word and its acknowledged meaning are equivalent. Substitution gives the sentence, 'Large fishlike marine mammals are *not* mammals'.[1] This statement is a contradiction. It requires no reference to evidence to establish its falsity. The same applies to the original positive assertion. The claim that 'whales are mammals' should be understood as a definition and analysed as such.

This approach works equally well with less obvious cases. For instance, it is not clear that the negative sentence, 'Radiation is *not* the emission of energy particles', is a contradiction. This is because the scientific meaning of the technical term 'radiation' is not so widely understood as the term 'whale'. By substituting the equivalent scientific definition of 'radiation' for that word in the negative version, we have the sentence, 'The emission of energy particles is *not* the emission of energy particles'. This is a contradiction. Thus, the positive claim is to be understood and treated as a definition.

Sentences which, in relevant contexts, are not contradictions when negated are regarded as empirical claims. For example, the statement that 'juveniles from unstable homes are *not* more likely to be delinquent', is not a contradiction. Evidence would be required to substantiate or refute such a claim.

Falsifiability

A claim is falsifiable when evidence makes a difference to whether one may believe it.[2] This normally presupposes that broad agreement exists about what counts as evidence but people do not always agree. For example, some count 'intelligence quotient' (IQ) as indicative of intelligence whilst others do not. Evidence of a different kind in each case would be required as a basis for claims about intelligence. To that extent, the competing claims would be controversial. Where broader agreement on what counts as evidence might exist, observations would uncontroversially determine what one is entitled to believe, for example, about unstable homes and juvenile delinquency. Falsifiability is a basis for selecting proposals for empirical research and avoiding unwise allocations of limited resources to futile projects. In different ways, the negation test and falsifiability distinguish claims about meanings from claims about facts. We now examine how various grounds support definitions and claims about the world.

DEFINITIONS

Definitions guide our attempts to interpret the world. Proceedings in British courts illustrate the importance of definitions. Consider a case where, against a background of domestic violence, a woman is charged with the murder of her husband. Provocation is a defence strategy which can reduce the murder charge to manslaughter. A characteristic of 'provocation' is that the danger must be imminent. Women who endure severe mental and physical cruelty over many years eventually get to the point where they inflict a physical remedy when the violent husband is vulnerable by virtue of sleep or drink. It is difficult to regard the danger to a woman in such circumstances as imminent, unless the background of domestic violence is considered inherently dangerous.

Precedent guides courts to determine when provocation occurs. Most case law suggests that provocation must be confrontational. Thus, killing someone who is asleep or incapacitated by alcohol is not a provoked act. Furthermore, case law rules out provocation not fitting confrontation patterns. Even worse, lawyers comply with these relatively fixed values. Nevertheless, natural justice and public sympathy recognise that danger can be inherent in circumstances which are not strictly confrontational. This was the basis of appeal in the case of Kiranjit Ahluwalia. Despite having suffered severe mental and physical cruelty from her husband for more than ten years, she was convicted of murder. She admitted having poured petrol on her husband's feet and set him on fire whilst he slept.[3]

Human beings adopt definitions and conventions for interpreting the world. Often these are taken for granted. This does not matter when people keep faith with the received view. It does matter when cultures collide. Serious academic discourse attempts to avoid communication breakdowns but academics sometimes disagree about the meanings of basic concepts.

Aspects of meaning

Designation, denotation and *connotation* are basic aspects of meaning. For example, the term 'snake' designates 'legless' and 'reptilian', summarising the essential characteristics of snakes. Such features help us to identify snakes and differentiate objects within our experience. The denotation of 'snake' lists all creatures which comply with the designation, including cobras, pythons and vipers. The connotation of 'snake' is more difficult. It comprises the associations brought to mind when using the word. One connotation of 'snake' is that snakes are slimy. In reality, most snakes are dry skinned, including those living in slimy environments. It is curious that something rarely observed can be part of what a word actually means. Whatever the context, statements employed as definitions are *tautologies*. The predicate is part of the subject term's meaning. So, it is appropriate to settle disputes about definitions by analysing the meaning of words.

Consistency

The negation test shows whether an assertion is a definition and that it is inherently consistent. Recognising that a negated sentence is contradictory can be tricky, especially where context is unclear. Consequently, definitions seem to depend upon states of affairs in the world, namely, that language usage is common or that definitions are conventional. However, an important distinction can be made between the world as a context to assist interpreting sentences and the world as a furnisher of evidence.

Failure to recognise the inconsistency in the sentence, 'Whales are *not* mammals', is to reject common language usage but not because one is blind to evidence or has found hitherto undiscovered evidence. The inconsistency in the sentence, 'Radiation is *not* the emission of energy particles', depends on our sharing concepts used by the scientific community. In this context, the claim is inconsistent but not because it does not square with our experience of the world. It is by virtue of contradiction. In both cases, the negation test must be conducted in the context of a culture or convention. Any belief, the negation of which is a contradiction in its appropriate setting, is an acceptable definition. Thus, *consistency* is a ground for accepting definitions.

Compatibility

To show that a definition is not contrary to others in the same framework of belief is a ground for accepting it. For example, the rules of a game need to be consistent in this sense. Also, laws of the land must be consistent. It would be absurd to be prosecuted under one law for an action which is legitimate under another in the same country. When a belief is a definition then, in the appropriate context, we would expect it to be self-consistent and *compatible* with other definitions in the web of belief.

CLAIMS ABOUT THE WORLD

Evidence inspires confidence in claims about the world and it can be enlisted in various ways as a ground for belief. It is cited in *observation statements*. Observations may correspond with an assertion. For example, observing a particular red post box corresponds directly with the assertion that 'the post box is red', on a one-to-one basis. The sentence describes a particular state of affairs. Evidence for general empirical claims is more difficult. Imagine trying to gather the evidence which corresponds with the assertion that 'all post boxes are red'. The entire evidence is hardly available and so it cannot strictly correspond with the generalisation. When evidence is incomplete it has to be evaluated. A feature of generalisations is that one counter-example is sufficient to reject them. For example, observing one yellow post box would justify rejecting the claim that 'all post boxes are red'. Consequently, only if every single post box were observed, would the absence of a non-red post box entitle us to conclude that in general post boxes are red.

It would be misleading to suggest that all observation statements are either particular or absolutely general. Consider the claim that 'all post boxes in Staffordshire are red'. This is both a generalisation and particular to the named area. It is customary to call such empirical claims *restricted* generalisations. Given time and patience, every post box in Staffordshire could be observed and there might be a direct correspondence between the observations and the assertion. Equally, one could take a sample of post boxes in Staffordshire and draw an appropriate conclusion based on the evidence.

The range and scope of observation statements can be listed as follows:

1 Particular claims correspond directly with respective observations.

2 Restricted general claims may correspond directly with respective observations or rest on an inference from a sample.

3 Absolutely general claims rest on an inference from a sample.

Interpreting falsifiability

Sometimes it is difficult to make observations required to furnish evidence, for instance, of molecular structures or the Atlantic Ocean floor. Not being able to see something is no ground for thinking that observations cannot make a difference to what we are entitled to believe. Professor Ayer's example that 'there are mountains on the other side of the moon' illustrates this point.[4] The moon always presents the same part of its surface to the earth and technology was not available in 1936 to see the other side. Since that time, human beings have been to the moon and observed for themselves. It is not that the moon mountains claim is now falsifiable but was not then. It always has been falsifiable because we agree on what counts as evidence for mountains and can recognise them. It would have been falsifiable to the Greeks two and a half thousand years ago, even though, as in 1936, uncorroborated. Empirical claims are identified by being in principle falsifiable. This implies that if a claim is false then, in principle, it is possible to obtain evidence to refute it. The fact that a claim is falsifiable does not mean that it should automatically be believed. Corroboration is required. For example, the claim that 'there is water on the surface of the planet Mars' is falsifiable but not the case, as recent observations by unmanned space vehicles have established beyond reasonable doubt. Similarly, the moon is not made of green cheese.

Correspondence

The observation of a single red post box corresponds directly with the assertion that 'the post box is red'. Even so, judgements are involved. To see that 'the post box is red', requires an observer first, to recognise that the object is a post box and second, to concede that it is red. In practice, most people are not conscious of making such judgements, based on the designations of 'post box' and 'red'. The respective definitions are implicitly agreed by those who participate in the English way of life.

In other situations, direct correspondence between what is believed and what is observed presents a difficulty. Consider the claim that 'the rock on the laboratory bench is radioactive'. Unlike the red post box, we cannot simply look. To the uninitiated, rapid clicks on a Geiger counter, though audible, would be unintelligible. However, in the context of radiation theory, they count as evidence. Although the observed clicks are not the radiation, there is a correspondence between their perceived rapidity and the alleged radioactivity of the rock. The difficulty is removed by familiarity with radiation theory. In this context, the observations provide a ground for the corresponding belief that 'the rock is radioactive'.

Consider the claim that 'everything in here is radioactive'. This restricted generalisation could be substantiated by Geiger counter evidence. It would require a series of readings to cover everything. On completion, if the total perceived evidence were to correspond with the claim that 'everything in here is radioactive' then there would be grounds for believing it. A single non-radioactive substance would render the restricted generalisation not the case because of the lack of direct correspondence.

Weight of evidence

Frequently, the scope of a restricted general claim is vast. In such cases it may be appropriate to draw a conclusion from a sample. For example, it would be impractical and uneconomic to establish direct correspondence by checking the blood pressure of everyone in the UK. Yet, for certain purposes, it would be helpful to know the numbers of British people who suffer from high blood pressure. Often, evidence supports a claim but is arguably insufficient to establish it beyond reasonable doubt. In such circumstances, one might refer to the 'weight' of evidence. If this were to lead one to be favourably disposed towards accepting the claim then, in common parlance, one might refer to such a claim as 'probable'. For example, observing people sleeping rough in a city might lead one to believe that there is a housing problem. Probability theory has a role to play in such cases. Consequently, observations, interpreted in the light of probability theory, may provide evidence which constitutes a ground for a belief in a claim about the world. This and related issues are discussed in subsequent chapters.

ENTAILMENT AND GROUND FOR BELIEF

Accepting premises logically forces acceptance of all that they validly imply. Whether a conclusion is a definition or a claim about the world, the fact that it follows from premises is one possible ground for believing it. Consider the following argument, comprised of definitions:

Example 9.1

	Because ,	
R₁	[History is ultimately about politics.]	
&	and because ,	
R₂	[Politics is ultimately about economics.]	
⇒	Therefore ,	
C	History is ultimately about economics.	

When evaluating such an argument, it is conventional to consider each sentence as a universal claim. Figure 9.1 shows that the inference is valid in terms of the key:

S = history
P = economics
M = politics

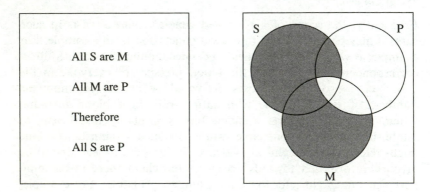

Figure 9.1   Predicate form and Venn diagram for Example 9.1

Thus, entailment provides one ground for accepting the definition that 'history is ultimately about economics' but what about the premises? Are they acceptable? These questions suggest that entailment shifts the ground for believing the conclusion back to the premises. In Example 9.1, it is not clear that the premises are acceptable. This casts doubt on whether entailment alone is a satisfactory ground for accepting that 'history is ultimately about economics'. However, in principle, entailment can be a ground for accepting a definition, provided that the argument is sound.

When a conclusion makes a claim about the world, its entailment by empirically substantiated premises is a ground for believing it. Evidence which directly substantiates the conclusion is not required. Consider the following argument:

Example 9.2

	Because ,
R₁	[Spent fuel rods from nuclear reactors are radioactive.]
&	and because ,
R₂	[Certain containers on ships from Japan to Britain hold spent fuel rods.]
⇒	Therefore ,
C	Certain containers on ships from Japan to Britain contain radioactive substances.

Again, entailment shifts the ground for belief back to the premises. Provided they can be substantiated empirically, the absence of evidence directly corresponding to the conclusion presents no difficulty.

Deduction of the unknown from what is known about the world is standard practice in police investigations. It is generally accepted that [people's finger prints appear on objects handled by them without gloves]. If the police established that [Peter's fingerprints were on the gun which killed the Dean] they would be entitled to conclude that Peter handled the gun which killed the Dean. Notice that entailment alone does not entitle the police to conclude that Peter killed the Dean. Other premises connecting Peter to the shooting would be required to develop the argument to the point where the latter conclusion could be validly drawn.

Entailment shifts the grounds for believing a claim back to the reasons for accepting the premises. In these circumstances, the basis for accepting a conclusion is conditional upon the grounds for accepting the reasons which entail that conclusion. If the potential infinite regress cannot be avoided then entailment cannot be counted as a ground for belief. Fortunately, this problem can be avoided because there are grounds, other than entailment, for accepting definitions and believing claims about the world.

DEFENDING CLAIMS AND SHIFTING GROUNDS

It is inappropriate to defend a definition as though it were a claim about the world and vice versa. It is relatively easy to spot a different approach to an issue or references to different material. It is more difficult to detect a subtle and fundamental shift in ground, where a claim about the world is defended as though it were a definition. Consider the case for determinism in Box 9.1.

Box 9.1 The case for determinism

> Human actions are events and because every event has a cause, it follows that human actions are caused. Since everything caused is not genuinely free, human actions cannot be genuinely free.

Central to the determinist's position is the claim that 'every event has a cause' but suppose there are random events with no assignable cause. Physicists tell us that electrons randomly change orbit. Furthermore, they claim that an individual occurrence of this kind has no assignable cause. A rebuttal might state that 'in time we will know what causes electrons to jump'. It may be replied that, when physicists say that electron jumps have no assignable cause they do not mean that the cause has not yet been found. Rather, they are claiming that it is inappropriate to look for causes of sub-atomic events. The response that 'sub-atomic occurrences are not genuine events' defends the determinist doctrine but only by excluding from the class of caused things all the counter-examples the physicist has in mind. This renders the cited evidence irrelevant. Now the doctrine is being defended as though it were a definition. The ground has shifted.

SUMMARY

1 When, in context, negation renders an assertion contradictory, the claim is a definition.
2 Definitions are claims about the meanings of words.
3 Aspects of the meaning of words include designation, denotation and connotation.
4 Grounds for belief in a definition include:
   a) Consistency, in so far as denial amounts to contradiction.
   b) Compatibility with other definitions within the web of belief.
5 Empirical assertions are claims about the world.
6 Negated empirical claims are not contradictory and must be in principle falsifiable.
7 Observation statements are particular, general in a restricted sense, or universal.
8 Grounds for belief in claims about the world include:

   a) Correspondence between an empirical claim and respective observations.

   b) Evidence from a sample interpreted in the light of probability theory.

9 Soundness affords resistance to serious criticism and influences methods for furthering knowledge in a given context but does not always matter.

10 It is inconsistent to defend a claim about the world as though it were a definition. To do so is to shift one's ground for believing it.

10 What counts as evidence?

In Chapter 9, various subtleties in the use and meaning of the word 'evidence' were discussed. We examined evidence as 'ground for belief' and considered how definitions offer standards for interpreting our experience of the world. Because it is naive to suppose that evidence can be simply collected, we now focus on the importance of context as well as some of the more practical aspects of what counts as evidence in different situations.

THE IMPORTANCE OF CONTEXT

The sixth definition of evidence in *The Oxford English Dictionary* is, 'Information, whether in the form of personal testimony, the language of documents, or the production of material objects, that is given in a legal investigation, to establish the fact or point in question'. Definition number eight is, 'A document by means of which a fact is established'.

These definitions are not inconsistent with the definition of evidence as 'ground for belief'. They suggest that the requirements of evidence and consequently the specification of what counts as evidence may differ according to the context in which the evidence is being used. The first alternative definition indicates that the legal profession has precise requirements concerning what is admissible in a court of law and that these requirements are so important that in legal usage the term 'evidence' is defined in accordance with these requirements. The word specifies the use to which evidence is to be put, namely to include anything which helps to establish a particular point. The second alternative definition raises questions about what counts as evidence in the context of a study of history, though contemporary historians rely on more than just documentary evidence. Such is the importance attached by historians to the quality of evidence that

Marwick writes, 'Essentially the special expertise of the historian lies in examining and assessing the "unwitting testimony" of the past' (Marwick 1970: 136). Barraclough refers to history as 'the attempt to discover, on the basis of fragmentary evidence, the significant things about the past' (Barraclough 1957: 29–30). The imperfect and fragmentary nature of evidence gives rise to many of the issues discussed below.

What counts as evidence in relation to a particular argument is often a source of confusion. In casual conversation, people often respond to a particular argument by citing evidence appropriate to a counter-argument. For example, when faced with the apparent accusation that discharges from the installation at Sellafield are at least in part to blame for the incidence of childhood leukaemia in the vicinity during the post-war period, one response is to refer to an apparent cluster of leukaemia cases in the vicinity before man discovered how to split the atom. This might be pertinent to a wider-ranging debate about the causes of leukaemia in general but it throws little light on the particular claim under discussion. If evidence is to be used effectively, it must be material to the specific issue being addressed.

THE ROLE OF OBSERVATION

We now address a common pitfall associated with the use of observations as evidence and thereby give an indication of the pervasive role of statistical analysis in the settlement of disputes in a variety of contexts. Consider the following hypothetical example:

Example 10.1

The Tasty Sweet Company markets packets of boiled sweets. On the packet is printed the statement 'Average contents: 35 sweets'. Having bought a packet of the sweets, a disgruntled consumer finds that it contains only 33 sweets and complains to the company. Following some unsatisfactory correspondence, the consumer decides to resort to litigation.

What would appropriately count as evidence in this example? The consumer would be unlikely to proceed far on the basis of the evidence provided from a single packet of sweets. The problem with this piece of evidence is that it may be regarded as an isolated case. Put another way, the problem is that to generalise on the basis of a sample of one single packet of sweets is of questionable legitimacy. So how many packets of sweets would the consumer need to purchase to make a convincing case and how far below thirty-five would the average need to be to convince a court that the Tasty Sweet Company's claim is fraudulent? These questions are addressed in Chapters 15 and 16, where appropriate concepts and techniques of statistical analysis are introduced.

The question of how many observations are needed to make a convincing case arises in many fields of study. Most national newspapers periodically publish opinion polls of the electorate's voting intentions, based on samples of the electorate. The degree of reliability attached to these will depend, amongst other things, on the number of people interviewed, which is one of the specific examples taken up in Chapter 15. Furthermore, the question of what constitutes a convincing case might have subtly different answers in different contexts. If one buys a second-hand car one wishes to be convinced that it will be reasonably reliable. Yet the strength of evidence is unlikely to be comparable with that required by a jury before they convict someone of murder.

Various considerations determine the type of information available to a researcher. Even within a particular discipline, alternative research methods can lead to different types of empirical study and hence use or generate different types of data. Although common usage tends to associate the word 'data' with numbers, this need not be so. Data (plural of datum) simply means whatever is given. At one extreme, empirical work may be highly quantitative, involving the application of sophisticated statistical techniques to numerical data; at the other it might involve the study of a cave drawing.

A feature of much research in the physical sciences is that a scientist designs an experiment to generate data required to test a particular hypothesis.[1] Within the human and social sciences, such a luxury is not always available. According to at least Professor Marwick's understanding of history, a task of the historian is to interpret whatever information is available, in a way which logically precedes the formation of any hypotheses (Marwick 1970).

Whether observation precedes or follows a hypothesis has serious implications. One difficulty is that the same observations may not be used both to generate a hypothesis and to test it. The Sellafield cancer-link controversy provides an example. Anything which is distributed randomly inevitably involves a certain degree of clustering. Consequently, to observe a cluster of leukaemia in a particular location and then hypothesise that there is something special about that particular location is dubious. It is not legitimate to cite the cluster which gave rise to the hypothesis as evidence in support of that hypothesis. Rather, if the existence of a cluster of cases near to a nuclear facility leads to the hypothesis that 'proximity to a nuclear facility is a factor contributing to higher than average incidence of leukaemia', then an appropriate procedure for testing such a hypothesis would be to see whether it is borne out in other locations.

CONCEPTUAL AND EMPIRICAL COUNTERPARTS

As a prerequisite for empirical work, where evidence is obtained from observations of the world, the researcher must have clear definitions of the concepts involved. Identifying empirical counterparts is not straightforward. Even a precisely defined concept can become elusive when attempts are made to measure it.

The difficulties faced by economists in defining and measuring unemployment illustrate these problems. The concept itself is not clear-cut. Different governments measure unemployment in different ways, making international comparisons difficult. Even within one country, definitions are changed and alternative definitions are published simultaneously. For example, at the time of writing, UK figures are published seasonally adjusted or unadjusted, including or excluding school leavers. The official definition can be changed for various political or economic reasons. The effect is reflected in the following comment:

> The unemployment figures ... have been subject to so many definitional and other changes over the last few years that it is unclear whether movements in the series reflect real effects or simply 'reclassifications' of individuals.
>
> ('Charter for Jobs', *Economic Report*, vol. 2, no. 7, May 1987)

In the 1980s, changes to the definition of unemployed to include only those claiming state benefit rather than those registered as seeking employment, and the removal of the need to register for men aged over sixty, between them reduced the official unemployment count by 340,000 (ibid. p. 5). Figures are also affected by various job creation programmes and training schemes. The combined effect of statistical changes and special employment and training measures introduced in the four years to 1983 was sufficient to cause the City Editor of *The Times* to write:

> Individually, many of these measures are sensible and desirable, most notably better training for the young.
>
> But in the context of a trebling of unemployment they smack of statistical chicanery. No single measure is sacred, but so many

changes obscure the trend of the labour market, which the figures are intended to show.

('City Editor's Comment', *The Times*, 4 August 1983)

If one is to make meaningful comparisons over a period of time, then a continuous, consistent, series of data is needed. These comments on UK unemployment statistics suggest that there have been so many changes to official definitions that limited reliable inferences may be drawn from official unemployment statistics alone.

Even when concepts can be defined precisely, empirical measures may be deficient due to problems of recording. With unemployment statistics, there are immense problems associated with the collection and processing of data from benefit offices so that considerable under- or over-recording is possible. Consider the social scientist seeking to understand the causes of high crime rates or the relationship between crime and unemployment. Available crime statistics refer only to crimes actually reported. This seriously understates the extent of crime and gives a distorted picture of both patterns of crime and trends in crime. There is no way of knowing the differing extents to which crimes are under-reported or the extent to which under-reporting is on the increase or decrease.

The same problems may become apparent in the physical sciences. Consider the difficulties facing the Black Committee, trying to establish whether there is a link between discharges from Sellafield and the incidence of childhood leukaemia in the neighbourhood. Although the Committee was able to identify specific types of leukaemia, epidemiological analysis also required that they considered cases occurring in people of a particular age group, during a particular time period and within specified geographical boundaries. The criteria selected for delineating specific regions, so that 'clusters' can be identified, are themselves critical. Finding out precisely when a person contracted such an illness may be impossible. In this case, the Committee, following accepted scientific procedures, treated time of diagnosis as the critical consideration. A consequence of such a procedure is that their data are affected by the proficiency of general practitioners and others in the geographical areas concerned. Furthermore, although doctors routinely notify cases of leukaemias to cancer registries, it has been suggested that some registries may miss up to 30 per cent of such cases and that up to 20 per cent of the data may contain errors.[2] There are many related problems. Some people may have lived in the area of interest when the illness was contracted but subsequently moved away. Officially recorded data may be so far removed from the researcher's original concept that doubt is cast on the conclusions. For instance, the number of leukaemias *diagnosed* in Seascale may not coincide with the number of leukaemias contracted there.

A further problem, which is particularly apparent for researchers in the human and social sciences, is that observable data do not correspond exactly to the concepts of theoretical analysis. Even the theoretical concepts can be open to a number of different interpretations or defined in a number of ways. Problems associated with the definition and measurement of poverty, homelessness and education are just a few examples. For instance, there is not general agreement on what constitutes poverty. Arbitrary measures can be used, such as income per head or number of square feet of living space. However, many sociologists would argue that poverty can only be defined in a particular social context. If an elderly person has insufficient income to buy a birthday card for a grandchild without sacrificing an item of her regular diet then, in late twentieth century Britain, this might be considered an example of poverty but this was probably not so fifty years ago.

SOURCES OF EVIDENCE

The appropriate source of information for any project, study or argument will be conditioned, at least in part, by the particular context and by the method of study chosen. It is also possible that a knowledge of potential sources of information may be instrumental in the formulation of a particular research strategy.

For some types of research, the source of data is already defined. The researcher is forced to take the data as it comes. However, this does not mean that it should be used unquestioningly. Business statisticians may find much data is generated internally by the routine operations of the business concerned. This would be typical, for example, in the case of stock control data where the data may correspond exactly to what is required so that it can be used reliably as the basis for reordering or rescheduling production. When referring to the data on discharges of radioactive waste, the Black Committee had to rely on data provided by British Nuclear Fuels. It would be a very creditable state of affairs if BNFL had managed to record every incident when radiation was discharged into the environment by any route and also measure the discharge accurately. In general terms, even if the concept or magnitude to be measured can be identified precisely, there is still a potential problem of measurement error.

Serious students of history distinguish between *primary* and *secondary* source material. Books, journal articles and other material already processed are considered secondary source material. Primary sources are the 'basic, raw, imperfect evidence' (Marwick 1970: 31). The wide variety of primary source material is indicated by the following quotation:

> Trade or population statistics, compiled by some governmental agency or by some interested private individual have long been accepted as important primary sources: recent advances in statistics have allowed for their more extensive and ambitious use by historians. The historian has learned to use the materials and, therefore, the tools of the archaeologist. Surviving factory installations, old brickwork, old machinery, are a valuable source for industrial history: we now, indeed, talk of 'industrial archaeology' to describe the systematic study of the remains left by an earlier industrial age. J. R. Green called the landscape a basic document; ... historians now supplement the inadequate gleanings of their own eyes with the revelations about landforms and earlier patterns of cultivation revealed by aerial photography.
>
> (Marwick 1970: 132)

Thus, primary source material can include documentary, statistical, archaeological, architectural and photographic evidence. The use and interpretation of different forms of evidence has spawned specialist literature. We aim to note only some of the more important characteristics of evidence in general. Of the various characteristics which influence the quality of primary source material, *authenticity* and *reliability* are particularly highlighted by Marwick. We can think of no reason why these same qualities should not be given high priority by practitioners in any discipline. The particular sources just referred to should not be regarded as the exclusive domain of historians. In fact, many, if not all of the above might alternatively be considered as sources for geographers, and practitioners of other disciplines also. Conversely, an old document may be a legal contract, requiring the expertise of a lawyer rather than a historian to interpret it. Although no one type of data source can be regarded as the exclusive domain of any particular discipline, many subject areas still rely heavily on certain types of source and avoid others. For much research in the social sciences, sources of evidence other than those mentioned above are also likely to be sought, some of the most common of which are considered below.

Published statistics

Most governments have agencies, such as the UK Central Statistics Office, which publish a wide variety of data, providing the bread and butter for many applied social scientists. Often, published data has been processed and reprocessed and may have been derived from a number of different original sources. Data on various economic indicators, such as output, employment and financial information, are abundantly available. Various social statistics covering education, crime and other topics of interest to sociologists, geographers, anthropologists and others are also available.[3] The United Nations Organisation for Economic Co-operation and Development (OECD) and the International Monetary Fund are amongst the various international organisations which publish data extensively.

Individual researchers or research organisations sometimes publish their data so that, provided no copyrights are breached and appropriate acknowledgements are given, others may use it, avoiding the need to replicate painstaking and detailed archival research. Nonetheless, the attractiveness of readily available data should not blind the researcher to the need to ensure that the empirical measures correspond to the precisely defined theoretical concepts. Data obtained for different purposes are only likely to be appropriate if certain key assumptions about what is measured are shared by both projects.

Experimental data

For some types of research, especially in the physical sciences, there is considerable potential for designing experiments to generate data for the testing of hypotheses. This particular research method is common, for example, amongst psychologists. Similarly, the desire prevalent amongst many economists to emulate the physical sciences has led to a body of research generally referred to as 'experimental economics'.[4] One advantage of an experimental study is the facility to control variables of interest and to exclude the effects of extraneous influences. However, if data about human behaviour are generated under artificial, experimental conditions then the researcher must be alert to the possibility that the subject(s)' behaviour is influenced, even if only subconsciously, by the unreality of the situation. Although researchers go to great lengths to simulate real-life conditions, there is inevitably a lack of correspondence between real-world behaviour and its experimentally-generated counterpart. This has implications for the extent to which the results of such experiments count as evidence in the context of real-life behaviour.

Surveys and questionnaires

Questionnaires and interviews are methods for collecting data which are widely used by sociologists, geographers, economists and political scientists among others. A well-known example is an opinion poll of attitudes or voting intentions. This ranges from a newspaper reporter who asks the opinion of perhaps six people in a local high street to a carefully conducted poll based on a well-compiled sample of respondents, following agreed procedures as outlined below and practised by some of the reputable polling organisations. Since questionnaire design and the planning of interview questions are specialised topics deserving and requiring detailed and careful attention, anyone planning to undertake such a study is recommended to consult the specialist literature.[5] Nevertheless, a few important points can be made now.

First, completed questionnaires only provide information relating to the interviewees' interpretation of the questions asked. Hence, all information acquired by this means is necessarily conditioned both by the design of the questions and by the respondents' interpretation of them. Even if the questionnaire designer has a clear, unambiguous notion of a theoretical concept on which information is required, it demands considerable skill in question design to ensure that the respondent interprets the question in the way intended. Second, once completed questionnaires are collected, they are usually coded and/or processed to transpose the information into a form suitable for computer and/or statistical processing. This introduces a whole set of additional problems, some of which are considered on pp. 119–20.

Observing behaviour

Watching and carefully observing the behaviour of people, animals or things can be a valuable source of data and is used in a variety of contexts, yet even this is not without its pitfalls.[6] The mere observation of people may lead them to modify their behaviour and if information about behaviour is to be published this may also have an effect. When journalists or TV cameras visit public demonstrations or political events, the fact that people can be noticed may lead them to behave unnaturally. How far is the behaviour of a large crowd in a street demonstration, or behind barricades in Northern Ireland, affected by the presence of 'impartial' reporters or television cameras? To take an even more extreme case, the treatment of prisoners of war may be affected by visits of impartial observers from the International Red Cross. It is frequently not possible to know how far or in what ways behaviour is modified in response to being observed.

These problems are not unique to one type of data source. In the early 1980s the British Government decided to pursue a particular type of economic policy known as monetarism. The money supply, as measured by a particular indicator, known as £M3, was monitored and its rate of growth was to be kept within predetermined and publicly announced bands. Once the policy was announced, the behaviour of £M3 became more erratic and proved almost impossible to control effectively. Thus, the social scientist, by merely trying to observe behaviour, can inadvertently affect it. If observed behaviour affects government or other action, the problem can be compounded even further.

'Participant observation', discussed further in Chapter 12 (see p. 157), occurs when, for example, a research sociologist chooses to live in the community which she is studying. Although data obtained by participant observation may appear to be qualitative rather than quantitative, many of the principles elucidated and the issues discussed in this and other chapters still apply. Most importantly, all of the problems associated with making an inference from a sample to a wider population apply, regardless of the extent to which data can be quantified. In fact, as the following section indicates, as data are prepared for computer storage or processing, the distinction between qualitative and quantitative data appears less than clear-cut.

THE CODING OF DATA AND THE ROLE OF STATISTICS

In various circumstances, evidence comprises a large number of individual items, which need to be sorted, catalogued and presented in an orderly form, sometimes using a computer. This section considers some points which should not be overlooked when handling such data.

First, even data which has been put onto a computer need not necessarily be quantitative. Computers can be used for storing names, addresses and any other information, as those who regularly receive 'junk mail' are painfully aware. Nevertheless, for convenience, information is often coded for entry into a computer data bank, so that what is originally qualitative data becomes converted into a set of numbers. For example, a person's gender may be coded as number 0 for a male or number 1 for a female. Geographic areas may be referred to by a series of numbers, so that even places of residence may appear in numerical form. Sometimes it is permissible to apply various statistical techniques to such numbers, treating them just as if they represented quantitative data, and on other occasions it is not. Such matters are considered in Chapters 15 and 16.

If coding data involves a process of categorisation, requiring judgement on behalf of the researcher, then the data loses its primary characteristic. Where the digits 0 and 1 are used as indicators of gender, any subsequent user of the data is able to convert the coded data into its original form. However, where addresses have been categorised into numbered regions, the original information is not retrievable. In the process of choosing the boundaries of regions, the researcher uses judgement in a way which could significantly affect how the coded data are interpreted. This is illustrated by reference to the cancer-link controversy. Each individual case of childhood leukaemia in the vicinity of Sellafield was carefully documented and it was noted in which area the case occurred. Consequently, an excess number of cases was recorded in the under twenty-five year old population of Millom Rural District and the under ten year old population of Seascale.[7] Had geographical criteria other than administrative boundaries been used, a different picture might have emerged.

There is a prevalent attitude that statistics are to be mistrusted and statistical analyses of all types are to be avoided. While there is merit in the suggestion that information should be treated with extreme caution, and checked for reliability and authenticity, we can find no reason for believing that information which is presented statistically should be regarded with any greater suspicion than any other form of evidence. The often-quoted sayings that 'one can prove anything with statistics', and that 'there are lies, damned lies and statistics' are sensibly regarded as a caution against being misled, but a caution to be applied to information or evidence of all forms. Even the evidence of one's own eyes has to be carefully interpreted. The way in which one perceives visual evidence is itself an area of research by psychologists, which has practical applications in, for example, the design of public transport maps. Caution is always required in identifying what may appropriately be regarded as evidence in the context of a particular argument.

CENSUS, POPULATION AND SAMPLE

When collecting data, a researcher will have to decide whether to enumerate every single item of a *population* by taking a *census*, or whether to rely on a *sample*. Although the terms 'population', 'census' and 'sample' enter into everyday usage, they have very precise meanings.

'Population' is used in a technical sense to refer to all items in the set of phenomena being studied. For example, it might refer to all people in a particular country, region, town, school, college or university. Use of the word, in this technical sense, is not restricted to people. It may alternatively refer to measurements of unemployment or national income for a set of countries, crime figures for different regions, aspects of flora or fauna or anything else thought worthy of study. If one wishes to be absolutely certain about the characteristics of a population as a whole then a census must be taken. This is a record of the relevant information for each individual member of the population. For anything other than a small population, a census is likely to be very expensive in terms of the researcher's time and money. It may also take a longer time to implement and organisational difficulties and the sheer bulk of information being handled may lead to errors. Under such circumstances, a relatively small sample, appropriately selected, may be preferable. For example, if one were interested in the average age of all employees in a large company, one option would be to obtain the age of every single employee, company regulations and data permitting. An alternative would be to select a sample of perhaps 100 employees and on the basis of information contained in the sample, an inference could be made about the average age of that company's total workforce. This would be an inductive inference, not a deduction. Consequently there would be a degree of uncertainty associated with it. To summarise:

A *population* is the total set of elements of interest for a given problem.[8]
A *sample* is a part of the population under study, selected so that inferences can be made from it about the population.
A *census* involves recording the relevant information for every element in the population.

By appropriate use of probability theory, it is often possible to make precise statements about the degree of reliability associated with inductive inferences. A rudimentary understanding of the theory of probability is presented in Chapter 13 as a necessary prerequisite for an appreciation of the theory of statistical inference.

SAMPLE SELECTION

In choosing a sample from a population, care must be taken in selecting the elements to include. Whenever conclusions about a population are drawn, based on information derived from a sample, a process of inductive reasoning is involved. If reliable inferences are to be made, then there are clear requirements that the sample must meet. This has given rise to an extensive literature on sampling methods, the importance of which is captured by the following:[9]

> The role of sampling methods is now generally recognised in all countries as permitting the study of characteristics and relationships by the selection, by rigorous methods, of part of a 'population' to be representative of the whole.
>
> (P. J. Loftus, Director, Statistical Office, United Nations)[10]

Provided that a sample has been selected according to rigorous methods derived from probability theory, then and only then is it referred to as a *random sample* or, to use an equivalent term, a *probability sample*. Only samples compiled in accordance with such procedures should be used as a basis for statistical inference. The simplest way to meet these requirements is to select a *simple random sample*. This is selected in such a way that every element in the population has the same chance of being selected. If this criterion has been met for a particular sample, then it follows that this sample has the same probability of selection as any other sample of the same size.

Some of the above points are illustrated by the following example. Daily and Sunday newspapers often publish opinion polls of people's voting intentions. These are used to draw an inference about the composition of the House of Commons, if a general election were to be held at the same time. Although we must stress that whereas most organisations which conduct such polls are reputable, some suspect polls have been known. The practice of conducting a telephone poll, for example, may consist of selecting a number of people from the telephone directory, telephoning them and, provided they can be contacted, including them in the sample. The most glaring fault associated with such a procedure is that not every member of the electorate is listed in the telephone directory. First, the directory usually lists only one member of the household; second, not every household has a telephone and third, some people who do have a telephone choose not to be listed in the telephone directory. If the population of interest is the total electorate then such a sample is not random and any inferences drawn from it about voters in general must be suspect.

Since the telephone poll example does not comply with the principles of sample selection, it can be used to illustrate why randomness is such an important criterion. Unless the proportion of the electorate which would vote for each party is the same amongst those contacted as it is for those not contacted, the results from the sample will not be an accurate reflection of the intentions of the whole population. They may overstate or understate the proportion which would vote for one party rather than another. Furthermore, the extent of over- or under-statement is generally not known and therefore cannot be corrected. Apart from giving suspect information, the results can have even more serious consequences. Many have claimed that published opinion polls actually affect the way people vote. For example, if they believe that their favoured party has little chance of winning then they may switch their vote to their second choice. If they are confident that their preferred party will win anyway then they may not vote at all. Although this example may be a little extreme, it illustrates the responsibility that falls on the shoulders of the social researcher.

Simple random sampling may be more difficult than it appears. For the opinion poll example, a person living in the Outer Hebrides must have the same chance of being selected as a person living in Westminster. Since electoral registers are compiled on a constituency basis this means that pollsters may have to travel to the Outer Hebrides and that account must be taken of the different numbers of voters registered in each electoral district. A common practice is to select a limited number of electoral wards at random and then to select a specified number of voters from each.

If the criteria for random sampling are to be met then it is necessary, in principle at least, that all elements in the population can be identified. In other words, a *sampling frame* should be made available. This is a listing of every individual in the population from which the sample is drawn. One method of ensuring a random sample would be to allocate a numbered ticket to each item in the sample frame, put a set of duplicate tickets in a tombola and blindly pick out the requisite number of tickets. The tombola part of the procedure could be bypassed by using electronically generated random numbers.

There are modifications to the procedure of random sampling which retain the features of a probability sample but are either easier to implement or improve the properties of the sample in a calculable way. If a sample amounting to, say, 1 per cent of a population were required, then a *systematic sample* could be compiled by choosing (randomly) a number between 1 and 99, selecting that item and then every one hundredth item in the list. For example, one might choose the 34th, 134th, 234th, ... people from an electoral register. If it is known that a population is composed of a number of subgroups, in given proportions, then a sample may be *stratified* so as to contain the same proportion of each subgroup. For example, if a population is composed of 50 per cent males and 50 per cent females, then a stratified sample would also contain 50 per cent males and 50 per cent females. Stratified samples may be compiled on the basis of gender, income, place of residence or any criteria that are available. The purpose of stratification is to improve the reliability of the inference drawn from the sample and this and related issues are discussed further in Chapter 16.[11] Poor stratification was one of the main factors blamed for the general failure of opinion polls to predict the 1992 general election result, as Box 10.1 illustrates.

Box 10.1 Opinion poll sampling techniques

Poor sampling blamed for failure of polls

By Philip Stephens, Political Editor

An exhaustive inquiry into the failure of opinion polls to predict accurately the outcome of the 1992 general election yesterday put most of the blame on the sampling techniques used by pollsters.

An independent report commissioned by the Market Research Society says a swing from Labour to Conservatives in the last days of the election campaign accounted for only between a fifth and a third of the error.

Introducing the report, Mr David Butler, a psephologist from Nuffield College, Oxford, said the failure of eve-of-election polls to predict Mr John Major's victory was the 'most spectacular in the history of British election surveys'.

A team chaired by Mr Butler and including representatives of two of the main polling organisations – MORI and ICM – singled out two crucial flaws in the way the opinion polls were collated.

• The quota and weighting systems used to select samples did not reflect with sufficient accuracy the social profile of the electorate.

• The systems, which take into account such factors as age, sex, social class and occupation, were not fully representative of the distribution of political support across the electorate.

The opinion polls, which were 4 percentage points away from the actual outcome for both the

Conservative and Labour parties, also suffered from the refusal of many voters to reveal their loyalties.

More Conservative than Labour voters declined to state their preference and the polls were not adjusted to take account of this.

The report says the final important factor was the late swing in support towards the Conservatives and the fact that Tory supporters proved more likely to register their votes on election day. Minor influences included the choice of constituencies for polling and interviews with people not on the electoral register.

The main polling companies said yesterday that they had already implemented the main recommendations of the inquiry in part or in full.

These include better techniques for selecting quota samples and weightings and new approaches to limit the number of 'refusals'.

But the report stresses that there is no single framework available to ensure that the mistakes are not repeated and companies should continually develop their research techniques.

The Opinion Polls and the 1992 General Election. Market Research Society, 15 Northburgh St, London EC1V 0AH. £25.

(*The Financial Times,* 6 July 1994, p. 10)

Sampling procedures which do not meet the criteria for a random sample still persist.[12] *Haphazard sampling* occurs where the researcher selects mainly on the basis of convenience. A common example is the use of volunteer samples for experiments. *Purposive sampling*, where the researcher uses subjective judgement to select elements which are 'representative' of the population and *quota sampling* are other examples of *non-random* or *non-probability* sampling methods. Although these may serve particular purposes, or be less costly to implement, there are serious limitations to their use as the basis for statistical inference.

If information derived from a sample is to provide evidence about a population then the procedure for sample selection must meet strict requirements, in accordance with the theory of probability. Even if this condition is met, one can never be certain that the population as a whole exhibits exactly the same characteristics as the sample. Thus, conclusions drawn on the basis of such evidence can never be reached with certainty. However, it often is possible to make statements about the degree of reliability of conclusions reached via a process of statistical inference and this is discussed in Chapter 15.

SUMMARY

1 What counts as evidence may depend on context.
2 In using observations as evidence, the number of observations required may depend on the context of the argument and will affect the strength of the case being made. Whether observation precedes hypothesis or hypothesis precedes observation has serious implications.
3 Theoretical concepts must be clearly defined and the relationship with their empirical counterparts must be understood. Theoretical measures may not have any obvious and uncontentious empirical counterpart. Empirical measures may also be deficient due to under-recording, changes in definition and methods of collection or processing.
4 Sources of evidence must be conditioned by context and method of study. Evidence may be classified as primary or secondary. Primary evidence may be documentary, statistical, archaeological or photographic. Authenticity and reliability are important criteria to be met. Major sources of evidence available to the social scientist include published statistics, experimental data, surveys and questionnaires and observation.
5 Data may need to be coded for further analysis. The distinction between quantitative and qualitative data is often based on a false dichotomy. Data coding often involves judgements which must be made explicit. Appropriate standards of care should be applied to evidence of all forms from all sources.
6 A *population* is the total set of elements of interest for a given problem. A *sample* is a part of the population under study, selected so that inferences can be made from it about the population. A *census* involves recording the relevant information for every element in the population.
7 Samples should be selected according to precise criteria, based on the theory of probability. Samples inappropriately selected may lead to misleading inferences.

11 Presenting and summarising evidence

Empirical evidence often comes in the form of numbers, sometimes consisting of a large set of data which may be difficult to interpret in its original form. A rudimentary facility for manipulating, presenting and interpreting such data is essential if it is to become the servant rather than the master. In recent years the proliferation of personal computers and associated software packages has been so great that it is no longer appropriate to discuss the handling of data other than in the context of recent developments in information technology. Anyone planning to do serious empirically based research, involving the use of quantitative data, is unlikely to do so without at the very least encountering a data base, spreadsheet or statistical package. These developments make it relatively easy to compute and publish sophisticated statistics which may be used or misused in support of a particular standpoint. Any student of the human or social sciences is likely to be bombarded with an increasingly complex array of statistics. When it is also considered that the drudgery of computation can now be taken over by machines, a strong case emerges for ensuring that any student of the human or social sciences develops an appreciation of the premises on which the use of statistics is based and is well versed in the pitfalls associated with the interpretation of statistical evidence.

The first two sections of this chapter consider some of the computing facilities available for the processing of data and present some shorthand notation which facilitates the discussion of statistical techniques and concepts. These are followed by a discussion of some of the conceptual issues involved in using statistics and an introduction to some elementary descriptive measures.

COMPUTER FACILITIES FOR DATA PROCESSING

Personal computers, such as those produced and marketed by IBM and its competitors, have a wide range of sophisticated applications to meet many of the research needs of the human and social scientist.

Data bases

A *data base package* can be thought of as similar to a very sophisticated filing system, capable of sorting, cross-classifying and selecting data according to criteria chosen by the user. For example, a researcher might have data pertaining to 1,000 individuals, with information on address, age, income, gender, educational attainment and race. Data base facilities would enable the researcher to obtain a listing of all males with income over £14,000 a year or a listing of all people of a certain race alongside their educational attainment. Data can be sorted and resorted according to any criteria and extended, updated or amended at will. Information from a questionnaire, for example, is often quite appropriately entered directly into a data base package, from where it can be further processed according to the individual needs of the research project. If a researcher is investing in the collection of an extensive data set, there are many advantages to inputting this directly into a data base where it is available for future work.

Statistical packages

Statistical packages tend to be of use at the other end of the research process. They are useful for calculating a range of statistics, both for describing features of the data and for purposes of inference, associated with estimation and hypothesis testing. Many statistics are complex to calculate and without computer facilities, many hours of time can be required and considerable scope for human error exists, even if the researcher is only working with a moderately sized data set. There is a danger, however, that a statistical package may be a sort of black box. Raw data is fed in and out comes a set of statistics to order. This places responsibility on the user, for the computer itself is incapable of distinguishing between good, bad or downright misleading applications of its output. Furthermore, although statistical packages can be very valuable to the serious researcher, they are quite useless when it comes to teaching or learning about how statistics are derived and how they may be interpreted.

Spreadsheets

Spreadsheet packages are designed for a range of applications. Conceptually, they are like a very large sheet of ruled paper (or graph paper) combined with a pencil, a rubber and a very powerful calculator.[1] They are used extensively in both education and business and have become an indispensable tool to many accountants, as well as finding increasing application in the teaching of some academic disciplines.[2] *Excel* and *Lotus 1-2-3* are two of the best-known examples of spreadsheets in the UK.

It is imperative that all work involving data should be kept neat and tidy. Apart from aesthetic considerations, there are strong practical reasons for this. One tiny slip in the transcription of a number, such as the misplacing of a decimal point, can have far-reaching consequences. Although a computer is most unlikely to make calculation errors, it only works on the data which has been input and is incapable of discerning a correct number from a quite ludicrous one. Furthermore, even after the completion of statistical work, there are often reasons to review the data for a suspected mistake, to see if a particular item stands out as unusual, or when all work has not been done on a computer, to look for calculation errors. An attractive feature of spreadsheets is that they enable and encourage the user to set out work in a very systematic and clear way.

From the perspective of the teacher or student of elementary statistics, spreadsheets have a number of pedagogic advantages. Spreadsheets can be programmed by the user to calculate a variety of specific statistics. The user inputs data (which is anyway required for any statistical application) and sets out the individual steps involved in each stage of the calculations. The routine, repetitive, calculations are then done on the computer, so that the student cannot avoid addressing every stage of the computation procedure but is spared the drudgery of repetitive calculations. A further advantage is that relatively realistic examples of application can be introduced at an early stage, so that students may gain a fuller appreciation of the variety of applications of individual techniques.[3]

Some examples of data or statistical calculation are presented in this and subsequent chapters via a spreadsheet. Although this serves to reinforce their pervasive application, the reader who wishes to work through this book with no access to computer technology is in no sense disadvantaged.

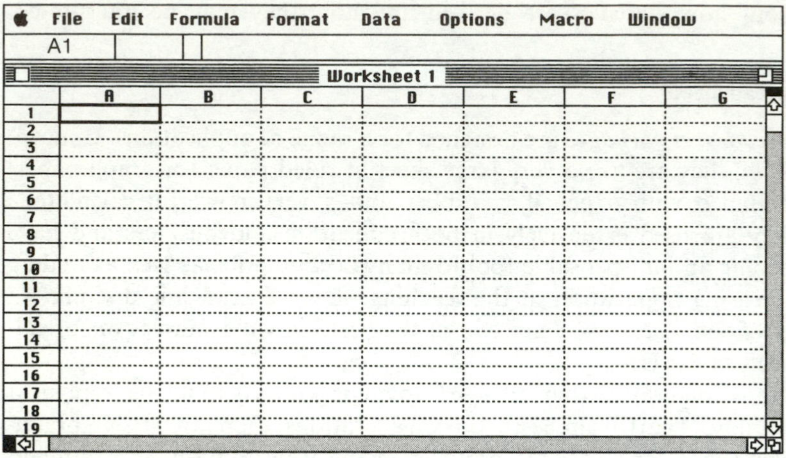

Figure 11.1   A blank Excel spreadsheet

Figure 11.1 is an example of a clean *Excel* spreadsheet, exactly as it appears on the screen of an Apple Macintosh. Rows are numbered and columns are indicated by letters. Hence, each individual *cell* is uniquely identified by a combination of a letter and a number. The user can enter numbers, labels (words) or formulae into any cell and can move around the spreadsheet at will. Computations can be done on individual cells, columns or groups of cells and most spreadsheets have a powerful collection of formulae for a variety of applications, which can be accessed by the user and applied to user-defined sets or subsets of data. Any spreadsheet package comes with a manual or user guide and in most cases a couple of hours of tuition or even self-instruction is quite sufficient to gain a basic competence.

NOTATION AND DEFINITIONS

Figure 11.2 is a spreadsheet containing information on the number of children per family, total family income and reported voting intention for fifteen families. This may have come, for example, from a sociological study, an economic study or a piece of political analysis, concentrating on voting intentions.

In this example, there are fifteen *observations*. The term observation is used to refer to a particular element of data. Thus, for the example

A	B	C	D
Family	*Children (Xi)*	*Income (Yi)*	*Voting (Zi)*
1	2	10,575	C
2	1	15,650	C
3	0	12,125	L
4	3	20,125	A
5	2	15,450	L
6	3	14,320	L
7	3	12,430	C
8	0	18,550	L
9	1	14,240	C
10	3	19,150	L
11	1	9,865	L
12	2	13,450	C
13	4	14,565	C
14	2	17,100	L
15	2	18,540	L

Figure 11.2 Family study

of Figure 11.2, an observation refers to a particular family.[4] A *variable* is a particular characteristic of interest, which may take different values. In this example there are three variables. Number of children per family and family income are *quantitative* variables in that they are magnitudes which can be expressed numerically. Voting intention, which is recorded as a letter, may be referred to as a *qualitative* variable. This illustrates the fact that data does not necessarily have to be in the form of numbers. However, it is convenient and useful, even for non-quantifiable data, to express it in a form that is easily *coded* for computer use. For example, the intention to vote Conservative is represented by the letter C, the intention to vote Labour by the letter L and any other party by A. In some cases, particularly if only two responses are possible, the researcher might even choose a number. Thus, the intention to vote Conservative might be recorded with the number 0 and the intention to vote Labour with the number 1. There are even statistical techniques which have been specifically devised for dealing with what is essentially qualitative data rather than quantitative data, especially in those instances where there are only two possible values. This further illustrates that in many cases statistical techniques can be applied to data which initially are not expressed in terms of numbers.

In Figure 11.2 the individual variables have also been assigned a letter, which is followed by a subscript. Thus, X refers to the number of children per family, Y refers to family income and Z refers to voting intention. Sometimes a subscript is used to denote an individual observation. A combination of letter for variable name and subscript for observation number can be used to refer to the value taken by a particular variable for a particular observation. X_i refers to the number of children in the 'ith' family so that, for example, $X_6 = 3$ denotes that family number 6 has three children.

The sigma notation, Σ

When processing data, there are certain operations which occur so frequently that it is convenient to have a shorthand notation to refer to them. The Σ sign, which is the Greek capital letter 'S', is conventionally used to mean 'the sum of'. When used correctly, it appears with a subscript and superscript and is preceded by a variable, which also carries a subscript, as follows:

$$\sum_{i=1}^{n} X_i \tag{11.1}$$

This reads, 'The sum of the individual values for X, starting with the first value and finishing with the nth value'. Since, for many applications, it is common to use the letter 'n' to refer to the number of observations, Expression 11.1 would typically mean, 'Add up all values of X, starting with the first value and finishing with the last value'. Where the summation is to occur over all values for a variable, as in Expression 11.1, it is common practice to omit the subscript and superscript entirely, so that an alternative expression, meaning exactly the same as Expression 11.1 would be:

$$\sum X_i \tag{11.2}$$

There are other applications where it may be appropriate to add up only a subset of the data. The instruction:

$$\sum_{i=2}^{6} X_i \tag{11.3}$$

would read, 'Add up the values taken by each observation on X, starting with the second and finishing with the sixth'. Applied to the data on the spreadsheet of Figure 11.2, this would give an answer of nine. One of the conveniences of using spreadsheets is that they have the in-built facility for doing such calculations.

There is nothing sacrosanct about the use of the letter 'X' to refer to a variable or of the letter 'i' as a subscript. Referring to the data of Figure 11.2, the expression ΣZ_i would be used to refer to the sum of all values of the variable Z. Where data come from observations at different points in time, the subscript 't' is often used to denote time period and in some applications – beyond the scope of this book – there may be occasion to sum over both individuals and time periods, so that two subscripts appear together.[5]

The advantages of the sigma notation really become apparent when undertaking operations more complicated than just adding a column of numbers. Consider the following examples:

$$\sum_{i=1}^{n} X_i^2 \tag{11.4}$$

$$\sum_{i=1}^{n} (X_i - 2)^3 \tag{11.5}$$

Expression 11.4 reads, 'Square each value for X, starting with the first and finishing with the nth value, then add up the results'. For Expression 11.5, read, 'Subtract 2 from each value of X, cube the result in each case and then add up all the answers'.[6]

MEASURES OF LOCATION

For the variable X, in Figure 11.2, there are fifteen individual bits of information to be assimilated. It is very difficult, especially for the casual observer, to interpret data in this form. Hence, various summary measures exist which encapsulate key features of a set of data in a single number. Instead of being presented with the information on all fifteen families, for many purposes it may be more useful to be given just one figure, for example, the average number of children per family. There is much less information for the brain to assimilate and for most people the average has a fairly straightforward interpretation, possibly conditioned by their own experience.

Before proceeding to discuss specific summary measures, it is necessary to consider the purpose for which these are to be used. There is an important distinction to be made between *descriptive statistics* and *statistical inference*. The average number of children for the fifteen families listed in Figure 11.2 may be used to convey information about those fifteen families only. Individual features of the population, such as the average number of children, are referred to only as a way of describing this particular set of data. To the human and social scientist, such application is limited. Very often, a summary measure is computed for the purpose of making an inference beyond the particular set of data from which it is derived. That is, it may be used as the starting point for a process of inductive reasoning. In this context, the fifteen families would be regarded as a sample, drawn from a wider population of families for the purpose of making inferences about that population. Such applications are called statistical inference. The conditions under which such inferences are useful or potentially misleading are the subject of Chapter 15. The remainder of this chapter is concerned with summary measures purely in a descriptive sense, as if to describe the results obtained from a census.

We begin with a group of measures which are often referred to as *measures of location* or *measures of central tendency*. These measures indicate a number around which the data are centred. Sometimes they are referred to as measures which 'typify' the data.

The arithmetic mean

The arithmetic mean is what most people, in casual usage, refer to as the average.[7] It is a single number encapsulating a large amount of information. For the fifteen families in Figure 11.2, one could gain an impression of typical family size by running an eye down the column of numbers, though when the number of families is large, this could have the disadvantage of 'information overload'. It may be just too much to assimilate. Taking the average family size condenses the information to a single number.

Although most people are familiar with how to calculate an average or arithmetic mean, Equation 11.6 gives the formula expressed using the Σ notation developed above and using the lower case 'n' to refer to the total number of observations in the sample.[8]

$$\bar{X} = \left\{ \sum_{i=1}^{n} X_i \right\} / n \tag{11.6}$$

The term, $\bar{X}$, is conventionally used to refer to the sample mean.[9] The right-hand side of Equation 11.6 reads, 'Add up every value of X, starting with the first and finishing with the nth, or last, and then divide the answer by however many observations there are'. Although such a complex formulation might seem pointless for such a conceptually simple notion as the arithmetic mean, it is indispensable for more complicated measures.

The median

This is a straightforward measure of location, easy to interpret and often used alongside or instead of the arithmetic mean. The median value taken by a variable is the middle value, when all values are arranged in ascending order. For the example of Figure 11.2, the median number of children, or median value taken by X, is the number of children in the eighth family, when reclassified in order of family size. For an even number of observations, the median is usually taken as the arithmetic mean of the middle two items. In a sense, it is more valuable than the mean as an indicator of 'typical' family size.

The mode

The mode only makes sense for data that can be classified into a finite number of discrete classes or groups. It is the group which contains the largest number of observations. For the data in column B of Figure 11.2, it would be that number of children which occurs most frequently, which for the fifteen recorded families is two. Data which can take a very large number of values, such as income, given in column C of Figure 11.2, first needs to be classified, say into those between £9,001 and £10,000, between £10,001 and £11,000, etc., before a mode can be calculated. The mode then depends not just on the values of the variable being considered, but also on which groupings are selected. For this reason, the mode is most commonly used for data which has already been presented in the form of a frequency distribution (see p. 138).

MEASURES OF DISPERSION

Measures of location do not give any indication of the extent to which the data are spread out. For the above example, an average of 1.93 children per family could have been derived from either a set of very different family sizes or a situation of very uniform family composition. A variety of measures exist which capture aspects of data spread. Figure 11.3 contains two sets of data, labelled A and B. Although the numbers are hypothetical and deliberately chosen to make a point, sets of data such as this could have been obtained from studies

A	B
2	4
4	5
6	6
8	7
10	8

Figure 11.3   Two sets of data in a spreadsheet

comparing the number of houses per acre in five regions of Argentina with five regions of Brazil or the ages of five children in each of two families. For both sets of data, the arithmetic mean is equal to six but set A is more spread out than set B. From a number of perspectives, one might be tempted to say that set A is twice as dispersed as set B. There are various measures which capture aspects of this dispersion.

Range and inter-quartile range

The *range* is the difference between the largest and smallest values for a set of data. For set A, the range is equal to $10 - 2 = 8$ and for set B the range is equal to $8 - 4 = 4$. Set A displays twice the range of set B. Although this measure is easy to calculate and gives exactly the information required for some purposes, its major deficiency is that it conveys information relating to only two observations from the data set. It is incapable of discerning between a situation where all values of the variable cluster at the extremes and a situation where most of the data cluster around the mean.

The *inter-quartile range* is obtained by reclassifying the data into ascending order, breaking it into two equal-sized groups and finding the median for each group. These two 'medians' are referred to as *quartiles*, since, along with the median for the original data set, they divide the data into four equal quarters. The difference between the upper and lower quartiles is referred to as the inter-quartile range. Since half of the original number of observations lie between the upper and lower quartiles, the inter-quartile range gives an indication of the degree of spread of the data, once all extreme values have been removed.

The variance and standard deviation

Both the variance and the standard deviation are single numbers, giving an indication of spread but derived from every single observation in the sample. The formula for calculating the *sample variance* is given as Equation 11.7:[10]

$$\text{Var}(X) = \left\{ \sum_{i=1}^{n} (X_i - \bar{X})^2 \right\} \Big/ n - 1 \qquad (11.7)$$

To calculate the variance, take each individual observation, subtract the mean and square the answer. The resulting numbers are then added up and the total is divided by the number of observations minus 1. At first sight, this seems a very complicated procedure but if set out clearly and neatly then the calculation can be reduced to just a few routine and repetitive steps, as shown for set A on the spreadsheet in Figure 11.4. The reader might confirm that the variance of the data in set B is equal to 2.5.

A	B	C
Data set A	*X– mean*	*(X– mean) squared*
2	–4	16
4	–2	4
6	0	0
8	2	4
10	4	16
30		40
	Variance:	10

Figure 11.4 Calculating a variance

The *standard deviation*, which for a sample is usually signified using the letter 's', is the square root of the variance. Thus, the standard deviation for data set A is 3.16 and the standard deviation for data set B is 1.58. Note that the standard deviation for data set A is twice that for data set B, once again reflecting the way that the first set of numbers is twice as spread out. Interpreting the standard deviation is largely a matter of practice. For any data set, the value taken by the standard deviation is influenced by the units in which the original variable is measured. Therefore interpretation must be in the context of the particular problem being considered. For example, if one compares the standard deviation of size of families in Argentina, Brazil, Chile and Denmark then the highest figure reflects the highest spread, the lowest figure the lowest spread and so on. Taken in isolation, however, the standard deviation is meaningless. It would be nonsense to compare, say, the figure for the standard deviation of family size in Brazil with the standard deviation of annual rainfall in Hong Kong since both are measured in different units.

To interpret the standard deviation, it is sometimes useful to know that at least three-quarters of the observations must lie within two standard deviations of the mean.[11] In many cases, the proportion is much higher, as for example with data that follows a 'normal distribution' as discussed in Chapter 14.

The coefficient of variation

A major disadvantage of the standard deviation, which has already been encountered, is that its value depends on the units of measurement used. A related concept, the coefficient of variation, usually signified by the letter 'C', measures the dispersion of a variable relative to its mean. For a sample, it is given by the formula:

$$C = 100(s/\bar{X}) \tag{11.8}$$

The coefficient of variation is the standard deviation divided by the mean and multiplied by 100 so as to give a percentage. Put simply, it is the standard deviation as a percentage of the mean.

FREQUENCY DISTRIBUTIONS AND HISTOGRAMS

An alternative way of making a set of data more digestible is to classify and display it in the form of a frequency distribution. For purposes of illustration, we introduce a new example, using data presented in Figure 11.5. This refers to the annual incomes of twenty-five graduates, five years after graduating.

Prior to compiling a frequency distribution, it is necessary to identify the range of the data and to decide on an appropriate specification of *classes*. For the data of Figure 11.5, the range of incomes is from £8,150 to £16,010. The researcher might decide on classes based on intervals of, perhaps, £1,000, so that the *class intervals* would be £8,000 to £8,999; £9,000 to £9,999 etc. Choice of

Income five years after graduation £
12,565
9,685
14,322
10,895
14,530
13,675
8,150
13,485
15,688
13,840
12,366
11,834
12,860
15,895
12,345
16,010
9,868
11,655
12,340
11,998
12,950
10,085
8,950
10,644
13,050

Figure 11.5   Graduate incomes

class interval is a matter of individual judgement, which may be affected by the purpose for which the study is to be used. Generally, the number of classes should be small enough that the results are easily assimilated and large enough to give a clear indication of distribution. It is then a straightforward procedure of working through the data and allocating each observation to the appropriate class, as

Class	Tally	Frequency
8,000–8,999	II	2
9,000–9,999	II	2
10,000–10,999	III	3
11,000–11,999	III	3
12,000–12,999	IĦI I	6
13,000–13,999	IIII	4
14,000–14,999	II	2
15,000–15,999	II	2
16,000–16,999	I	1

Figure 11.6   Frequency distribution for graduate incomes

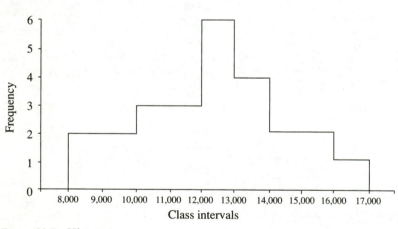

Figure 11.7   Histogram

in Figure 11.6. At this stage it is useful to check that no observations have been missed, which can be done by adding up the column of *frequencies*, where the term frequency refers to the number of observations in each class.

The information contained in a frequency distribution can usually be presented to greater visual effect using a *histogram*. The histogram for the frequency distribution of Figure 11.6 is shown as Figure 11.7. Class intervals are indicated along the bottom of the diagram and frequencies are indicated by vertical distances. In terms of visual impact, histograms have much to offer and not surprisingly they appear frequently in newspapers and in more technical publications.

An alternative visual presentation is the frequency polygon, which is a graph joining the mid-points of the top of each bar on the histogram. The frequency polygon can be thought of as a graph showing the frequency associated with each class.

Once a table of frequencies has been obtained, various related tables, indicating cumulative frequencies, cumulative percentages and relative frequencies, can be derived and are shown in Figure 11.8.

A	B	C	D	E	F	G
Class	*Fq.*	*Cum.fq.(a)*	*Cum.fq.(b)*	*Cum.%(a)*	*Cum.%(b)*	*Relative fq.*
8,000–8,999	2	2	25	8	100	0.08
9,000–9,999	2	4	23	16	92	0.08
10,000–10,999	3	7	21	28	84	0.12
11,000–11,999	3	10	18	40	72	0.12
12,000–12,999	6	16	15	64	60	0.24
13,000–13,999	4	20	9	80	36	0.16
14,000–14,999	2	22	5	88	20	0.08
15,000–15,999	2	24	3	96	12	0.08
16,000–16,999	1	25	1	100	4	0.04

Figure 11.8   Calculation of cumulative and relative frequency distributions

The *cumulative frequency distribution* indicates the number of observations in each class, up to and including the class being considered. It can be compiled for the data in either ascending order, as in column C, or in descending order, as in column D. The same information may also be expressed as a percentage, giving the cumulative percentage distributions shown in columns E and F. Any of these four forms of cumulative distribution may be shown on a graph and since such graphs have a number of applications in the social sciences, they are frequently encountered. The graph of the cumulative frequency distribution is generally referred to as an *ogive* and is shown with the

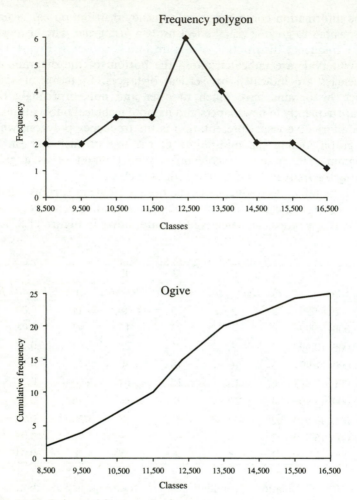

Figure 11.9   Ogive and frequency polygon

frequency polygon in Figure 11.9. When the cumulative frequency distribution is expressed in percentage terms, which is particularly common with data on income distribution, then the graph is referred to as a *Lorenz curve*. This can be a useful device for indicating degrees of inequality, comparing the extent of inequality in different countries and indicating the effects of income tax on income distribution, as illustrated in Figure 11.10.

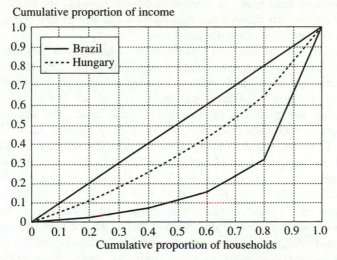

Cumulative proportion of income

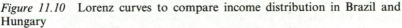
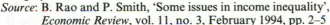

Cumulative proportion of households

Figure 11.10   Lorenz curves to compare income distribution in Brazil and Hungary
Source: B. Rao and P. Smith, 'Some issues in income inequality',
   Economic Review, vol. 11, no. 3, February 1994, pp. 2–5

The table of *relative frequencies*, given as column G of Figure 11.8, indicates the proportion of observations in each class. Each relative frequency is calculated by dividing the frequency for that class by the total number of observations. If one individual observation were to be selected at random from the twenty-five, then each relative frequency could be interpreted as the *probability* that the observation selected would be from that class. For example, if one of the twenty-five were selected at random then there would be a 0.04 probability that the person would have an annual income of between £16,000 and £16,999 and a 0.08 probability that the income would be between £8,000 and £8,999. This particular interpretation of relative frequencies is important in the development of probability theory, as discussed further in Chapter 13.

ALTERNATIVE FORMS OF VISUAL PRESENTATION

The histogram is just one way of presenting data to good visual effect. Most elementary statistics books include at least one chapter on this topic and although it is inappropriate to give a lengthy treatment here, anyone who plans to present a case supported by much data may be advised to become acquainted with the use of bar charts, pie charts, pictograms and scatter diagrams.

Bar charts are identical in construction to histograms but are used in situations where frequencies refer to qualitatively distinct categories. For example, a geographer or town planner might wish to portray the number of vehicles using a particular stretch of road each day, comparing the numbers of different vehicle types. An economist, geographer, politician or sociologist may be interested in an international comparison of unemployment rates for selected countries. Indeed, as an indication of the general level of interest attached to such comparisons, these are often given in the quality Sunday newspapers. An example is given in Figure 11.11a.

Pie charts are used to give visual impact to composition. British Nuclear Fuels are keen to educate the public to the fact that only a small proportion of the radiation received by a member of the public in a year comes from the nuclear industry and consequently the diagram of Figure 11.11b appears quite frequently in their publications. The composition of the House of Commons could similarly be shown by a pie chart where a segment for each political party is drawn in proportion to the number of seats held by that party and there are numerous other applications of relevance to most academic disciplines.

A *pictogram* shows exactly the same information as a bar chart but different sized pictures symbolising the magnitude being measured are used instead of bars. The Black Report includes a full page diagram in which cylinders of different sizes are used to signify the comparative extent of waste discharges from different nuclear installations in the UK (Black 1984: 9). Part of this is reproduced in Figure 11.11c. Other applications might include the drawing of dole queues of different lengths to symbolise different unemployment rates or piles of coins of different sizes to signify differences in the degree of public spending on different services.

Where the relationship between two variables is of interest then the *scatter diagram* is a useful device. Figure 11.12 is an excellent example of a scatter diagram used to good effect. The authors were interested in a possible relationship between increases in unemployment and early retirement and had evidence relating to nine different countries. The two variables of interest are plotted along the two axes and a position is marked for each observation according to the value taken by the two variables. For example, the position marked for Germany indicates that an increase in unemployment of approximately 5 per

a) International comparisons
   Unemployment rate: males aged 25–54

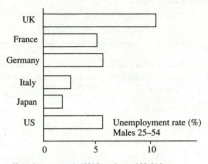

Unemployment rates in 1984 for males aged 25–54 from
OECD labour force sources (Italian data are for 1983,
males aged 25–59)

b) Composition of UK imports by value, 1992

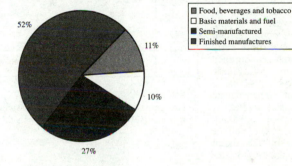

c) UK unemployed (millions)

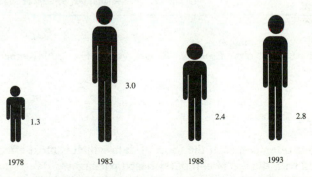

Figure 11.11 Alternative ways of presenting data
Sources: a) 'Charter for jobs', *Economic Report*, vol. 1, no. 1, September 1985
        b) *Annual Abstract of Statistics*
        c) *Employment Gazette*

cent was associated with an increase in early retirement of somewhere between 11 and 12 per cent. The use to which the information was put is captured well by the accompanying text.

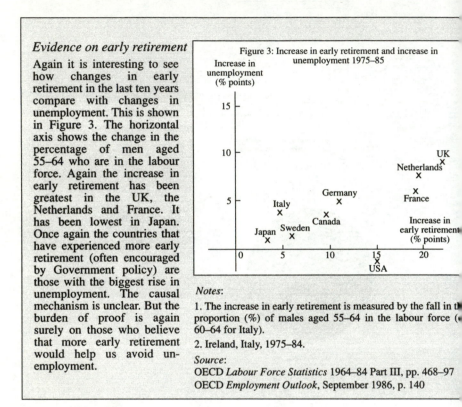

Evidence on early retirement

Again it is interesting to see how changes in early retirement in the last ten years compare with changes in unemployment. This is shown in Figure 3. The horizontal axis shows the change in the percentage of men aged 55–64 who are in the labour force. Again the increase in early retirement has been greatest in the UK, the Netherlands and France. It has been lowest in Japan. Once again the countries that have experienced more early retirement (often encouraged by Government policy) are those with the biggest rise in unemployment. The causal mechanism is unclear. But the burden of proof is again surely on those who believe that more early retirement would help us avoid unemployment.

Figure 3: Increase in early retirement and increase in unemployment 1975–85

Notes:

1. The increase in early retirement is measured by the fall in the proportion (%) of males aged 55–64 in the labour force (55–60–64 for Italy).

2. Ireland, Italy, 1975–84.

Source:
OECD *Labour Force Statistics* 1964–84 Part III, pp. 468–97
OECD *Employment Outlook*, September 1986, p. 140

Figure 11.12   Scatter diagram
Source: 'Charter for jobs', *Economic Report*, vol. 2, no. 2, November 1986, p. 3

SUMMARY

1   Evidence often comes in the form of data which is most effectively handled with the use of computer-based packages.

2   A *data base package* is a type of sophisticated filing system, capable of sorting, cross-classifying and selecting data according to criteria chosen by the user.

3 *Statistical packages* are used for calculating a range of statistics which describe features of data and for purposes of inference, associated with estimation and hypothesis testing.

4 *Spreadsheets* are a means of handling, manipulating and transforming data.

5 The term *observation* is used to refer to a particular element of data.

6 A *variable* is a particular characteristic of interest, which may take different values.

7 The Σ sign is used to mean 'the sum of'. It usually appears with a subscript and superscript. $\sum_{=1}^{n} X_i$ reads, 'The sum of the individual values for X, starting with the first value and finishing with the nth value'.

8 *Descriptive statistics* is concerned with measures which merely summarise aspects of a set of data.

9 *Statistical inference* is concerned with making inferences about a wider population on the basis of information contained in a sample.

10 *Measures of location* or *measures of central tendency* indicate a number around which data are 'centred'. They include the mean, median and mode.

11 *Measures of dispersion* indicate the extent to which data are spread out. They include the range, inter-quartile range, variance, standard deviation and coefficient of variation.

12 A *frequency distribution* is a way of classifying and displaying data. This can be expressed in diagrammatic form using a *histogram*.

13 Other forms of displaying data include the cumulative frequency distribution, Lorenz curve, bar chart, pie chart and pictogram. The way in which two variables appear to be related can be displayed using a scatter diagram.

12 Furthering knowledge

In the process of furthering knowledge, deductive and inductive reasoning interact in various ways. Students and researchers sometimes adopt methods which largely exclude one or the other. Such positions are extreme. They are considered now as a preliminary to identifying a balanced approach to furthering knowledge, which acknowledges and utilises the interconnectedness of argument and evidence.

DEDUCTIVE METHOD AND REALITY

Deductive methods typically suspend the acceptability requirement for premises. They are akin to suppositional reasoning in that the defence of premises is considered unimportant. In this sense, deductivism is naive. It fails to get a grip on the world it seeks to understand, whether the world of concepts and ideas or the world of substantive things. Even so, some practitioners within some academic disciplines at various times have attempted to further knowledge by methods largely based on deductive reasoning.

The economist, David Ricardo, made substantial contributions to political economy by using what were essentially deductive methods.[1] His approach was to build economic models and draw conclusions from them. For example, by making quite restrictive assumptions about the conditions under which two commodities are produced in two different countries he deduced that economic welfare would be increased in both countries if each specialised in the production of the commodity which it could produce comparatively cheaply and traded this for the other commodity, produced by its trading partner. Despite the fact that countries inevitably produce more than two commodities, so that the assumptions are quite unrealistic, the analysis was meticulous and sophisticated. It was even couched in terms of geometry. The reasoning involved was valid. The conclusions were entailed by the premises but required the insight of a mind such as Ricardo's to make them explicit. Furthermore, by setting out his analysis in terms of an example where the two commodities were wine and cloth, Ricardo managed to contextualise the argument, so that although the reasoning was at an abstract and general level, the reader was encouraged to make the association with the contemporary trade disputes between Britain and Portugal. This 'theory of comparative advantage', albeit with slight modifications, is still taught to economics students and used, even today, as the basis for arguing the case for free trade as opposed to protectionism. The Ricardian method – or Ricardian 'vice', as it has been called by at least one critic – was extended to many areas of public policy.[2] Ricardo used it, for example, to argue the case for the repeal of the corn laws and his analysis of the factors responsible for the distribution of income formed an important basis for the arguments in favour of a land tax.

It was noted earlier that deductive reasoning makes explicit what is already implied in the premises. Thus, in a very real sense, one can only get out of a deductive argument what one puts into it. Ricardo's stated premises were unrealistic in some ways but also there were certain ideas which were taken for granted by the community of economists concerning, for example, the meaning of 'free trade'. It could be argued that Ricardo 'put into the premises' precisely what he intended to get out of them.

Deductivism is considered by some to be naive. It has two features which make this so. First, the suspension of independent support for the premises and, second, one only gets out what one puts in. The effect is to disconnect method from the world it seeks to explain. This lack of grip on the world can be avoided by finding an alternative means of applying the benefits of deductive method without going to the other extreme of requiring that all premises be in principle well grounded.

INDUCTIVE REASONING

Inductive reasoning is commonly used in everyday life, in business and in furthering knowledge. A child goes to bed at night knowing that it will be light the next morning. She is unlikely to have been subjected to complicated theories about the earth rotating every twenty-four hours. Even if she has, it is unlikely that this will be the basis for her optimism about the next day. More simply, she knows that it will be light in the morning because it always is. On the basis of past experience, the child has extrapolated forward from known, observed cases to the as yet unknown. Learning from experience is part of the human condition.

Businessmen also learn from their experience. If sales have risen rapidly every week for six months, the sales manager might be inclined to ensure that he has sufficient stocks to meet a similar increase in sales the following week. If he is more sophisticated he might draw a graph of sales figures up to the present and use this to extrapolate forward. Had he been trained in a business school he might go one step further and use a model to predict the next week's sales on the basis of previous performance. However, an astute businessman will be aware that whatever has been causing sales to increase until now may well not do so tomorrow. He will realise that the observed cases cannot be projected forward with certainty.

More broadly, the pursuit of knowledge based on arguing from evidence uses premises which are observations of particular instances. Inductive modes of reasoning have the following structure:

[Observation statement 1]
[Observation statement 2]
[Observation statement 3]
. . . .
. . . .
[Observation statement n]
Therefore generalisation.

The particular observations reveal a pattern of events and the inductive inference projects this pattern forwards into future or unwitnessed cases. Inductive reasoning commonly occurs in the social sciences and many consider it reliable.

THE PROBLEM OF INDUCTION

Sensibly used, inductive inferences are an important part of the learning process. Their use has the advantage of taking evidence seriously and yet there are always risks in going beyond the available evidence. Consider the story told by Bertrand Russell,[3] presented in Box 12.1. The gruesome end to the story shows that inductive inferences are inherently unreliable. Conclusions based on projections beyond what has already been observed are not guaranteed.

Box 12.1 Russell's inductivist chicken

One day a chicken hatched. By chance, it stumbled upon corn and water. It was a happy chick. The next day it happened again and again the next. Being an intelligent chicken, it considered the possibility that the supplies might stop and wondered whether it would be necessary to take precautions. It decided to investigate the world to see whether, given a large number of cases and a wide variety of conditions, there were grounds to suppose that the pattern of events so far witnessed would continue into the future. The benefit would be that no precaution against the non-supply of corn and water need be taken. After months of careful observations and noting that differences in weather, configurations of stars, beings encountered, mood and many other things did not stop the supplies, the chicken concluded that the world truly was a wonderful place. The very next day, everything changed. It was 24 December.

Box 12.2 illustrates a further point about inductive reasoning.[4]

Box 12.2 Projecting patterns in a series of numbers

An IQ test question asked, 'What is the next number in the series 1, 2, 3, 4, 5 . . .?' Most would say '6' because there is a rule which describes a pattern in the series such that the next number is the current number plus 1. However, there is another rule which describes the observable pattern equally accurately. It is:

$$((K - 1) \times (K - 2) \times (K - 3) \times (K - 4) \times (K - 5)) + K$$

where the Kth number is K in every case; for example, the third number is 3 and can be calculated by substituting 3 for K throughout. It should be possible, therefore, to use the formula to identify the sixth number. When '6' is substituted for 'K' throughout, the answer is 126. Would a candidate giving this answer in a test be marked correct?

This shows that more than one generalisation may accurately describe a given pattern. Empirical grounds do not help establish which one should be accepted. Uniformities in the world cannot be discovered with certainty by naive inductive inference.

Inductive reasoning which generates conclusions claiming more than the evidence warrants are less than reliable. Intuitively, this seems unscientific. Going beyond available evidence is a leap in the dark, a huge presumption about the uniformity of nature. Sometimes this problem can be addressed by couching statements in terms of probability. Under some circumstances, this strategy can have considerable pay-off. In other instances it may be quite misleading. These issues are discussed further in Chapter 13.

INDUCTIVE METHOD AND THEORY

In a strict sense, inductive inferences are not logical at all. Yet, they still make sense and constitute a method of reasoning, which plays a role in scientific inquiry and academic debate. Sir Francis Bacon's reaction to exclusively deductive methods is legendary. He was convinced that evidence should make a difference to what we are entitled to believe about the world. This position is attractive in so far as it makes strong overtures towards objective knowledge, although the issue concerning what counts as evidence needs to be addressed and clear, agreed definitions are required. There are ways, other than the naive rejection of theory, to respond to the Baconian requirement that evidence matters. Some scientists believe that theoretical entities do exist. For example, the notion of a molecule was posited as a theoretical entity. The molecular approach used by natural scientists was considerably developed before it was possible to make observations of actual molecules. Scientists were not daunted by being unable to see molecules. Energy and resources were allocated to devising the means of doing so. The electron microscope made this possible. One could take a critical view of this development and complain that scientists designed the electron microscope with the theory built into it, such that whatever was seen could be construed as molecular. On the other hand, it is a serious attempt to balance the need for theory and the requirement to give proper weight to evidence.

Striking an appropriate balance between theory and observation raises a problem fundamental to the furthering of knowledge. Theories offer stories in terms of which observed phenomena can be interpreted and understood. Molecular theory tells us that physical matter comprises groups of atoms which combine in various ways to form the fundamental units of chemical compounds that take part in chemical reactions. According to the theory, molecules oscillate rapidly when excited. In such a world, differences in temperature are described as differences in the level of molecular excitation. Our experiences of heat and cold are described differently. Hot things burn, people perspire in hot climates and shiver in cold weather. Hence, there are two accounts of temperature differences – the one a theoretical story and the other an observed story. Each account describes a different type of event. There is a gap between the theoretical, excited molecules and the observed heat.

The discrepancy between the two stories makes it difficult to see how statements couched in theoretical terms can be made to confront the evidence, as the falsifiability of empirical claims requires. Because theories are employed to explain observed phenomena, furthering knowledge about the world depends on a theory's capacity to generate testable hypotheses. This capacity is considerably diminished if the gap between theory and what is observable cannot be bridged. Ryan (1970: Chapter 4) mentions several cases where the problems in making links between theory and observation have proved so difficult that the key concepts have been discredited. Such concepts include the 'luminiferous ether', now abandoned by astronomers and physicists; the 'unconscious', rejected by many psychologists as unscientific; and the Marxian term, 'alienation', criticised for not generating testable hypotheses with sufficient rigour.

There are two particular approaches to furthering knowledge worth mentioning. *Realists* and *instrumentalists* respond differently to the gap between theory and observation. From a realist perspective, theoretical entities exist. Thus, in principle, there is no reason why there should be a gap between theory and observation. If there is a difficulty then the realist would say that the problem is a practical one, as in the earlier example concerning molecules. Instrumentalists do not consider the theory–observation gap problematic. Popper describes their view of theory as 'an instrument for the deduction of predictions of future events' (Popper 1983: 111).[5] The economist, Professor Milton Friedman, is frequently described as an instrumentalist.[6] His ideas had a considerable influence in the approach to economic policy followed by the British and United States Governments during the 1980s. Other social scientists also take this stance, including the sociologist, Max Weber.[7] His theory of *ideal types* supposes that features of the social world can be explained by reasoning about entities, which could never have existed. The 'rational man' of economic theory is such an entity. To instrumentalists, whether such entities exist is of no consequence. Provided the theory adequately predicts future events, it continues to be a basis for research. If not then the theory should be abandoned. A persistent criticism of instrumentalist theories and methods is that they fail to contribute substantively to our knowledge and understanding of the world.[8] Realists accept that theory has a role in furthering knowledge because they suppose that the theory–observation gap can be bridged. Instrumentalists, not worried by the gap, concede that observations determine which theories should be believed. The difference in method is a matter of emphasis.

A BALANCED APPROACH TO METHOD

Social scientists today are rarely naive deductivists or naive inductivists. Much reasoning and most investigations combine deductive and inductive inferences, although some people have leanings towards one rather than the other. Consider the following statement from the late Lord Kaldor, economic adviser to the Labour Government of Harold Wilson:

> one should subordinate deduction to induction, and discover the empirical regularities first, whether through a study of statistics or through special inquiries that include 'informal conversations with the owners or executives of small businesses'.
>
> (Kaldor 1985 p. 8)

He clearly sees a role for deduction and induction but, in the context of 'discovering methods and policies to improve the performance of the economy', he considers it appropriate to 'subordinate deduction to induction'. His view and that of Friedman could be located on a crude but perhaps helpful spectrum of methodological positions, which is presented in Figure 12.1.

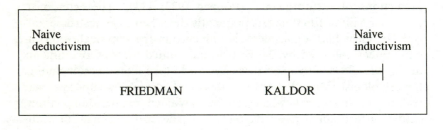

Figure 12.1   Methodological positions

The hypothetico-deductive method

The *hypothetico-deductive* method is an approach to research which involves both deductive and inductive reasoning. It is neither naive deductivism nor naive inductivism. This approach begins with a hunch or conjecture. This may be a response to an observed event, a spark of imagination or a combination of both. The next stage is to use deductive reasoning to generate propositions or *hypotheses*, which are in principle testable. To test an hypothesis, the researcher attempts to establish whether it is borne out by the evidence. The results of the test will have implications for the original conjecture, which is evaluated accordingly. The essential features of the hypothetico-deductive method are set out in Figure 12.2. Deductive inferences take researchers from conjecture to testable hypotheses. Then inductive inferences support the hypotheses to a greater or lesser extent and thereby may corroborate the original conjecture. This approach to research is used by many social scientists and may be consistent with a variety of realist and instrumentalist positions.

CONJECTURE → HYPOTHESES → TEST → EVALUATION

Figure 12.2   The hypothetico-deductive method

A sociologist may claim that females, when faced with the technology of microcomputers, have greater learning difficulties than males. This is as yet mere conjecture. Much discussion about what counts as a learning difficulty and how to detect it accurately in any particular instances would need to take place. For example, learning ability would have to be distinguished from a preparedness to work hard or for long hours and be measured by more sensitive means than the marks from an end of semester test. Such discussion aims to bridge the theory–observation gap. When agreement about the meanings of key concepts is established, testable hypotheses are derived. Evidence is sought which will refute or substantiate the sociologist's claim. This method of research combines deductive and inductive styles of reasoning, so that researchers approach the furthering of knowledge with both theoretical and empirical rigour.

OTHER APPROACHES

Empirical research in the social sciences is difficult. There are moral objections to methods which in relevant ways fail to respect the dignity of those being studied. Individuals attach meaning to their behaviour by having intentions, motives and purposes. For example, crying may signify happiness or sorrow. Consequently, accounts of human actions are at best incomplete if the psychological states that accompany them are ignored. Any serious attempt to understand human behaviour has to identify the meanings of actions observed. The cultural context in which behaviour occurs can provide clues about the meaning of actions. Language is another clue, where the accurate interpretation of intentions requires an appreciation of the ways in which words are used to capture key features of experience.[9] Several approaches have been made along these lines to furthering knowledge about human beings.

Participant observation

Participant observation is an attempt to get an insider's view of what people are doing in a given situation. Acquiring such knowledge is achieved by joining in the community and sharing the language of the culture concerned. Difficulties are encountered when trying to understand one culture in terms of another. The researcher's involvement amounts to learning the rules by which participants interpret each other's actions. This provides information that would be valuable in itself and also because what is observed in these terms could be used to test hypotheses.[10] Objectivity and detachment are a problem. If the observer participates completely then a detached analysis may be impossible. Yet, if researchers remain detached, their remoteness could result in something important being overlooked. It is no easy matter to achieve a satisfactory balance but there could be circumstances in which such an approach to furthering knowledge would be justified. For instance, evidence witnessed by police officers in disguise has led to the successful conviction of football hooligans. Another well known example of these methods has been the studies with gorillas and chimpanzees presented for television by David Attenborough.

Philosophical approaches

Taking seriously the dimension of meaning in which people live requires an approach that addresses how people think about what they do. Philosophers have been engaged in such activities for more than two and a half thousand years. Peter Winch (1958) argued that the methods of philosophy rather than science are appropriate for the understanding of people and society because they address the problems of interpretation and specifically the meaning of human actions. The merit of such philosophical approaches is that they seek to take account of those aspects of nature that are characteristically human. The detachment of philosophical analysis would be regarded as a beneficial disposition for social researchers.[11]

Hermeneutic approaches

Techniques for establishing authentic interpretations of written works have been developed over hundreds of years in the study of biblical, literary and legal texts. This approach to examining meaning in people's lives is called *hermeneutics*.[12] During the twentieth century the methods have been more widely applied in the social sciences, putting a central focus on the problem of interpretation. This school of thought locates individual and group behaviour in the context of a tradition or convention. Trigg describes Gadamer's hermeneutic position[13] in these terms:

> Individuals are placed firmly in their social context, and the subject does not give meaning to his or her activities. Instead, meaning is generated by tradition, and self-reflection must be parasitic on it. Gadamer asserts that 'history does not belong to us, but we belong to it'.
>
> (Trigg 1985: 199)

One problem associated with this holistic approach to furthering knowledge concerns the reliability of interpreting one tradition from the standpoint of another. Following the philosopher Wittgenstein, Gadamer considers that the linguistic world in which others live need not inhibit the researcher's understanding of context. It is possible to take the world of others into our own by broadening our horizons or, for the purposes of analysis, by making appropriate assumptions. In so far as this can be done, the researcher has access to empirical data about human behaviour.

Participant observation and hermeneutic methods enrich the quality of information about society. The aridity of purely behaviourist accounts of human actions is avoided by providing more information, though of a different kind. Providing data about what people do for its own sake is an acceptable form of research in the social sciences but this activity is not the same as the testing of hypotheses about human behaviour. Data provision and hypothesis tests are not mutually exclusive alternatives for the researcher. The two different activities are compatible and authentic data can be part of a research design based on hypothesis tests.

BIAS AND PREJUDICE

Openness contributes to the furthering of knowledge because research is subject to the scrutiny of colleagues. Declaring theoretical assumptions is one way in which openness manifests itself. This reveals something of the scholar's world view as a framework for research design and sets the standards for what counts as evidence. Permitting anything relevant, especially context, to have its bearing on the outcome of research is another sign of openness. It is more subtly present when the researcher qualifies findings with phrases such as 'at the present state of knowledge' and 'as far as we can tell', because they allow for as yet unknown data to influence the results. Yet another indicator of openness is the adoption of methods that can be replicated by others. This means that even those who do not share a researcher's theoretical stance can, for the purposes of inquiry, double check the findings by repeating the experiments.

By contrast, *bias* and *prejudice* tend to inhibit the furthering of knowledge. The terms are used interchangeably to refer to a range of methodological misdemeanours but most fall into two broad categories. One set of difficulties arises from what might be called *preferred belief*. This involves rejecting all else in favour of a specific theoretical position. Such researchers bring a self-inflicted narrowness of mind into their work which is tantamount to imposing one's own ignorance on others. Durkheim advised good researchers to admit such bias so that its effect on their work can be assessed by others.[14]

Prejudging the outcomes of experiments is in some ways more serious and, as a policy for furthering knowledge, is fundamentally flawed. On the one hand, there is the presumption that evidence makes a difference to what one is entitled to believe and, on the other, there is an implication that evidence does not matter because the desired results are forced either by faulty sampling or even by inventing data. It is difficult to imagine that anyone would seriously attempt such things but it does happen, as some of Professor Burt's work on the association between race and IQ illustrates.[15] Safeguards against such deception include good research design and sound methods for sampling, statistical analysis and testing. They should become an integral part of any inquiry and feature in critical appraisal. These practical concerns are discussed in subsequent chapters.

SUMMARY

1 Naive deductivism suspends the acceptability requirement for premises in order to further knowledge.
2 Naive inductivism relies on evidence without theory to further knowledge.
3 Realism presumes that theoretical entities exist.
4 Instrumentalism or operationalism uses theories as instruments in order to establish coherent ways of thinking about society.
5 Balanced approaches to furthering knowledge combine deductive and inductive inferences. Researchers may have leanings towards one or the other.
6 Hypothetico-deductivism confronts what can be thought by what is experienced.
7 Furthering knowledge about the social world requires:
   a) The specification of theoretical assumptions about world views and what counts as evidence.
   b) The formulation of testable hypotheses.
   c) The adoption of methods adequate for obtaining accurate data, reliable estimates and hypothesis tests.
   d) The recognition of knowledge limits and that as yet unknown data could, when available, influence any findings to which they may be relevant.

13 Probability and uncertainty

Inductive reasoning is often concerned with projecting from known cases to as yet unknown cases. Any inductive argument is subject to the problem of induction. Although this cannot be ignored, an understanding of probability frequently permits one to use inductive reasoning. Various concepts of probability and various situations involving uncertainty are discussed on pp. 164–7 in order to distinguish contexts where the theory of probability is appropriately applied from those where it is inappropriate or misleading. This is an essential prerequisite for the theory of statistical inference. It is also a fundamental basis for actuarial work, as the following example indicates:

Example 13.1

Insurance companies aim to set premiums that are low enough to be competitive but high enough to yield an acceptable margin for profit. An unknown female customer, aged twenty-two, having just passed a driving test and owning a brand new 1.4 litre Ford Escort applies for fully comprehensive cover. The company will quote a premium, basing its quotation on the accident record of other drivers. The company has records on 1,000 newly qualified female drivers aged 20–25 with 1.4 litre cars, which show that on average eighty of these make a claim each year, with the average settlement amounting to £4,000. The relative frequency of an accident, amongst this particular set of drivers, is 80/1,000 or 0.08. For any one of these drivers, selected at random, there is a probability of 0.08 that she will make a claim. In the absence of further information about the new customer, the company might infer that there is also a 0.08 probability that she will make a claim and set the premium to reflect this. It must also reflect the size of the typical claim, which, so far, has averaged £4,000. The company estimates that the expected value of a claim is £4,000 times 0.08, which amounts to £320. Adding a margin for administrative costs, profit and possibly inflation, say 20 per cent, the company might offer a quotation of £384.

In Example 13.1, when estimating the probability of an individual driver having an accident, the company is projecting from the known evidence concerning previous cases to the unknown outcome for the new driver. As the new driver's record unfolds it will form part of the data available for the future estimation of probabilities and calculation of premiums. Having illustrated a practical sense in which probability calculations are important in everyday life, we now consider further aspects of probability theory.

PROBABILITY CONCEPTS AND DEFINITIONS

Some of the basic concepts in the theory of probability are most effectively explained using simple examples. The concept of probability is relevant to any activity or process that leads to a number of possible outcomes where the actual outcome is not known in advance. We consider two very simple examples:

Example 13.2

Consider the process of rolling a die and observing the number on top. The six possible outcomes are for the number on top to be either 1, 2, 3, 4, 5 or 6.

Outcome is a technical term, used in probability theory in a precise way. The crucial point about an outcome is that, although there may be many possible outcomes to a process, only one outcome will actually occur. For any such process, the set of all possible outcomes is referred to as the *sample space*. Thus, the sample space for the above example consists of the numbers 1, 2, 3, 4, 5 and 6.

Sometimes the outcome of a process is a number, as in the above example. In other situations the outcomes are not immediately specified as numbers but can be converted into numerical form by assigning numbers to them.

Example 13.3

There are three white balls and one black ball in a bag. A ball is selected at random and its colour noted.

The two possible outcomes to this process are 'white' or 'black'. One may allocate numbers to each of these outcomes such that if a white ball is selected we might say that outcome number 0 has occurred and if a black ball is selected then outcome number 1 has occurred. In

technical terms, one defines a *random variable*, which we may arbitrar-
ily call X, to take the value of 0 if a white ball is selected and 1 if a
black ball is selected.

Sometimes it is useful to refer to specific collections, or groups, of
outcomes from a particular process and for such purposes one uses
the term 'event'. An *event* consists of a collection of one or more
outcomes from a process. For instance, in the die rolling experiment
of Example 13.2, we may define the following events:

Event A	X is greater than or equal to 3.
Event B	X is less than or equal to 3.
Event C	X is 1 or 2.
Event D	X is 3, 4 or 5.
Event E	X is 6.
Event S	X is any number between 1 and 6 inclusive.

An event may consist of just one outcome, such as event E, in which
case it is called a *simple event*; or it may consist of more than one
outcome, such as events A, B, C, D and S, in which case it is referred
to as a *composite event*.

Sometimes it is necessary to consider two or more events at the
same time. Two events are said to be *mutually exclusive* if there are no
outcomes common to both. Events C and D are mutually exclusive;
events A and B are not mutually exclusive.

ASSIGNING PROBABILITIES

In Example 13.1 it was shown how previous driving records are used
to infer a probability for a particular driver having an accident. Note
that the probability is expressed as a number. Using the terms introduced above, the newly qualified driver will undertake the process of
driving for one year and there are two possible outcomes. Either she
will have an accident or she will not. We could define a random
variable, X, to take the value 0 if the new driver has an accident-free
year and to take the value 1 if she has an accident. The insurance
company is assigning a probability of 0.08 to the outcome that X
equals 1 and, by implication, 0.92 to the outcome that X equals 0.
Thus, a probability, expressed as a number, specifies the likelihood of
a particular outcome or event occurring.

Probabilities are assigned according to a set of basic rules, or
postulates. On the basis of these, mathematicians and statisticians
have derived a further set of rules and theorems which, taken together,
comprise a comprehensive body of analysis, loosely referred to as

probability theory. Fortunately, quite considerable progress can be made with just two postulates, which can be expressed in quite straightforward terms:

Postulate 1: A probability is a number between 0 and 1 inclusive.
Postulate 2: An event which *must* occur is assigned a probability of 1.

There is a convention to let a capital letter P denote probability and to denote the probability of an event, say event A, occurring as P(A). Note that this does not mean P multiplied by A. Rather, the expression must be treated as a whole and interpreted as above. Similarly, in Example 13.2, the probability of rolling a six, denoted as event E, is written: $P(E) = 1/6$.

Another convention is to let the letter 'S' denote the entire sample space. Referring to the same example, recall that we defined event S as X being any number between 1 and 6 inclusive. Since there are only six faces on a die, event S must occur and so it follows that $P(S) = 1$. An alternative, more formal way of writing Postulate 2 would be to state that $P(S) = 1$.

Two extensions to the notation enable one to encompass situations involving two or more events. *P(A and B)* means the probability of both event A and event B occurring together. *P(A or B)* means the probability either of event A occurring or of event B occurring or of them both occurring together.[1]

The addition theorem

For the die-rolling Example 13.2, there are six possible outcomes. Each of these is a simple event and they are all mutually exclusive. Event A, defined above as X being greater than or equal to 3, is a composite event comprising four outcomes. The probability of event A occurring is calculated by adding the probabilities of the individual mutually exclusive outcomes of which the composite event is comprised. Thus, the probability of event A occurring is equal to $1/6 + 1/6 + 1/6 + 1/6 = 4/6$ or $2/3$. This is an illustration of the *addition theorem* of probability. It is usually expressed in terms of events rather than outcomes and is stated as follows: *For mutually exclusive events, the probability of one or another occurring is given by the sum of the individual probabilities.* Formally, one may write:

$$P(A \text{ or } B) = P(A) + P(B) \tag{13.1}$$

Although the notation P(A or B) means 'the probability of event A occurring or of event B occurring or of both occurring', when events are mutually exclusive they cannot both occur together.

For non-mutually exclusive events, the addition theorem becomes a little more complicated and can be written formally as:

$$P(A \text{ or } B) = P(A) + P(B) - P(A \text{ and } B) \qquad (13.2)$$

Where the last term in brackets on the right-hand side refers to the probability of both A and B occurring together.[2]

INTERPRETING PROBABILITIES

From the two postulates set out above, one can often derive the probabilities associated with each individual outcome in a process. Postulate 2 asserts that an event which must occur has a probability of 1. In the die-rolling experiment, the composite event, S, that X will be equal to one of the numbers, 1, 2, 3, 4, 5 or 6, must occur and therefore has a probability equal to unity. Knowledge of the process includes the fact that all six outcomes are equally likely. Hence, the probability of any one outcome occurring is equal to 1/6. Probabilities derived from prior knowledge of the process involved are sometimes called *a priori probabilities*.

In Example 13.1, the probability assigned to the event of an individual driver having an accident was arrived at in a different way. It was derived from empirical data. Probabilities derived in this way are referred to as *empirical probabilities*. They are based on the relative frequency with which the event has already occurred in observed data. This concept has limitations. In Example 13.1, the probability was calculated using data from the records of existing drivers and it was inferred that these would be appropriate for calculating probabilities associated with other drivers. Once the probability is projected beyond the known data then a process of inductive reasoning is involved and there is the danger that unforeseen circumstances may render the inductive inference inappropriate. Changes to the driving test or dramatic changes in weather patterns, for example, may result in the accident records of new drivers being very different from those of their predecessors. In other words, there is the problem of induction.

Both *a priori* and empirical probabilities are *objectively* determined. A different person, assigning probabilities in the same circumstances, would assign the same numbers. Sometimes, probabilities are assigned on a *subjective* basis.[3] For example, an individual student, of nervous disposition, might consider that the probability of passing a particular end of semester examination is 0.2. The tutor's assessment for the same student might be 0.9. Both numbers would be obtained subjectively and hence have a slightly different status than objective probabilities. That does not imply that they are necessarily useless. In deciding how much credibility to attach to them one would consider the authority of the person making the assessment, the information on which the assessment was based, the degree of confidence with which the claim was made and anything else which might be relevant.

Perhaps the least problematic interpretation of probabilities, for our purposes as social scientists, is the 'frequency' interpretation, whereby a probability is defined as: *The limit of the relative frequency of the occurrence of an attribute in an infinite sequence of events.*[4] When dealing with known physical processes, such as the process of rolling a die, this interpretation does not appear to present any problems. However, for empirical probabilities, there is the problem that one cannot infer the limit of the relative frequency from a finite number of observations. Thus, the problem of induction arises.

DEGREES OF UNCERTAINTY

'Uncertainty' is a broad term which covers a range of types of situation. The die-rolling experiment, as in Example 13.2, is at one extreme. There is a finite number of outcomes and each possible outcome is known. Furthermore, because the process is known and understood, the probability associated with each outcome can be calculated. The only element of uncertainty is in which of the specified outcomes will occur. The 'frequency' interpretation of probability fits this case well.

However, there are some problems where even though the entire sample space can be delineated, the probability of a particular outcome occurring is unknown. Reconsider Example 13.1. Empirical probabilities, calculated from data generated in the past, are allocated to the outcome that a driver will or will not have an accident, despite that particular driver never having driven before. By using such empirical probabilities, the insurance company is assuming that the new driver will behave in a similar way to previous drivers and will also be subjected to a similar set of external influences. By classifying drivers according to their age, sex and occupation and cars according to their power, insurance companies may be confident that they have taken sufficient factors into consideration when calculating probabilities.

None the less, if external influences were to change adversely, then the probability that the new driver has an accident would be increased. It is likely that the insurance company, having set many premiums on the basis of probabilities calculated from past records, will be faced with more claims than it anticipated. In this case, there is an additional element of uncertainty which arises because of the problem of induction.

Now consider an insurance company asked to quote a premium to cover the first manned space flight to Mars. Let us initially suppose that the terms of the policy are explicit: the company pays up if the craft does not return to earth but otherwise it incurs no liability. The two possible outcomes are known but there is little basis for calculating probabilities. It would certainly have no empirical data. But the situation could be even worse. Suppose that the terms of the contract are that the insurance company reimburses all travellers for any loss incurred, however caused. To delineate the sample space, the company needs to know all the possible causes of loss. In this latter case, not only does the company have no basis for allocating probabilities to each outcome; it does not even know what the outcomes are. Yet a further element of uncertainty has been introduced. It is examples like this which some writers call true uncertainty. If the insurance company still wishes to set a premium it is likely to guess the probability of loss occurring. But, in this case, it is difficult to interpret such a 'probability' as anything other than what it is – a guess!

One should be wary of figures purporting to represent the probabilities of different outcomes, without knowing the basis on which these have been derived. For example, the nuclear industry is often required to reassure the general public on the safety of its installations. Hence, one often comes across statements such as, 'there is a probability of less than one in a million of an accident occurring' in a particular plant or from a particular process. But where do these figures come from? One might presume that if any potential cause of a nuclear accident can be identified then the authority concerned takes every possible measure to eliminate any risk from that particular cause. Yet accidents do happen. According to Patterson (1986) there have been over 200 reported serious incidents at nuclear installations. Patterson documents many of these with what, if not for their seriousness, would be amusing stories. Excerpts from two of these are reproduced in Box 13.1. In both cases the causes are bizarre. Surely, no-one could have foreseen them. In such situations, probabilities are impossible to arrive at.

Box 13.1 When probabilities cannot be calculated

The Brown's Ferry candle incident

The candle was in the hand of an electrician in the cable-spreading room under the control room of the Brown's Ferry station in Alabama, which had just become the world's largest operating nuclear station. . . . At 12.30 pm on 22 March 1975 the electrician and his mate were checking the airflow through wall-penetrations for cables, by holding the candle next to the penetration, when the draught blew the candle flame and ignited the foam plastic packing around the cable-tray. The electrician could not put out the fire.

The temperature rise was noticed by the plant operator, who flooded the room with carbon dioxide and extinguished the fire beneath the control room – but the fire had already spread along the cables into the reactor building. . . . The fire continued to burn for seven hours, affecting hundreds of cables. According to the US Nuclear Regulatory Commission the fire knocked out all five emergency core-cooling systems on Unit 1. Repairs to the station kept it out of service for eighteen months, and entailed over $40 million in the cost of replacement electricity output alone.

Source: Patterson (1986: 150–1)

The Rancho Seco lightbulb

On 28 March 1978 . . . a 25-cent light bulb proved to be almost as hazardous as the notorious candle at Brown's Ferry. A technician was replacing the bulb behind a lighted push button on the control panel of the Rancho Seco nuclear plant near Sacramento, California. He dropped the bulb; and it fell into the control panel, shorting out one of the main electrical connections to the reactor's instrumentation. Spurious signals about pressure, temperature, water level and flow, and other important data began flooding into the reactor's main control computer. . . . The reactor pressure shot up and the reactor scrammed itself. . . .

By the time the short-circuited power had been restored, seventy minutes after the hapless technician had dropped the lightbulb, the cooling system temperature had fallen to below the technical specification limits. . . .

The particular sequence of events at Rancho Seco did not, as it happened, involve any safety hazard, although it certainly might have written off some pretty expensive equipment. But it provided a startling demonstration of the fragility of the link between a reactor and its operators, if the link could be reduced to futility by a 25-cent light bulb.

Source: Patterson (1986: 166–7). Reprinted from *Nuclear Power* by Walter C. Patterson (Penguin Books 1976, 2nd edn 1983),
Copyright © Walter C. Patterson 1976, 1980, 1983, 1986

PROBABILITY DISTRIBUTIONS

A *probability distribution* consists of each possible value that a random variable can take along with the probability of the random variable taking that particular value.

For the die-throwing process of Example 13.2, the random variable, X, may be any of the values 1, 2, 3, 4, 5 or 6. The probability to be assigned to each outcome in the sample space is 1/6. The probability distribution for this process is set out in Figure 13.1.

X	P(X)
1	1/6
2	1/6
3	1/6
4	1/6
5	1/6
6	1/6

Figure 13.1   Probability distribution for Example 13.2

Although compiling a probability distribution is sometimes straightforward, the procedure is more complicated when dealing with composite events. Since composite events consist of more than one individual outcome, derivation of the probability distribution requires one to use the addition rule of probability. In such circumstances, it usually helps to begin by setting out the entire sample space for the process under discussion. Consider Example 13.4:

Example 13.4
A coin is tossed three times in succession. The random variable, X, is defined as the number of heads. Using H to denote a head and T to denote a tail, the sample space is set out in Figure 13.2.

HHH   HHT   HTH   HTT   THH   THT   TTH   TTT

Figure 13.2   Sample space for Example 13.4

For Example 13.4, there are eight possible outcomes, each of which is equally likely. Consequently, the two probability postulates imply that each has a probability of 1/8. We draw up a probability distribution for our initial process, as set out in Figure 13.3 and to facilitate discussion, we assign a letter to each of the eight outcomes (or simple events).

Outcome		*Probability*
HHH	A	1/8
HHT	B	1/8
HTH	C	1/8
HTT	D	1/8
THH	E	1/8
THT	F	1/8
TTH	G	1/8
TTT	H	1/8

Figure 13.3   Probability distribution for Example 13.4

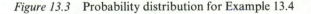

Now we can compile a probability distribution for X, the total number of heads. Examination of the sample space reveals that X can be 0, 1, 2 or 3. To compile the probability distribution for X we assign the probabilities associated with each of these possible values. In the first and last cases, this is straightforward. X taking the value 0 coincides with event H occurring and X taking the value 3 coincides with event A occurring. In both cases, the associated probability is 1/8. The composite event of X taking the value 1 consists of the three mutually exclusive simple events,

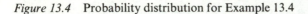

X	P(X)
0	1/8
1	3/8
2	3/8
3	1/8

Figure 13.4   Probability distribution for Example 13.4

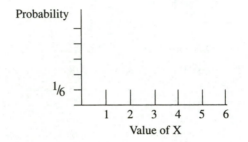

Figure 13.5   Probability distribution for rolling a die

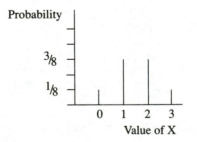

Figure 13.6   Probability distribution for the number of heads from three tosses of a coin

D, F and G. Following the addition theorem, the probability of this composite event occurring is derived by adding the probabilities of each of the simple events, D, F and G occurring. Thus, the probability of obtaining one head is equal to $1/8 + 1/8 + 1/8 = 3/8$. By similar reasoning, the probability of obtaining two heads is also 3/8. The probability distribution for X can now be set down as in Figure 13.4.

A probability distribution can be displayed in the form of a diagram. List all the possible values that the random variable can take along a horizontal line and above each value draw a vertical line, the height of which indicates the probability of the random variable taking that particular value. Figures 13.5 and 13.6 show the probability distributions for Examples 13.2 and 13.4.

JOINT PROBABILITIES

In practical applications of probability, one often studies situations involving more than one random variable and it may be important to know whether or not the random variables are independent of each other. If the value taken by each random variable does not influence the probability distribution for the other then they are independent. Conversely, if the value taken by one of the random variables influences the probability distribution for the other, then they are not independent.

Consider the process of rolling two dice. Define a random variable, X, as the number on top of the first die, define Y as the number on top of the second die and define Z as the sum of X and Y. Since the number obtained from rolling one die cannot influence the number obtained from rolling a different die, X and Y are independent. However, once the first die has been rolled, this limits both the set of available outcomes for Z and the probability of Z taking any particular value. The random variables X and Z are therefore non-independent.

The notion of independence also carries over to events. Two events are said to be independent if the occurrence of one has no effect on the probability of the other occurring.

For the process of throwing two dice, define event M as a number 1 coming up on the first die, event N as a number 2 coming up on the second die and event Q as the total on the two dice being equal to 8. Events M and N are independent events exactly because X and Y are independent random variables. But now consider the events M and Q. Once event M has occurred, event Q cannot possibly occur since the total on two dice cannot be equal to 8 if there is only a 1 on one of the dice. M and Q are clearly not independent. Events N and Q are not independent either. Once a number 2 has been thrown on the first die, the probability distribution for Z is different from what it was before the first die was thrown. It is possible to obtain a total of 8 but the probability of doing so is different.

The multiplication thorem for independent events

For two independent events, the probability of them both occurring together is given by the product of the probabilities for them each occurring separately.

Formally, this is written as follows:

$$P(A \text{ and } B) = P(A) * P(B) \qquad (13.3)$$

A general version of the multiplication theorem covers both independent and non-independent events but involves the concept of conditional probability, which we do not discuss.[5]

For the process of rolling two dice, events M and N are independent. The probability of obtaining a 1 on the first die and a 2 on the second die can therefore be calculated using the multiplication theorem. For the process of rolling one die we know that $P(M) = 1/6$ and $P(N) = 1/6$. Therefore:

$$P(M \text{ and } N) = P(M) * P(N) = 1/6 * 1/6 = 1/36 \qquad (13.4)$$

The probability of rolling a 1 followed by a 2 is $1/36$.

KEY FEATURES OF PROBABILITY DISTRIBUTIONS

Just as there are descriptive measures which summarise information about a given set of data, there are analogous concepts which convey information about the probability distribution for any random variable. Here we are concerned with the mean and variance of a random variable, which are illustrated with reference to Example 13.3. There are three white balls and one black ball in a bag. A ball is selected at random and then replaced. X is defined to take the value 0 if a white ball is selected and 1 if a black ball is drawn. If this experiment were repeated many times then one would obtain a large series of values for X. We could treat these as a set of data and apply the formulae of Chapter 11 to calculate the mean, variance and standard deviation. If we did this for an extremely large set of data (millions and millions) then we would obtain the mean, variance and standard deviation of the random variable generating the data. Thus, the mean of a random variable can be thought of as the average value that the random variable would take if the process generating it could be repeated an infinitely large number of times. In fact, we can never repeat any experiment an infinite number of times. The best we can do is to repeat it a large number of times, in which case, the best we can hope for, by this method, is to obtain approximations for the mean, variance and standard deviation. Fortunately, there is another method that can be used, provided that one can specify the precise process by which the random variable is generated, or what amounts to the same thing, provided that one knows the probability distribution associated with that random variable.

The mean of a random variable

The mean of a random variable, X, is usually referred to as 'the expected value of X', written E(X) and commonly denoted by the Greek letter, μ. As is the case with the notation for probabilities, the expression E(X) does not mean E multiplied by X. It defines a particular operation to be applied to X. The operation is to find the expected value, which for a discrete random variable, is achieved by applying the formula:[6]

$$E(X) = \Sigma \, XP(X) \tag{13.5}$$

Suppose we wish to calculate the expected value for the random variable defined in Example 13.4 as the number of heads obtained from three tosses of a coin. The probability distribution is set out in the first two columns of Figure 13.7.

X	P(X)	XP(X)	X–E(X)	(X–E(X))^2	((X–E(X))^{2}P(X)
0	0.125	0	−1.5	2.25	0.28125
1	0.375	0.375	−0.5	0.25	0.09375
2	0.375	0.75	0.5	0.25	0.09375
3	0.125	0.375	1.5	2.25	0.28125
–	–	1.5	–	–	0.75

Figure 13.7 Worksheet for calculation of the mean, variance and standard deviation of a random variable

Formula 13.5 is applied by multiplying each value of X by its associated probability and then summing the resulting products. This is done in the third column of Figure 13.7 to give E(X) = 1.5.

Variance and standard deviation of a random variable

The variance of a random variable, X, denoted Var(X) and standard deviation, denoted σ, are calculated using the formulae:

$$\text{Var(X)} = \Sigma \{X - E(X)\}^2 P(X) \tag{13.6}$$

$$\sigma = \sqrt{\Sigma \{X - E(X)\}^2 P(X)} \tag{13.7}$$

Application of these formulae requires that the expected value of X is subtracted from each individual observation to obtain $\{X - E(X)\}$. The resulting numbers are squared, multiplied by their associated probabilities and then added up. Once again, a systematic approach is strongly recommended and the working is set out in Figure 13.7. In this example, the variance of X equals 0.75. The standard deviation is obtained by taking the square root. Thus, σ equals 0.866.

SUMMARY

The following concepts have now been introduced:

1 Process, probability, outcome, sample space, random variable, event, simple event, composite event, mutually exclusive event, addition theorem.
2 *A priori* probability, empirical probability, subjective probability.
3 Probability distribution, independent and non-independent events and random variables.
4 Multiplication theorem.
5 Mean, variance and standard deviation of a random variable.

14 Probability theory applied

We now extend the analysis to consider situations where a variable is measured on a continuous scale. For example, suppose we are interested in the weight of a new-born child. In principle, this could be measured to an infinitely high degree of precision. Consequently, there are an infinite number of weights that could be recorded. It would be silly to try and list all the possible weights that the child might take and even more silly to try and assign a probability to each. Because the child's weight can take any value over a continuum of values it is called a *continuous random variable*. By contrast, the examples considered in the previous chapter were all of *discrete* random variables, since they have a discrete number of possible outcomes.

CONTINUOUS RANDOM VARIABLES AND PROBABILITIES

Other examples of continuous random variables include the specific gravity of a pint of beer, the height of a tree, the petrol consumption of a car in miles per gallon, the life expectancy of a child born in a certain country in a certain year and the rate of price inflation. There are also situations where the number of possible outcomes is so large that although the variable is strictly discrete, it may be treated as if it were continuous. Examples include the population of a particular country, the number of crimes per year in a certain town and the number of people unemployed.

Probability distributions for continuous random variables cannot be specified in the same way as for discrete random variables. Since there are an infinite number of possible values that a continuous random variable can take, the probability of it taking any one value precisely is virtually zero. Reconsider the example of the weight of a new-born child. Although the probability of the child being *exactly* six pounds seven ounces is virtually zero, there is a definite and finite probability that the child will weigh between (say) six pounds seven ounces and six pounds eight ounces. Although we cannot define the probability that the child will have a specific weight, we can define the probability that the child's weight will lie within a specified band of weights. The concept of a probability distribution is replaced by a related but slightly different concept known as a probability density function.

The *probability density function* (pdf) indicates the probability with which a random variable lies within any specified range of values. Although the pdf has extensive application to particular examples of interest to social scientists, it is most effectively introduced via a simplified example. Consider a large, traditional clock face, with the hour hand removed. The face is conventionally numbered except that at the top both the numbers zero and twelve occur together. The clock mechanism has been removed so that the hand can spin freely. Define the random variable, X, to take the value determined by the hand on the clock, once it has been given a good spin. X may take any value between zero and twelve, measured to many decimal places. Since there is an infinitely large number of values that X could take, we treat X as a continuous random variable and represent the possible outcomes of the process by means of a probability density function. This is shown as Figure 14.1.

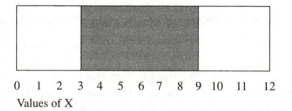

0   1   2   3   4   5   6   7   8   9   10   11   12
Values of X

Figure 14.1   Simple probability density function

When interpreting the diagram of a pdf, meaning is attached to positions along the horizontal axis and to the *area* underneath the pdf between any two points along the horizontal axis. This is unlike many types of diagram, where meaning is attached to both horizontal and vertical distances.The possible values that X may take are indicated along the horizontal axis. In this case, the numbers from zero to twelve are shown. The diagram is drawn such that the area underneath the pdf, between any two numbers, indicates the probability of X taking a value between those two numbers. The complete area underneath the pdf is defined to be equal to unity, since from the second postulate of probability theory, the probability assigned to an event which must occur is unity. The probability of X taking a value between, say, three and nine is given by the area underneath the pdf between these two values. This is measured by the shaded area in the diagram. As the total area equals 1, the shaded area is equal to 0.5.

THE NORMAL DISTRIBUTION

The normal distribution, sometimes called the Gaussian distribution, is an example of a probability density function for a continuous random variable which has many practical applications. An example is shown in Figure 14.2. It is symmetrical and bell shaped.

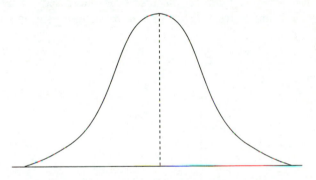

Figure 14.2   The normal distribution

There are many real world phenomena which have probability density functions which look just like it. For example, if one were to select at random any male from the adult population of any racial group and measure that person's height, one would have a random variable that is continuous and whose probability density function looks extremely like that of Figure 14.2. The same would apply if one selected women rather than men, chose weight as a variable rather than height, or measured the height of oak trees. Furthermore – and perhaps even more importantly – there is a theorem in statistics, called the central limit theorem, which enables one to make extensive use of the normal distribution, even in cases where a variable is not normally distributed.

The central limit theorem

Consider one of the simplest random processes: a coin is tossed and X is defined to take a value of zero if it comes up heads and a value of one if it comes up tails. The probability distribution for X and its associated diagram are shown together in Figure 14.3a. This does not resemble a normal distribution. Now redefine the process such that the coin is tossed not once but three times. Let $\bar{X}$ be the average value taken by X. The probability distribution for $\bar{X}$ is shown, with its associated diagram, in Figure 14.3b.

Although the diagram of Figure 14.3b also differs from the bell-shaped normal distribution, its resemblance is at least a little closer. Now suppose the coin is tossed not three times but five times. Then ten times. The resulting probability distributions, along with their associated diagrams, are shown in Figures 14.3c and d. Note how the probability distributions more closely resemble the normal distribution as the number of tosses is increased. This is no coincidence. It illustrates a powerful and important result in statistical theory:

The central limit theorem: Even if a variable, X, is not normally

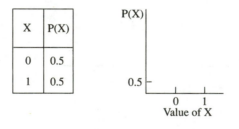

Figure 14.3a   Probability distribution for one toss of a coin

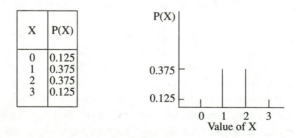

Figure 14.3b   Probability distribution for three tosses of a coin

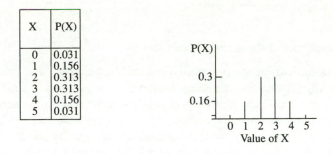

X	P(X)
0	0.031
1	0.156
2	0.313
3	0.313
4	0.156
5	0.031

Figure 14.3c Probability distribution for five tosses of a coin

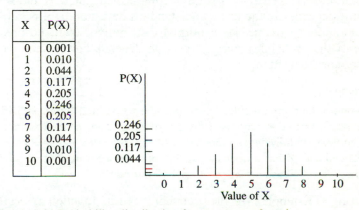

X	P(X)
0	0.001
1	0.010
2	0.044
3	0.117
4	0.205
5	0.246
6	0.205
7	0.117
8	0.044
9	0.010
10	0.001

Figure 14.3d Probability distribution for ten tosses of a coin

distributed, the mean of a number of Xs, $\bar{X}$, will be approximately normally distributed, with mean, μ and variance, σ^2/n. The approximation improves as the number, n, increases.

The number of times an experiment needs to be repeated in order for the probability density function for the mean to resemble a normal distribution as closely as in the above example depends on the probability distribution for X. There is no simple rule determining how large this number must be before an acceptable approximation is obtained. For most practical applications in the human and social sciences, twenty-five would probably be considered a reasonable compromise between the costs of obtaining large amounts of data and the requirement for precision.

Some properties of the normal distribution

The normal distribution is symmetrical and bell shaped. The mean of a normally distributed random variable – or of any continuous random variable – may be interpreted in the same way as the mean of a discrete random variable, although it is not possible to calculate it in quite the same way. Nevertheless, conceptually, the mean of any random variable can be thought of as the average value that the random variable would take if the process generating it were repeated a large number of times.

Although the formula for the probability density function associated with the normal distribution is quite complicated, the only terms on which it depends are the mean and standard deviation. If it is known that a random variable has a normal distribution, then the precise shape of the probability density function depends only on the mean and standard deviation.

Example 14.1

Define a random variable, X, as the mark obtained by an individual student, selected at random, from all students taking an examination in Argument and Evidence. On the basis of previous experience it is believed that X has a normal distribution with a mean of (say) 55 per cent and a standard deviation of (say) 10 per cent.

Referring to Example 14.1, the probability density function associated with an individual student's mark could be represented by Figure 14.2. Because we know the shape of the normal probability density function, we can calculate the probability of the student obtaining a mark between 45 per cent and 55 per cent, between 35 per cent and 45 per cent or between any other pair of numbers that we select.

For any variable which is known to have a normal distribution, there is a probability of just over two-thirds that any observation on that variable, chosen at random, will be within one standard deviation of the mean. This is expressed formally and more precisely as follows.

If X has a normal distribution, with mean, μ, and standard deviation, σ, then:

$$P(\mu - \sigma < X < \mu + \sigma) = 0.6826 \tag{14.1}$$

This is read as, 'the probability of X exceeding the mean *minus* one standard deviation and being less than the mean *plus* one standard deviation is equal to 0.6826'.

The following statements also apply:

$$P(\mu - 2\sigma < X < \mu + 2\sigma) = 0.9540 \tag{14.2}$$
$$P(\mu - 3\sigma < X < \mu + 3\sigma) = 0.9974 \tag{14.3}$$

This means that there is a probability of approximately 0.95 that X lies within two standard deviations of the mean and a probability of approximately 0.997 that X lies within three standard deviations of the mean. This implies that, in Example 14.1, there is more than a two-thirds probability that the individual student selected will score between 45 per cent and 65 per cent.

The examples so far considered have examined the probability of a random variable taking a value within a range defined by exact multiples of the standard deviation either side of the mean. It is also possible to derive the probability of X occurring between any pair of numbers. This is achieved by using a specific example of the normal distribution, introduced below.

THE STANDARD NORMAL DISTRIBUTION

The standard normal distribution is a normal distribution for a random variable, conventionally called Z, which has a mean of zero and a standard deviation of one. Its probability density function is shown in Figure 14.4.

Its distinguishing feature is the particular set of values that appear on the horizontal axis. Because the standard deviation is equal to one, in effect, the horizontal axis is measured in terms of numbers of standard deviations either side of the mean. From knowledge of the formula generating the probability density function it is possible to calculate directly the probability of Z taking a value between any pair of numbers. Since the calculations are complex, a short-cut procedure has been devised, based on the use of *standard normal tables*. It will subsequently be shown how use of the tables can be extended to *any* normally distributed random variable, regardless of the value taken by the mean and standard deviation. Since the central limit theorem enables one to apply theory based on the normal distribution, even if a particular variable is not normally distributed, standard normal tables are a most valuable item in the tool kit of any serious researcher.

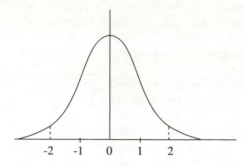

Figure 14.4   The standard normal distribution

Standard normal tables appear as Table A.1 in Appendix III. Consider the left-hand columns of Table A.1. The first column indicates a particular value along the horizontal axis of Figure 14.4. The second column gives the probability of Z taking a value between 0 and the particular number chosen. For example, the probability of Z taking a value between 0 and 1.4 is equal to 0.4192. The remaining columns of Table A.1 are used if one wishes to consider values along the horizontal axis of Figure 14.4 which are measured to more than one decimal place. The table is used as just indicated except that one only uses the second column if the second decimal place is zero (as with 1.40). Otherwise, one uses the column according to the value taken by the second digit after the decimal point. For example, the probability of Z occurring between 0 and 1.68 is found by looking down the left-hand column to find the row corresponding to 1.6 and then moving across to column 8. The answer is 0.4535. A little practice is recommended at this stage.

Although these tables only give probabilities associated with Z taking values between zero and a particular number, a little ingenuity enables one to extend their use to a much wider range of applications. Calculation of the probability of Z occurring between a pair of numbers that does not include zero is achieved by breaking down the problem into two parts, each with zero as one of the limits. This is illustrated by Examples 14.2 and 14.3:

Example 14.2

Calculate the probability of Z occurring between − 0.4 and 1.2.
This is made up of two parts, shown as the shaded areas of Figure 14.5.

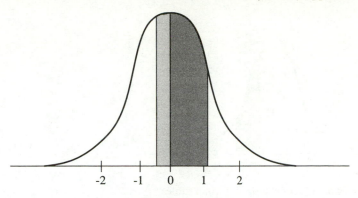

Figure 14.5   Use of standard normal tables (1)

The probability of Z lying between -0.4 and 1.2 is an area which is equal to the probability of Z occurring between 0 and -0.4 plus the probability of Z occurring between 0 and 1.2. The second of these components is straightforward and the probability, which can be read directly from Table A.1, is equal to 0.3849. To calculate the probability of Z occurring between 0 and a negative number one uses the fact that the normal density function is symmetrical, so that the probability of Z occurring between 0 and -0.4 is the same as the probability of Z occurring between 0 and 0.4, given as 0.1555 in the table. Thus, the probability of Z occurring between -0.4 and 1.2 is equal to $0.3849 + 0.1555 = 0.5404$.

Example 14.3

Calculate the probability of Z occurring between 0.4 and 1.3.
This problem can also be broken down into two parts, shown in Figure 14.6.
The probability of Z occurring between 0.4 and 1.3 is indicated by the area of darker shading. This is equal to the total shaded area minus the area of light shading. Formally:

$$P(0.4 < Z < 1.3) = P(0 < Z < 1.3) - P(0 < Z < 0.4)$$
$$= 0.4032 - 0.1555$$
$$= 0.2477$$

Standard normal tables would be of little use unless they could be applied in a wider range of circumstances than just to a random variable with a mean of zero and a standard deviation of one. Fortunately, because the normal distribution is completely defined by

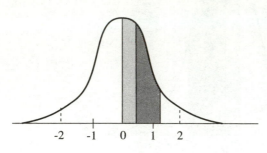

Figure 14.6   Use of standard normal tables (2)

its mean and standard deviation, it is possible, by way of a fairly straightforward transformation, to use the standard normal tables for any normally distributed random variable, provided that the mean and standard deviation are known.

If X has a normal distribution, with a known mean, equal to μ, then it follows that $X - \mu$ has a normal distribution with a mean of zero. It also follows that if $X - \mu$ has a standard deviation equal to σ then $(X - \mu)/\sigma$ has a standard deviation equal to one. Thus, there is a precise relationship between *any* normally distributed random variable, X, and the random variable which has a standard normal distribution, Z. This relationship is restated as follows.

If X has a normal distribution with mean, μ, and standard deviation, σ, then $Z = (X - \mu)/\sigma$ has a standard normal distribution with a mean of zero and a standard deviation of one.

This simple, but very powerful result enables one to use the standard normal tables for a wider class of problems.

Using the information from Example 14.1, it is assumed that an individual student, chosen at random, will achieve an examination mark which may be treated as a random variable, X, having a normal distribution, with a mean of 55 per cent and a standard deviation of 10 per cent. Suppose we wish to calculate the probability that X lies between 55 per cent and 60 per cent. It may help to reconsider the diagram of the probability density function for X alongside that for Z. These are placed together in Figure 14.7.

The probability of the student's mark being between 55 and 60 is represented by the shaded area in Figure 14.7a. This is exactly the

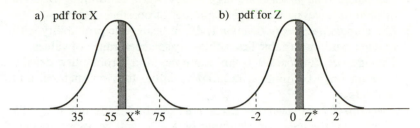

Figure 14.7 Probability density functions for X and Z in Example 14.1

same as the shaded area in Figure 14.7b. To use standard normal tables, it is necessary to know the value of the point z*, which is the equivalent to the point x*, which is 60 per cent. By applying the transformation, we find z* = (60 − 55)/10 = 0.5. Thus, the probability of X being between 55 and 60 is the same as the probability of Z being between 0 and 0.5. Using Table A.1, the answer is 0.1915. More formally, our working would be as follows:

$$
\begin{aligned}
P\{55 < X < 60\} &= P\{(55-\mu)/\sigma < (X-\mu)/\sigma < (60-\mu)/\sigma\} \\
&= P\{(55-55)/10 < Z < (60-55)/10\} \\
&= P\{0 < Z < 0.5\} \\
&= 0.1915
\end{aligned}
$$

The probability of the student's mark being between 55 per cent and 60 per cent is equal to 0.1915.

Understanding what is assumed, involved and implied in making statements about the probability of something lying between certain values is crucial if one is to conduct, understand or interpret hypothesis tests involving real-world data and phenomena. For example, in the context of nuclear waste reprocessing at Sellafield, probabilities of nuclear accidents and of individuals contracting cancer have frequently been mentioned. In making statements about the average level of pollution on the beach at Ravenglass, inferences are made on the basis of the results from a relatively small number of sand samples and statements about the reliability of such estimates would be couched in terms of probabilities. The next chapter examines such inferences.

SUMMARY

1 *Continuous random variables* take values over a continuum. *Discrete random variables* have a discrete number of possible outcomes.

2 The *probability density function* (pdf) indicates the probability with which a random variable lies within any specified range of values.

3 The *normal distribution* is an example of a probability density function for a continuous random variable. It is symmetrical and bell shaped.

4 *The central limit theorem*: Even if a variable, X, is not normally distributed, the mean of a number of Xs, $\bar{X}$, will be approximately normally distributed, with mean, μ, and variance, σ^2/n. The approximation improves as the number increases.

5 The standard normal distribution is a normal distribution for a random variable, conventionally called Z, which has a mean of zero and a standard deviation of one. The probability of Z being within any specified range can be calculated from standard normal tables.

6 If X has a normal distribution with mean, μ, and standard deviation, σ, then $Z = (X - \mu)/\sigma$ has a standard normal distribution with a mean of zero and a standard deviation of one.

15 Estimation and reliability

This chapter is concerned with using samples to provide information about the wider population from which they are drawn. The first three sections consider the issues involved in making inferences about the population mean and standard deviation and subsequent sections discuss the reliability of such inferences. The terms sample and population are used precisely as defined in Chapter 10 and it is assumed throughout that where a sample is referred to, it is a 'random sample'. The importance of this cannot be overstated. Some powerful procedures are derived which can be of great help in the furtherance of knowledge – but applied in inappropriate circumstances they can be misleading or dangerous.

The formulae for the population mean and standard deviation of a finite set of data, consisting of N elements, given in Chapter 11 and the mean and standard deviation calculated from a known probability distribution, given in Chapter 13, are restated in Table 15.1.

Table 15.1 Formulae for population mean and standard deviation

	Mean (μ)	Standard deviation (σ)
Finite data	$(\Sigma X_i)/N$	$\sqrt{\Sigma(X_i - \mu)^2/N}$
Probability distribution	$E(X)$	$\sqrt{\Sigma\{X - E(X)\}^2 P(X)}$

Example 15.1 is a typical situation which illustrates the issues with which we are concerned. The information of interest to the researcher may be the mean and standard deviation of family income. This would give her an indication both of the 'typical' family income and of the degree of spread around this. The latter information may be important in indicating the proportion of such families in extreme poverty. The reliability of the researcher's conclusions would be

critical, for example, if they were to be used as the basis for policy recommendations. In this case, perhaps, the researcher might engage in arguments about the operation of the Child Support Agency:

Example 15.1

A researcher is interested in the income of all single-parent families in the UK. Since it would be too expensive to collect data from every element in the population, that is, every single-parent family in the UK, she confines herself to a random sample of 100 such families. On the basis of information contained in the sample, inferences are made about all single-parent families in the UK.

ESTIMATORS AND THEIR PROPERTIES

An *estimator* is a formula, which may be applied to data from a sample, for the purpose of inferring the value taken by a population parameter. We confine attention to two estimators of the population mean: a single observation, X_i, selected at random and the mean, $\bar{X}$, derived from a sample of observations. Selecting at random just one observation would be the simplest way to estimate the population mean. For Example 15.1, the researcher could select just one single-parent family, record its income and use this as an estimator for the population mean income. A second possibility would be to take a *sample mean*, calculated from all observations in the sample. Following generally accepted conventions, we use a lower case letter 'n' to refer to the number of observations in the sample and $\bar{X}$ to refer to the sample mean. The formula is given by Equation 15.1:

$$\bar{X} = (\Sigma X_i)/n \qquad (15.1)$$

Note that this is the same as the formula for the population mean, μ, calculated from a finite set of data, given in Table 15.1, except that the formula for the population mean includes an upper case 'N', referring to the total number of elements in the population.

In the first case one is using an individual X_i as an estimator for μ. Since X_i is being drawn at random from the population, it is a random variable, though as yet we know nothing about the features of its probability distribution.[1] For purposes of illustration, assume that we know that the random variable, X, has an approximately normal distribution, so that the probability distribution for X_i might look something like that shown in Figure 15.1.[2] The expected value of X_i is equal to μ and the standard deviation is equal to σ.

The second estimator that we are considering is the sample mean, $\bar{X}$.

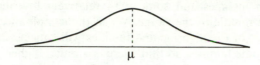

Figure 15.1   Probability distribution for X_i

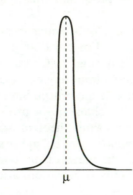

Figure 15.2   Probability distribution for $\bar{X}$

Since the sample is to be selected at random, the sample mean is also
a random variable. This point is often the source of confusion. Once
the actual sample has been selected, then the sample mean is fully
determined and will be a precise number. However, if the sample is
chosen at random, then the exact value taken by the sample mean will
depend on which specific elements in the population are chosen. In
the context of Example 15.1, the sample mean will depend on exactly
which families happen to enter the sample. Since the sample mean is a
random variable, its potential values can be represented by a probability distribution as shown in Figure 15.2. Notice that although the
areas underneath the curves of Figures 15.1 and 15.2 are the same, the
diagram of Figure 15.2 is much more condensed. When selecting just
one individual observation, it might be a family with high income, or
one with low income, or one somewhere in the middle of the range.
However, when 100 families are chosen at random it is unlikely that
all 100 will be selected from the bottom end of the income scale, just
as it is unlikely that they will all be selected from the top end of the
income scale. It is far more likely that there will be some families with

relatively high incomes and some with relatively low incomes and some near the middle of the range. When the sample mean is calculated, the effect of the high income families will cancel out the effect of the low income families, so that there is a much higher probability that the sample mean will be closer to the population mean than would be the case if only a single observation were taken. Consequently, the probability distribution for the sample mean has a smaller standard deviation than the probability distribution for an individual observation.

The probability distribution for a sample mean is sometimes referred to as its *sampling distribution*. For our example, we assumed that the individual X_is each have a normal distribution and $\bar{X}$ was taken to have a normal distribution without any explanation being offered. In fact, this is justified because of the central limit theorem, explained in Chapter 14. Regardless of the shape of the probability distribution for the individual X_i, the central limit theorem assures us that $\bar{X}$ has a probability distribution which can be approximated by a normal distribution. Furthermore, the mean of the sampling distribution for $\bar{X}$ is equal to μ and its standard deviation, also given by the central limit theorem, is expressed as:

$$\sigma_{\bar{x}} = \sigma/\sqrt{n} \tag{15.2}$$

where $\sigma_{\bar{x}}$ is used to denote the standard deviation of the sampling distribution for the mean. This gives formal confirmation to the result gained intuitively above, that the probability distribution for the sample mean has a smaller spread than the probability distribution for an individual observation selected at random.

For example, suppose we know that the income of one-parent families has a standard deviation of ten and we have a sample of 100 such families. The standard deviation of the sampling distribution of the mean can be calculated as follows:

$$\sigma_{\bar{x}} = \sigma/\sqrt{n} = 10/\sqrt{100} = 10/10 = 1$$

Equation 15.2 also indicates that the spread of the probability distribution for the sample mean varies inversely with the number of observations in the sample.[3]

Properties of estimators

We have considered two possible estimators for the population mean: an individual observation, X_i, which is a random variable, having a distribution with a mean of μ and a standard deviation of σ; and a sample mean, $\bar{X}$, calculated from n observations, which is also a random variable, with a mean of μ and a standard deviation of $\sigma/\sqrt{n}$. To decide which estimator is most appropriate, we consider three desirable properties, referred to as unbiasedness, efficiency and consistency.

If an estimator is to be *unbiased*, then there must be no systematic tendency to either overstate or understate the parameter being estimated. Consequently, the mean of its sampling distribution is equal to the population parameter being estimated.

In the context of estimating the mean, an estimator is unbiased if the mean of its sampling distribution is equal to the population mean, μ. This helps clarify why so much emphasis is placed on the notion of a 'random' sample. Suppose, for Example 15.1, that instead of choosing a random sample of one-parent families, one had chosen the entire sample from Kensington. If incomes in Kensington are generally higher than most other places, then the sample mean would have a probability distribution centred somewhere to the right of the population mean, μ. This does not imply that for any particular sample chosen from Kensington the sample mean will *necessarily* overstate the population mean, but it does imply that there is a greater probability of overstatement than of understatement.

If two estimators are both unbiased, then the one with the smaller standard deviation is said to be more *efficient*.[4] It is shown above (see pp. 188–9) that the standard deviation of the probability distribution for the sample mean, $\bar{X}$, is less than the standard deviation of the probability distribution for an individual observation, X_i, and that the standard deviation of $\bar{X}$ is inversely related to the sample size. Consequently, the sample mean is a more efficient estimator than an individual observation. Since the standard deviation of the sample mean is inversely related to sample size, larger samples provide more efficient estimators than smaller samples. Unless there are other factors to be considered, more efficient estimators are to be preferred to less efficient estimators. Technically, more efficient estimators are said to be *better* than less efficient estimators.

The third property to be discussed is consistency. An estimator is *consistent* if, as the sample size increases, the difference between the estimate and the population parameter being estimated approaches zero. In terms of the previous two properties, a consistent estimator becomes more efficient as the sample size increases and is either unbiased or has a degree of bias which approaches zero as the sample size increases.

Thus, provided a sample is randomly selected, the sample mean is an unbiased and consistent estimator of the population mean. The larger the sample size, the better the estimator.

PROBABILITY STATEMENTS ABOUT THE SAMPLE MEAN

Standard normal tables, explained in Chapter 14, can be used to make probability statements about a sample mean. Furthermore, by virtue of the central limit theorem, one is not confined to situations where the original variable follows a normal distribution – provided that the sample size is reasonably large and that the underlying probability distribution for the variable in question is not too far from being symmetrical. Applying the theory of the standard normal distribution: if $\bar{X}$ has a normal distribution, with mean μ and standard deviation $\sigma_{\bar{X}}$ then $Z = \{\bar{X} - \mu\}/\sigma_{\bar{X}}$ has a normal distribution with mean 0 and standard deviation equal to 1. The analysis of Example 15.2 illustrates an application of this important result:

Example 15.2

Suppose that X is a random variable with a mean of £60 and a standard deviation of £10. We could be saying, suppose we know that one-parent families have an average income of £60 per week, with a standard deviation of £10. We have access to a sample of 100 observations. What is the probability of the sample mean lying between 58 and 62?

Formally, we wish to find:

$$P\{58 < \bar{X} < 62\}$$

Because of the central limit theorem, it may be assumed that $\bar{X}$ has a normal distribution with a mean of μ and a standard deviation equal to $\sigma_{\bar{X}}$.

$\sigma_{\bar{X}}$ can be calculated, using Equation 15.2, as follows:

$$\sigma_{\bar{X}} = \sigma/\sqrt{n} = \sigma/10 = 10/10 = 1$$

Applying the transformation to a standard normal distribution:

$$\begin{aligned}
P\{58 < \bar{X} < 62\} &= P\{(58 - 60)/1 < Z < (62 - 60)/1\} \\
&= P\{-2 < Z < 2\} \\
&= P\{0 < Z < 2\} + P\{-2 < Z < 0)\} \\
&= 0.4772 + 0.4772 = 0.9544
\end{aligned}$$

There is a probability of 0.9544 that the sample mean will be between 58 and 62.

The analysis of Example 15.2 demonstrates how one can make precise probabilistic statements about the value that a sample statistic will take, based on a knowledge of the sample size and of key aspects of the underlying population. The implications of being able to make such statements are quite far-reaching – as is demonstrated subsequently.

ESTIMATING THE STANDARD DEVIATION

A mysterious feature of the problems posed so far is that the standard deviation has been assumed to be known. In any practical application, this is unlikely to be the case. Instead, the standard deviation would be *estimated*. At first sight one might expect that a sensible procedure would be to apply the formula for the population standard deviation, as set out in Table 15.1, to a sample of data and use this to estimate the population standard deviation. Unfortunately, the formula for the standard deviation of a population, when applied to a sample of data, is not an unbiased estimator of the population standard deviation. It gives an underestimate. If one is using data from a sample for the purpose of estimating the standard deviation of the population, then it is appropriate to use the *sample standard deviation*, which is defined as:

$$s = \sqrt{\{\Sigma(X - \bar{X})^2\}/(n - 1)} \tag{15.3}$$

This differs from the population formula in that $n - 1$ is used in the denominator instead of N. The sample standard deviation, s, is an unbiased estimator of the population standard deviation, σ.

Suppose, for example, that we wish to estimate the mean and standard deviation of marks for a particular examination, using the marks obtained by a sample of four students. The marks are 68, 50, 60 and 62. The sample mean, $\bar{X}$, is calculated and used to estimate the population mean, μ. The sample standard deviation, s, is calculated, to estimate the population standard deviation, σ. The working is set out as Table 15.2.

The standard deviation of the sampling distribution for the mean, $\sigma_{\bar{x}}$ can also be estimated using the formula:

$$s_{\bar{x}} = s/\sqrt{n} \tag{15.4}$$

Applying Equation 15.4 to the data of Table 15.2, $s_{\bar{x}} = 3.74$.

Having shown how to estimate both the sample standard deviation and the standard deviation of the sample mean, we are now equipped to make what may seem like an astounding claim. We can make statements about the degree of reliability of our own estimates!

Table 15.2 Calculation of sample standard deviation

	X	X − X̄	(X − X̄)²
	68	8	64
	50	− 10	100
	60	0	0
	62	2	4
Σ	240	0	168

$$s = \sqrt{168/3} = 7.48$$

THE RELIABILITY OF ESTIMATES

When a sample statistic is used as an estimator for a population parameter then the estimate is referred to as a *point estimate*. That is, it is a single number, with no indication of the extent to which one would expect the estimate to vary from the parameter. The major disadvantage of point estimates is that one has no knowledge about their reliability. In this section we introduce the idea of an *interval estimate*, or *confidence interval*, which consists of an upper bound and a lower bound with a statement about the probability with which the parameter being estimated lies inside the interval. For example, one might have information from a random sample of coal-miners who retired last year. A confidence interval for the mean retirement age of all coal-miners would consist of two numbers, say 51 and 55, together with a statement about the probability of the population mean being between them. For example, 'We are 95 per cent confident that the average retirement age of all miners in the UK in the year in question was between 51 and 53 years'.

The attractiveness of such a proclamation is that it incorporates both an estimate and a statement about the degree of confidence with which the proclamation is held. That is, it incorporates both an estimate and an indication of just how reliable that estimate is thought to be.

The theory underlying the concept of a confidence interval is based on the normal distribution. The following analysis is appropriate either for variables that are normally distributed or where the sample is sufficiently large that the central limit theorem can be applied.[5] It is this second case which underlies so many applications and potential applications in the human and social sciences. The simplest example of a confidence interval is the confidence interval for a population mean.

CONFIDENCE INTERVAL FOR A POPULATION MEAN

The particular procedure for calculating the confidence interval depends on whether the population standard deviation is known or has to be estimated.

Confidence interval when the standard deviation is known

From knowledge of the normal distribution, we know that there is approximately a 0.95 probability that an individual observation, X_i, will lie within a range of 2 of its standard deviations, that is, within 2σ either side of the population mean.[6] Turning this around, we can say that there is a 0.95 probability of the population mean lying within 2σ either side of an individual observation. Hence, the *95 per cent confidence interval* for the population mean is the interval:

$$X_i - 2\sigma \text{ to } X_i + 2\sigma \tag{15.5}$$

For example, we might have observed one coal-miner who retired last year and noted that his retirement age was 52. If we knew that coal-miners' retirement age followed a normal distribution with a standard deviation of 4 then we could state with 95 per cent confidence that the retirement age of all miners who retired last year was between 44 and 60. The range 44 to 60 would be the 95 per cent confidence interval. Note that in this example the estimate is based on just one observation and conditional on the assumption that the underlying population can be represented by a normal distribution. We established above that estimators derived from samples are better than estimators derived from a single observation and that larger samples are preferred to smaller samples. Applying the central limit theorem, a confidence interval for the population mean is given as:

$$\bar{X} - 2\sigma_{\bar{X}} \text{ to } \bar{X} + 2\sigma_{\bar{X}} \tag{15.6}$$

where $\bar{X}$ is the sample mean and $\sigma_{\bar{X}}$ is used to denote the standard deviation, assumed known, of the population mean. For example, if 52 was the mean age of 100 retiring coal miners then the 95 per cent confidence interval would be the range, $52 - (2 \times \frac{4}{10})$ to $52 + (2 \times \frac{4}{10})$ that is, 51.2 to 52.8. Using a larger number of observations enables one to derive a narrower and consequently more useful confidence interval. A further illustration, with more detailed calculations, is given in Example 15.3.

Example 15.3

We have a sample of 100 observations on a random variable, X.
The standard deviation of X is known to be equal to 30.
The sample mean is calculated to be 80.

a) Calculate the standard deviation of the sampling distribution for the mean.

b) Obtain a 95 per cent confidence interval for the population mean, μ.

SOLUTION:

$$\sigma_{\bar{x}} = 30/\sqrt{100} = 3$$

The 95 per cent confidence interval is the range

$$\bar{X} - 2\sigma_{\bar{x}} \text{ to } \bar{X} + 2\sigma_{\bar{x}}$$

which is   80 − 2(3) to 80 + 2(3)

which is   74 to 86

We are 95 per cent confident that the population mean lies between 74 and 86.

The concept of a 95 per cent confidence interval should be interpreted exactly as in Example 15.2. It is a statement about the degree of accuracy to be attributed to the estimate. If one were to conduct the whole procedure many times using different random samples, then one would probably calculate a slightly different confidence interval each time. On approximately 95 per cent of those occasions one would expect the true parameter to lie inside the confidence interval. To put this another way, any experienced researcher, provided that he or she does not make any errors in calculation and provided that the decision to rely on the central limit theorem was justified, would expect that on most occasions the true population parameter would lie inside the estimated confidence interval but would be prepared to accept that on perhaps one occasion out of twenty they would be wrong.

Under certain circumstances, 95 per cent confidence may not be good enough. For example, in situations where public health is involved, such as estimating the time that it is 'safe' for a product to be left on the shelf before the average concentration of bacteria reaches a certain level, then a much higher degree of confidence may be demanded. Referring to the normal distribution tables, there is a probability of 0.997 that a random variable lies within three of its standard deviations either side of the mean. Thus, one could define the 99.7 per cent confidence interval as $\bar{X} - 3\sigma_{\bar{x}}$ to $\bar{X} + 3\sigma_{\bar{x}}$. For Example 15.3 one would be 99.7 per cent confident that the population mean is between 71 and 89. Greater degrees of confidence can be gained by using wider confidence intervals, so that there is a trade off between degree of confidence and precision. However, unless every item in the population is included, in which case one no longer has a sample but a census, there is still the possibility that the population parameter might lie outside the confidence interval. This is another manifestation of the problem of induction. One cannot make inductive inferences with certainty – no matter how sophisticated the underlying probability theory may be. For research in the humanities and social sciences, as well as in many other areas, a 95 per cent confidence interval is usually accepted as a sensible compromise between reliability and precision when inferences are to be made from a sample.

Confidence intervals when the standard deviation is unknown

In any practical application, σ is unlikely to be known. Consequently, any practical application of the theory of confidence intervals requires that the population standard deviation be estimated and this introduces some additional complications.

It is argued above that where the probability distribution of X_i can be treated as approximately normal, there is a probability of approximately 0.95 that the population mean will lie within $2\sigma_{\bar{X}}$ either side of the sample mean. When σ is replaced by its estimate, s, this result does not necessarily apply. An intuitive explanation for this is that an extra degree of uncertainty is introduced into the calculations, so that one should no longer have the same degree of confidence in the resulting interval. To take account of this, a slightly wider interval should be calculated. The confidence intervals derived from a single observation or from a sample mean are given respectively by Formulae 15.7a and 15.7b:

$$X_i - ts \text{ to } X_i + ts \tag{15.7a}$$

$$\bar{X} - ts_{\bar{X}} \text{ to } \bar{X} + ts_{\bar{X}} \tag{15.7b}$$

where $s_{\bar{X}}$ is an estimate of the standard deviation of the sampling distribution for $\bar{X}$ and t is a number a little bit bigger than 2, carefully chosen so as to compensate for the additional uncertainty associated with having to estimate σ. To see where t comes from it is necessary to look more closely at the theory underlying the confidence interval.

The t-distribution

In constructing the confidence interval with σ known we took an interval 2σ either side of the point estimate. The number 2 came from the fact that there is a probability of 0.95 that the standard normal variable, Z, lies between -2 and $+2$. Formally, standard normal tables inform us that $P(-2 < Z < 2) = 0.95$. Using the knowledge that $(X - \mu)/\sigma = Z$ has a standard normal distribution, it is argued that $P(X - 2\sigma < \mu < X + 2\sigma) = 0.95$.

Unfortunately, $(X_i - \mu)/s$ does not have a standard normal distribution, so when σ is replaced by s, the transformation to Z cannot be justified. In fact, $(X - \mu)/s$ has a probability distribution known as a *students' t-distribution with n $-$ 1 degrees of freedom*. The theory underlying this need not concern us. What matters is that if σ is not known but has to be estimated then, when calculating a confidence interval for the mean, use of the normal distribution is not justified. To calculate a confidence interval for the mean when using an estimate for the standard deviation, it is necessary to substitute a value from the t-tables into the Formulae 15.7a and 15.7b using n $-$ 1 degrees of freedom.

The shape of the t-distribution looks rather like the normal distribution, though it takes a slightly different form depending on its 'degrees of freedom'. For purposes of the applications considered in this chapter, the degrees of freedom is equal to n $-$ 1 where n is the number of observations used to estimate s.[7] When the sample size is very large, then the t-distribution becomes indistinguishable from the normal distribution. Even for a sample as small as six, the t-distribution looks very similar to the normal distribution, as indicated in Figure 15.3.

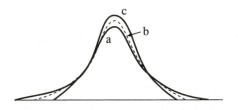

Figure 15.3   The students' t-distribution
Notes: a) Shows t-distribution for approximately five degrees of freedom
      b) Shows t-distribution for approximately eight degrees of freedom
      c) Shows normal distribution

A set of t-tables is given in Table A.2 in Appendix III. Different books may present these in slightly different forms. The tables in Appendix III are presented in a way appropriate for the applications here, whilst preserving those features that would enable them to be used more widely. The first column represents the 'degrees of freedom'. As already indicated, for the applications in this chapter there are $n - 1$ degrees of freedom. To calculate a 95 per cent confidence interval, the appropriate value of t is to be found in the third column. For low numbers of degrees of freedom the numbers are larger than 2, but as the number of observations gets larger, the t-distribution resembles the normal distribution more closely.[8] Consider Example 15.4 as an illustration:

Example 15.4

Referring to the data of Example 15.3, we know the examination marks for four students and we believe that examination marks can be very closely approximated by a normal distribution. It has already been calculated that $\bar{X} = 60$ and $s_{\bar{x}}$ equals 3.74. In this example $n = 4$. Therefore, the number of degrees of freedom is 3 and so the value from t-tables is 3.18. The 95 per cent confidence interval is:

$$60 - (3.18)(3.74) \text{ to } 60 + (3.18)(3.74)$$

which is approximately 48 to 72. We are 95 per cent confident that the average examination mark, for the whole population of students from which our random sample was drawn, is somewhere between 48 and 72.

If one obtained a confidence interval as wide as that in Example 15.4 then one might reasonably respond, quite correctly, that this does not tell us much. But this is an excellent illustration of just why confidence intervals can be so informative. A statement along the lines, 'I estimate the average examination mark to be 60' may seem impressive. However, this particular estimate has such a wide band of uncertainty associated with it that it is unlikely to be of much practical use. It is only by calculating the confidence interval that this is revealed.

WHAT WE CAN AND CANNOT LEARN FROM OPINION POLLS

In this section we indicate how the concept of a confidence interval can be applied to a population proportion. Although this is discussed with specific reference to public opinion polls, the method is applicable in all situations where the information of interest can be expressed as a proportion.

In the context of opinion polls, one may be interested in the proportion of the UK electorate which would vote for a particular party or which has a particular view on a certain issue. In the context of the childhood leukaemia controversy, one might be interested in the proportion of workers at Sellafield who have received doses of radiation above the recommended minimum in the last twelve months or the proportion of male workers who are planning to start families.

In all of these examples there are only two possible outcomes, which are sometimes, though not always appropriately, referred to as 'success' or 'failure'. In the language of probability theory we are concerned with a random variable which has only two possible outcomes. An example already encountered is the process of tossing a coin and observing whether the outcome is heads or tails. It is a general feature of all such processes that they have a particular type of probability distribution, called the *binomial distribution.*

The normal approximation to the binomial distribution

We return to the coin tossing experiment to show how the theory developed in Chapter 14 can be extended to more practical applications. Figure 14.3 shows how $\bar{X}$ has a probability distribution which approximates to the normal distribution, with the approximation improving as n increases. This is despite the fact that the random variable, X, has a probability distribution very unlike a normal distribution. Indeed, this example was used as an illustration of the central limit theorem. Exactly the same analysis can be applied to any 'proportion'.[9] For reasons of consistency, we define the population proportion as ρ – the Greek letter 'rho' – and the sample proportion as the letter 'p'. For example, by conducting an opinion poll on an appropriately selected sample, one may obtain a proportion, p, who declare an intention to vote Conservative and this may be used as an estimate of the underlying population proportion, ρ. The proportion p is an unbiased estimator for ρ for the same reasons that $\bar{X}$ is an unbiased estimator for μ. The standard deviation of the sampling distribution for p is given as:

$$\sigma_p = \sqrt{\{\rho(1 - \rho)\}/n} \tag{15.8}$$

Provided that the sample is only a small proportion of the total population, this can be estimated using equation 15.9:[10]

$$s_p = \sqrt{\{p(1 - p)\}/(n - 1)} \tag{15.9}$$

For example, if $n = 64$ and $p = 0.3$ we calculate s_p as follows:

$$s_p = \sqrt{\{p(1 - p)\}/(n - 1)} = \sqrt{\{0.3(0.7)/63} = \sqrt{0.00333} = 0.0578$$

95 per cent confidence interval for a population proportion

A 95 per cent confidence interval can be calculated for p in much the same way as for μ, provided that the sample size is reasonably large. For small samples, the normal approximation to the binomial distribution may not be appropriate and a different procedure must be followed.[11] A confidence interval for p is given by Formula 15.10, where z is the number obtained from standard normal tables, according to the degree of confidence required:

$$p - zs_p \text{ to } p + zs_p \tag{15.10}$$

For a 90 per cent confidence interval $z = 1.64$ and for a 95 per cent confidence interval, $z = 1.96$. As a useful rule of thumb, which also avoids implying a spurious degree of accuracy, 1.96 can be rounded to 2.0, so that the 95 per cent confidence interval for the population proportion may be stated as:

$$p - 2s_p \text{ to } p + 2s_p \tag{15.11}$$

Example 15.5, derived from an opinion poll conducted for *The Observer* newspaper, illustrates how the theory of confidence intervals can be applied to give an indication of how much credibility should be attached to any particular poll:

Example 15.5

What proportion of voters think that Britain should give up its nuclear deterrent as part of an overall arms deal between the Soviet Union and the United States? This question was part of an opinion poll conducted for *The Observer* newspaper by Harris.[12] According to *The Observer*, '1,044 respondents at 100 sampling points were interviewed on 21–22 February'. Of these, 48 per cent thought that Britain should give up its nuclear deterrent.

Using Example 15.5 for illustration, to make inferences about the proportion of the electorate as a whole who share this opinion one would calculate a confidence interval, which first requires an estimate of the standard deviation of the population proportion. From Equation 15.9:

$$s_p = \sqrt{\{p(1 - p)\}/(n - 1)} = \sqrt{\{0.48(0.52)\}/1043} = 0.015$$

By substituting the estimate for s_p into Formula 15.11 a 95 per cent confidence interval for the population proportion is given as follows:

$$0.48 - 2(0.015) \text{ to } 0.48 + 2(0.015)$$
$$= 0.48 - 0.03 \text{ to } 0.48 + 0.03$$
$$= 0.45 \text{ to } 0.51.$$

Converting these proportions into percentages, we conclude that we are 95 per cent confident that between 45 per cent and 51 per cent of the electorate believe that Britain should give up its nuclear deterrent as part of an overall arms deal between the Soviet Union and the United States.

The importance of sample size

When calculating the confidence interval for a proportion, the underlying probability distribution is binomial. Under such circumstances the sampling distribution of p approximates to a normal distribution. The approximation increases with sample size and for any given sample size the approximation is at its best when p is equal to 0.5 and gets progressively worse as p gets closer to zero or to unity. Taking account of both of these considerations, it is generally acceptable to rely on the normal approximation to the binomial distribution provided that both np and $n(1 - p)$ exceed five.

Since the sample size enters into the formula for the standard deviation of the sample proportion, it has an influence on the width of the confidence interval. In fact it is possible to do the calculations backwards, so that if one wishes to specify a certain width for the confidence interval, one can calculate the sample size required. It is no coincidence that most political opinion polls published in the British press are based on just a little over 1,000 respondents.

SUMMARY

1   An estimator is a formula, which may be applied to data from a sample for the purpose of inferring the value taken by a population parameter.
2   Unbiasedness, efficiency and consistency are desirable properties for an estimator to have.
3   An estimator is *unbiased* if the mean of its sampling distribution is equal to the population parameter being estimated.

4 If two estimators are both unbiased, then the one with the smaller standard deviation is said to be more *efficient*.

5 An estimator is *consistent* if, as the sample size increases, the difference between the estimate and the population parameter being estimated approaches zero.

6 The sample statistics for the mean and standard deviation are used as estimators for the population mean and standard deviation.

7 The sample mean, $\bar{X} = (\Sigma X_i)/n$ is an unbiased and consistent estimator for the population mean, μ.

8 The standard deviation of the sample mean is given by $\sigma_x = \sigma/\sqrt{n}$.

9 The sample standard deviation, $s = \sqrt{\{\Sigma(X_i - \bar{X})^2\}/(n - 1)}$ is an unbiased, consistent estimator for the population standard deviation, σ.

10 A *confidence interval* consists of an upper bound and a lower bound with a statement about the probability with which the parameter being estimated lies inside the interval.

11 The exact procedure for calculating a confidence interval depends on whether the standard deviation of the underlying probability distribution is known or has to be estimated from a sample. The latter is more common.

12 A confidence interval for a population mean, when the population standard deviation, σ, is known, is given as:

$X_i - 2\sigma$ to $X_i + 2\sigma$ using an individual observation as an estimator.

$\bar{X} - 2\sigma_{\bar{x}}$ to $\bar{X} + 2\sigma_{\bar{x}}$ using the sample mean as an estimator.

13 A confidence interval for a population mean, when the standard deviation is not known, is given as:

$X_i - ts$ to $X_i + ts$ using an individual observation as an estimator.

$\bar{X} - ts_{\bar{x}}$ to $\bar{X} + ts_{\bar{x}}$ using the sample mean as an estimator.

14 t is a number obtained from the students' t-distribution and s is the sample standard deviation.

15 A probability distribution with only two outcomes is referred to as a binomial distribution. It is common to refer to the two outcomes as 'success' and 'failure' and to denote the proportion of successes as ρ and p for the population and sample respectively.

16 For a binomial distribution, the standard deviation of the sampling distribution for p is given by:

$$\sigma_p = \sqrt{\{p(1 - p)\}/n}$$

Provided that the sample is only a small proportion of the total population, this can be estimated using:

$$s_p = \sqrt{\{p(1 - p)\}/(n - 1)}$$

17 A 95 per cent confidence interval for a population proportion can be approximated by:

$$p - 2s_p \text{ to } p + 2s_p$$

16 Testing hypotheses

A hypothesis is an idea or hunch about the world. It might concern a claim about an individual variable, such as the degree of pollution in the River Trent, or it might be concerned with the relationship between two or more variables. Examples of the latter include the claim that the incidence of childhood leukaemia is related to the proximity of nuclear installations; that the level of crime is related to the level of unemployment; and that the incidence of child mortality in Victorian Britain was related to the level of spending on sewer construction.

Most hypotheses are prompted by a combination of inspiration and experience of the world. A hypothesis about some aspect of the world is sometimes referred to as an *empirical hypothesis*. The idea that nuclear installations are somehow connected with increases in the incidence of leukaemia in children is an example. This hypothesis has been suggested because people have observed an apparently high incidence around certain installations. The origin of a hypothesis does not affect its susceptibility to investigation in principle, though it may affect the way in which it is investigated. The apparently high incidence of leukaemia near Sellafield prompted the cancer-link hypothesis referred to above. The hypothesis is testable but, as pointed out by Taylor and Wilkie (1988), given that the observations near Sellafield were the origin of the hypothesis, it is methodologically unsound to use the same set of data as the basis for testing the hypothesis. Rather, the appropriate procedure, following the hypothetico-deductive method referred to in Chapter 12, is to deduce something else which one would expect to observe, if the hypothesis were to be substantiated. In this case, one would expect to observe clusters near to other nuclear installations.

Not all types of hypothesis are testable. For hypotheses such as 'angels sing' there is nothing observable, even in principle, that could, if seen, show them to be false. Other hypotheses are testable in principle but as yet no-one has managed to find a way of doing so. 'There is life in other galaxies' is an example. Where hypotheses are testable, testing can occur in a variety of ways. Hypotheses which involve general statements about a whole population are often tested by using information contained in a sample selected at random from that population.

Although hypothesis testing occurs in a variety of situations, the basic principles can be elucidated by concentrating on hypothesis tests about the mean value taken by a single variable. For example, we may believe that a local river has been polluted. To put this into context, there might be a firm which is pouring waste products into the river but claiming that despite this the river is clean. Potentially, the belief that the river is polluted can be substantiated by measuring the degree of acidity/alkalinity of the water. Scientists tell us that this can be determined in a laboratory by the pH measure of the water. Clear, unpolluted water has a neutral pH measure of 7.0 and the pH is lower or higher than 7 if the liquid is respectively acid or alkaline. One way to test for pollution would be to collect a number of phials of water and have them tested at a laboratory. On the basis of the average pH measure of the water portions, it may be possible to say something about the average pH measure of the river and hence decide whether or not the river is polluted.

FORMULATING A HYPOTHESIS TEST

The first step is to specify the possible conclusions from the test. Formally, this is done by specifying a *null hypothesis*, H_0, and an *alternative hypothesis*, H_1, which must be true if the null hypothesis is false. The river pollution test might be formulated as follows:

$H_0: \mu = 7$
$H_1: \mu \neq 7$

The possible results of the test are to accept H_0 and by implication reject H_1 or to reject H_0 and by implication accept H_1.

In formulating a hypothesis test, it is important to consider exactly how the null hypothesis is framed. Notice that in the river pollution example the null hypothesis does not correspond directly to the empirical hypothesis that the river is polluted. In deciding what is appropriate as the null hypothesis, it is useful to think of the analogy with a case in the British criminal courts. The null hypothesis is 'innocent'. The alternative hypothesis is 'guilty'. The convention is to accept the null hypothesis unless sufficient evidence is found to reject it. The *burden of proof* lies with the prosecutor to persuade the jury to reject the null hypothesis. Unless a sufficiently compelling case is offered, the null hypothesis is not rejected. Notice that a person is found 'guilty' or 'not guilty'. Either sufficient evidence is available for a verdict of 'guilty' to be returned or the finding is 'not guilty'. In the second case, the finding is not 'innocent'. This is because of where the burden of proof lies. To fail to make a sufficiently compelling case that someone is guilty is not the same as making a compelling case that he or she is innocent. The same approach carries over into scientific work. The appropriate null hypothesis is that the river is unpolluted. The burden of proof falls on the scientific investigator to amass a sufficiently strong case that the null hypothesis is appropriately rejected.

Potential errors

One potential mistake is to reject the null hypothesis when it accurately describes a state of affairs in the world. This is known as a *Type I error*. The other possible mistake is to fail to reject the null hypothesis when it does not accurately describe a state of affairs in the world. This is to make a *Type II error*. In deciding on a criterion for rejecting H_0, the researcher should be aware of the risks of making each of these potential errors. As a matter of terminology, the risk associated with making a Type I error is called the α *risk*, the risk of making a Type II error is the β *risk*. Either of these risks can be reduced but only at the expense of increasing the other. In testing for river pollution, one could decide to accept H_0 if the laboratory results indicate a mean pH value between 4 and 10. This would give a fairly small probability of committing a Type I error but the probability of making a Type II error may be unacceptably high. Alternatively, the limits may be narrowed down to, say, 6 and 8, thereby reducing the probability of a Type I error, but increasing the probability of a Type II error. In general terms, a wider interval is associated with a lower α risk and a narrower interval is associated with a lower β risk. In formulating a criterion for rejecting the null hypothesis it is usual to do so in such a way as to fix the probability of a Type I error to be acceptably small. If scientific claims are to be taken seriously, then the scientist must carry a weighty burden of proof. For the statistical testing of hypotheses, the scientific equivalent of the lawyer's 'beyond reasonable doubt' conventionally is taken to mean that there is no more than about a one in twenty chance of being wrong. Hence, the criterion for rejecting the null hypothesis is usually determined in such a way that the probability of a Type I error is set at 0.05.

THE LOGIC OF HYPOTHESIS TESTING

According to probability theory, if the null hypothesis accurately describes a state of affairs in the world then the sample mean will have approximately a normal distribution, centred on the population mean, μ. This is because of the central limit theorem. Hence, there is a probability of 0.95 of the sample mean lying within 2 of its standard deviations (i.e. $2\sigma_{\bar{x}}$) either side of μ. We can draw the probability distribution for the sample mean, $\bar{X}$, under the assumption that the null hypothesis is true. This can be related to the theory of the standard normal distribution. Recall that if $\bar{X}$ has a normal distribution, with mean, μ and standard deviation, $\sigma_{\bar{x}}$, then the standard normal variable, Z, which is equal to $(\bar{X} - \mu)/\sigma_{\bar{x}}$, also has a normal distribution, but with a mean of 0 and a standard deviation of 1. The two distributions are shown, side by side, in Figure 16.1.

Probability density function for $\bar{X}$
(Null hypothesis accurately describes situation)

Probability density function for Z
(Null hypothesis accurately describes situation) $Z = (\bar{X} - \mu)/\sigma_{\bar{x}}$

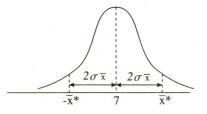

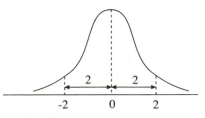

Figure 16.1   Sampling distribution of test statistic

The logic of the hypothesis test is as follows: if the null hypothesis accurately describes a state of affairs in the world then 95 per cent of the time $\bar{X}$ will be somewhere between the two critical points, marked on the diagram as $\bar{x}^*$. Another way of expressing the same condition is to state that 95 per cent of the time Z will be between -2 and $+2$. To be precise, it will be between -1.96 and $+1.96$, according to the normal distribution tables.

CONDUCTING THE TEST

To derive a procedure for conducting a hypothesis test, based on the theory of the normal distribution, it is necessary to know the standard deviation of the sample mean. Unfortunately, in practical applications, it is unlikely to be known. Just as is the case with the construction of confidence intervals, $\sigma_{\bar{x}}$ has to be estimated, using the sample data. Nevertheless, it is useful to begin by examining how a hypothesis test would be conducted in a situation where $\sigma_{\bar{x}}$ is known, since this provides a useful introduction to the situation more widely encountered in practice.

Hypothesis testing when the standard deviation is known

Following the logic set out in the previous section, since $\bar{X}$ is assumed to have a normal distribution, the standard normal variable, Z, could be calculated according to the formula:

$$Z = (\bar{X} - \mu)/\sigma_{\bar{x}} \tag{16.1}$$

Statisticians often refer to this as the *test statistic*. This is quite an apt expression. It is a statistic because it is a single number calculated from sample data and it is used to conduct the test in the following way: if Z lies between the values -2 and $+2$ then the evidence is consistent with the null hypothesis and so it is not rejected. Conversely, if Z lies outside this range then the null hypothesis is rejected. Such a criterion is referred to as a *statistical decision rule*. This expression is also appropriate since it indicates precisely on what basis the decision whether or not to reject the null hypothesis is being made. Example 16.1 is expressed in terms of X and Z to enable the reader to follow the procedure just outlined. A contextualised example is given on p. 211.

Example 16.1

400 observations have been obtained on a variable, X, appropriately selected to meet the criteria for a random sample, as set out in Chapter 11. The standard deviation of X is known to be 9. Using the sample data, the sample mean is calculated to be 48. This is to be used to test the following hypothesis:

$H_0: \mu = 50$

$H_1: \mu \neq 50$

To calculate the test statistic, first it is necessary to calculate the

standard deviation of the sample mean, $\sigma_{\bar{x}}$, which is equal to $\sigma/\sqrt{n}$.
In this example, $\sigma/\sqrt{n} = 9/20 = 0.45$
From Equation 16.1, the test statistic equals $(48 - 50)/0.45 = -4.44$
Since this lies outside the critical limits of -2 and $+2$, set by the statistical decision rule, the null hypothesis is rejected.

Example 16.1 is interesting in that prior to conducting the test, one might have suspected that the sample mean was sufficiently close to 50 that the difference could have been explained by the particular observations selected for the sample. It could. But there is a probability of less than 0.05 of this being the case.

Hypothesis testing when the standard deviation is estimated

If $\sigma_{\bar{x}}$ is not known but has to be estimated, then the transformation from X to Z may not be justified and consequently the theory of the normal distribution does not apply. Instead, it is necessary to make the transformation:

$$t = (\bar{X} - \mu)/s_{\bar{x}} \qquad (16.2)$$

Although the transformation *procedure* appears to be the same as when σ is known, the *test statistic*, t, does *not* have a normal distribution but instead has a students' t-distribution, with $n - 1$ degrees of freedom.

The logic of the hypothesis test with unknown $\sigma_{\bar{x}}$ is equivalent to that in the situation where $\sigma_{\bar{x}}$ is known. If the null hypothesis is an

Probability density function for $\bar{X}$
(Null hypothesis accurately describes
situation)

Probability density function for t
(Null hypothesis accurately describes
situation) $t = (\bar{X} - \mu)/s_{\bar{x}}$

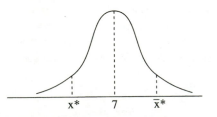

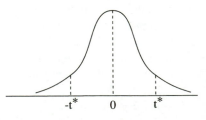

Figure 16.2   The students' t-distribution

accurate description of the state of affairs being investigated then 95 per cent of the time, $\bar{X}$ will fall somewhere between the two critical points, marked in Figure 16.2 as x*. Another way of expressing the same condition is to state that 95 per cent of the time t will fall between $-t*$ and $+t*$, where t* is the number obtained from t tables using n − 1 degrees of freedom.

Conducting a hypothesis test where the standard deviation is estimated involves a procedure similar to that where the standard deviation is known but using the test statistic given by Equation 16.2 and a statistical decision rule based on critical limits for t* obtained from students' t-tables, using n − 1 degrees of freedom.

Example 16.2

A river is believed to be polluted. On the basis of the mean pH measure from sixteen portions of water, we intend to test the null hypothesis that the river is unpolluted against the alternative hypothesis that it is polluted. The test would be formulated as follows:

$H_0: \mu = 7$
$H_1: \mu \neq 7$

Suppose results from the laboratory are as follows:

Sample size: 16
Sample mean: 6.85
Sample standard deviation: 0.16

We calculate the sample standard deviation, $s_{\bar{x}} = s/\sqrt{n}$:

$s/\sqrt{n} = 0.16/4 = 0.04$

There are sixteen observations, so there are fifteen degrees of freedom.

Hence, t* = 2.13

To conduct the test, we calculate the *test statistic*, $t = (\bar{X} - \mu)/s_{\bar{x}}$:

$t = (6.85 - 7.0)/0.04 = -0.15/0.04 = -3.75$

The *statistical decision rule* is to reject H_0 if t lies outside the range $-t*$ to $+t*$. Since -3.75 lies outside the range -2.13 to $+$ the null hypothesis is rejected.

We have found a *statistically significant* level of pollution in the river.[1]

INTERPRETING THE TEST RESULTS

In conducting a hypothesis test, we began by assuming that the null hypothesis accurately described a state of affairs in the world and specified critical limits such that were it to do so, there would be only a 5 per cent chance of rejecting it; in other words, only a 0.05 probability of making a Type I error. By rejecting the null hypothesis we could be mistaken, but the probability of this happening is acceptably small. If the null hypothesis is rejected it is legitimate to claim that one has found something that is *statistically significant*. In the context of Example 16.2 one might claim that the mean differs from 7.0 *at the 5 per cent level of significance*. Alternatively, one might state that there is a *statistically significant* level of pollution. Although this terminology leaves the significance level of the test unspecified, there is a convention that unless otherwise stated it is taken to be equal to 0.05. If a 5 per cent chance of making a Type I error were considered to be too high or too low then it could be adjusted by setting a different value for the α risk. In the social sciences there are often situations where the researcher, having found statistically significant results at the 5 per cent level, conducts the test again, the second time specifying an α risk of 0.01. If the null hypothesis is rejected at this higher level of significance then the results are sometimes referred to as *statistically very significant*.

The previous discussion should help to clarify why zero pollution is specified as the null hypothesis. In order to establish that there is a significant level of pollution, one first specifies the null hypothesis that there is no pollution. Failing to reject the null hypothesis tells very little, but rejecting the null hypothesis means that the evidence is sufficiently strong that, at worst, there is only a 5 per cent chance of being mistaken in concluding that the river is polluted.

The power of a test

In failing to reject the null hypothesis, we could be committing a Type II error. However, it remains the appropriate decision unless we have sufficiently strong evidence to decide otherwise. Similarly, in the court case, a verdict of not guilty is returned unless there is sufficiently strong evidence to the contrary. The decision to reject the null hypothesis is a strong one. The decision not to reject it merely indicates that there is insufficient evidence to do otherwise.

In adopting a particular statistical decision rule, the critical limits are set to determine a value for the α risk rather than the β risk. For Example 16.2, suppose that the actual pH of the River Trent were equal to 6.99. Strictly, this indicates a level of pollution and failing to reject H_0 would be to commit a Type II error. Yet, with $\alpha = 0.05$, the probability, β, of making such an error is very high. Conversely, had the actual state of the River Trent been so poor that the average pH for the entire river were equal to 6.00, then β would be very small. For a severely polluted river, the test is very powerful whereas for a river that is only slightly polluted there is not a very high probability that the null hypothesis will be rejected, so the test is much weaker. Statisticians refer to the number $1 - \beta$ as the *power* of the test.

The p-value of a test

If a particular phenomenon is found to be statistically significant at the 5 per cent level, the researcher may feel pleased that his hunch has been supported by the evidence. If the results are found to be statistically significant at the 1 per cent level there might be a case for even greater celebration. Not unnaturally, the researcher may be curious to know just how stringent a test could be applied before the test statistic coincides with the critical limit and the null hypothesis can no longer be rejected. *The p-value is the probability of obtaining a test statistic equal to or more extreme than the result obtained, given that H_0 accurately describes the world.* A very low p-value would correspond to a situation when H_0 was rejected. A p-value of 2 would indicate a situation on the borderline between rejecting and not rejecting H_0 at the 5 per cent level, for a test using a large sample.

One-sided and two-sided hypothesis tests

For Example 16.2 the *empirical hypothesis* is that the river is polluted. It has not been specified whether the pollution is believed to be acid or alkaline and consequently the hypothesis could have been confirmed had the sample mean pH value been significantly *less* or significantly *greater* than 7.0. Both possibilities were accounted for by specifying the alternative hypothesis as H_1: $\mu \neq 7.0$.

Now suppose that the investigator believed that the firm was pouring an alkaline substance into the river, which would result in the pH value being greater than 7.0. In formulating a hypothesis test, the appropriate null hypothesis remains H_0: $\mu = 7.0$. However, if the sample mean was a number less than 7.0, this would *not* be consistent with the empirical hypothesis and consequently the null hypothesis should *not* be rejected. Formally, this situation is encompassed by specifying the test as follows:

H_0: μ = **7.0**
H_1: μ > **7.0**

Under the assumption that the test statistic has a t-distribution, there is only one critical limit for the test. If the probability of a Type I error is set at 0.05, then we read from the students' t-tables that provided the number of degrees of freedom is large, $t^* = 1.64$. Note that t^* for a one-sided test is smaller than for a two-sided test.

OTHER APPLICATIONS

Hypothesis tests can be conducted in a wide variety of circumstances. The particular computations may differ but the general principles remain the same. A test statistic is derived and a null hypothesis is rejected or not, according to a criterion which is specified, based on a knowledge of the sampling distribution of the test statistic, which for the applications in this section is either a normal distribution or t-distribution. A further class of tests is considered in the next section. The examples are chosen to indicate the variety of circumstances in which hypothesis tests are conducted. Having gained an appreciation of the basic principles, the reader may be in a better position to understand some of the statistical analysis as presented and interpreted in many journal articles in the social sciences.

Example 16.3 concerns a different type of application of a hypothesis test for a mean:

Example 16.3[2]

Two skulls are found 100 miles north of the previously known limits of a civilisation known to have existed about 1500 BC. If one had knowledge of the characteristics of the known population, for example, if one knew the mean, μ, and standard deviation, σ, of skull widths for the known civilisation, one would test the hypothesis that the sample came from the same population. If it does, then the sample mean, $\bar{X}$, will have a sampling distribution with mean equal to μ and standard deviation equal to $\sigma/\sqrt{n}$, which in this case equals $\sigma/\sqrt{2}$.

Testing hypotheses about a proportion

In Chapter 15 it was shown that where a variable can take one of only two possible values then it has a binomial distribution and that provided the sample is sufficiently large, the binomial distribution can be approximated by the normal distribution. This can be applied to specify and conduct hypothesis tests about the population proportion. In general, one specifies a null hypothesis that a population proportion is equal to p. If this is the case then the sample proportion, p, will have a sampling distribution which is approximately normal with a mean of ρ and a standard deviation equal to $\sqrt{\{\rho(1 - \rho)\}/n}$. Example 16.4 concerns a practical application.

Example 16.4

An electrical appliance manufacturer claims that its product is so reliable that only one in forty will develop a serious fault within the first twelve months. A sample of 200 reveals that seven are faulty. Does this provide sufficient grounds for rejecting the manufacturer's claim?

Differences between means and proportions

Often, a social scientist may wish to know whether two different populations exhibit the same or a different· key characteristic. For example, one might wish to know whether public schools achieve better examination results than state schools. Such a difference could be identified by recording the average number of A-level passes achieved by 100 students drawn at random from each sector and testing for a statistically significant difference. Similarly, a sociologist may wish to know if there is a difference between males and females in learning ability in a particular area. In general terms, if one has a sample drawn from one population with a mean which we refer to as $\bar{X}$, and a sample from a second population with a mean of $\bar{Y}$, then provided that $\bar{X}$ and $\bar{Y}$ each has a normal distribution, the test statistic $\bar{X} - \bar{Y}$ has a normal distribution with a standard deviation equal to $\sqrt{\sigma_1^2/n_1 + \sigma_2^2/n_2}$ where σ_1 and σ_2 are the standard deviations of the two populations. Some slight complications are introduced where σ needs to be estimated and where the sample size is small but the procedure can be modified to accommodate these.

By similar procedures, it is possible to test for statistically significant differences between proportions. For example, one might be interested to know if the proportion of females voting for a particular party is different from the proportion of males or if there is any difference between the proportion of Ford motor cars which break down within the first year as compared with the proportion of Rover cars.

The relationship between variables

So far, the examples of hypotheses referred to have all involved tests about the mean value taken by a single variable or proportion. Correlation and regression are branches of statistics which are concerned with the relationship between two or more variables. Recently, for example, a number of studies have examined the relationship between income at a certain age (e.g. at age 30) and number of years spent in full-time education. One might find, for example, that based on a sample of 100 people, one additional year in education adds £1,000 to annual income by age 30. But how reliable is this? With a little extension to our theoretical framework, we could test to see if the study's findings are statistically significant and calculate confidence intervals for the effect of education on income.

DOES THE DATA FIT THE THEORY? THE CHI-SQUARE TEST

This section is concerned with what has appropriately been described as 'one of the most widely used of all the statistical tests available to the behavioural scientist'.[3] This is, at least in part, because it has application in situations where one has information about attributes, such as gender, which are not expressed in numerical form.

The chi-square test, written χ^2 and pronounced KY as in sky, is often referred to as a test of 'goodness of fit'. If one begins with a set of data, classified into a frequency distribution or into a contingency table and has an idea, or hypothesis, about how the data should be distributed, then the χ^2 test is used to see if the *observed frequencies* match the *expected frequencies* sufficiently closely for the hypothesis to be accepted. There are two particular ways in which this test is commonly used. First, one may test whether a set of data follows a particular theoretical distribution. For example, a historian may have collected data on the number of days holiday taken by 100 farm workers living in a particular parish in 1840 and wish to know whether her sample came from a population where the number of days holiday can be treated as a normally distributed random variable.[4]

The second common set of applications of χ^2 concerns their use with contingency tables. Suppose, for example, one had information on 100 people, all of whom were classified as smokers and non-smokers and as heavy drinkers or not. The χ^2 test could be used to see if there is any association between these two classifications. Perhaps one might ask the question, 'Do smokers tend to be heavy drinkers?' The null hypothesis is that there is no association and the alternative hypothesis is that an association exists. Detailed examples of both types of application are given in the next two sections.

The χ^2 distribution

The χ^2 distribution is another example of a 'sampling distribution'. It has a probability density function which assumes a certain shape, depending on the 'degrees of freedom'. If a variable has a χ^2 distribution, then statistical tables can be used to find the *critical value* such that there is a given probability (say 0.05) of the variable exceeding that value. The shape of the probability density function depends on the number of degrees of freedom, which in turn depends on the particular type of application. Figure 16.3 shows the approximate shape of the χ^2 distribution for various degrees of freedom. Referring, for example, to χ^2_{10}, which is the short-hand way of writing χ^2 with ten degrees of freedom, the critical limit, x*, is defined such that there is a probability of 0.05 that a value greater than x* could be generated from any process that has a χ^2 distribution. Critical values of χ^2 for different numbers of degrees of freedom are given in Table A.3 of Appendix III. The reader should confirm, for example, that the value of χ^2 for five degrees of freedom, at the 1 per cent significance level is 15.1.

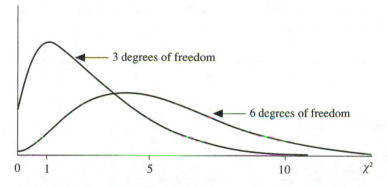

Figure 16.3   The chi-square distribution

In general, if there are n possible frequencies, or categories, then we define O_i as the number of observations in category i and E_i as the expected number of observations in category i, where E_i is determined according to the particular hypothesis being tested. The χ^2 statistic is defined as follows:

$$\chi^2 = \Sigma\{(O_i - E_i)^2/E_i\} \tag{16.3}$$

The null hypothesis is that the observations *do* come from a population which exhibits the expected frequencies. To apply the χ^2 test, the test statistic (16.3) is calculated and compared with the critical value read from the tables for the appropriate number of degrees of freedom and for the chosen level of significance. The statistical decision rule is to reject the null hypothesis if the test statistic is greater than the critical value.

GOODNESS OF FIT

The first set of applications concerns whether data could have been generated by a particular process and hence correspond to a particular probability distribution. A simple example would be to test whether a die is 'fair'. If a fair die is rolled, say 600 times, then the 'expected' number of sixes is 100. However, one would be unlikely to achieve exactly that outcome. To test if a particular die is 'fair', one would take the *observed frequencies*, compare these with the *expected frequencies* and use the χ^2 test to see if the observed frequencies differ significantly from what is expected. For this test, the number of degrees of freedom is the number of categories (six) minus one. The first three rows of Table 16.1 contain a hypothetical set of results for such an experiment.

Table 16.1 Observed and expected results from tossing a die 600 times

Outcome	1	2	3	4	5	6
Expected frequency	100	100	100	100	100	100
Observed frequency	110	95	90	105	90	110
$O_i - E_i$	10	−5	−10	5	−10	10
$(O_i - E_i)^2$	100	25	100	25	100	100
$(O_i - E_i)^2/E_i$	1.0	0.25	1.0	0.25	1.0	1.0

Applying Equation 16.3 to the data of Table 16.1, the test statistic is calculated as $\chi^2_5 = 4.5$. From the tables, χ^2_5 * for a 5 per cent test is 11.1. The null hypothesis that the die is fair is not rejected.

A more practical application is the test for normality, whereby the χ^2 test is used to see whether a set of data could have come from a population which is normally distributed. The null hypothesis would be that the underlying population *does* follow a normal distribution. A set of expected frequencies is calculated, using tables from the normal distribution and the χ^2 statistic is calculated, in accordance with Equation 16.3. Though the procedure can be a little involved because the mean and standard deviation of the hypothesised normal distribution need to be estimated, the logic of the hypothesis test follows the same pattern as described above.

ASSOCIATIONS BETWEEN ATTRIBUTES

Figure 11.2 contains information on fifteen families, according to number of children, income and voting intention. This is presented in the form of a contingency table in Table 16.2, focussing on the possible association between family size and voting intention.

Table 16.2 Contingency table relating voting intention to family size

Number of children	0	1	2	3	4
Number of families	2	4	4	4	1
Observed number of families voting Conservative (O_i)	0	2	2	1	1
Expected number of families voting Conservative (E_i)	0.8	1.6	1.6	1.6	0.4

An interesting question would be, 'Is there any association between family size and voting intention?' This could be approached by specifying the null hypothesis that there is no such association. Hence, under the null hypothesis, the expected number of people in each category is in proportion to the total number of people with that number of children and the total number of people with that particular voting intention. For example, if there were no association between the two groups of attributes, then out of a sample of fifteen, if four have two children and six intend to vote Conservative, then the number of people who have two children and intend to vote Conservative, is *expected* to be equal to $\frac{4}{15}$ times six, which is equal to 1.6. Although this is just the sort of question for which the χ^2 test was designed, unfortunately we are immediately – and quite deliberately – faced with one of its major limitations. The test is not reliable in circumstances where any of the expected frequencies is less than five. Hence, its application is restricted to fairly large samples. This fact needs to be considered at the early stages of designing a research project. Detailed explanation of the test is developed with reference to the following example:

Example 16.5

A sociologist is interested in whether females experience greater difficulties than males in learning to use statistical packages. All students taking a course in the use of such packages are given an examination and the results are to be used as an indicator of the students' level of difficulty in this area. There are 150 students who take the examination and the results are presented in Table 16.3. Do females find it more difficult to learn to use computer packages? The null hypothesis is that there is no relationship between gender and examination score. The alternative hypothesis is that there is such an association.

Table 16.3 Contingency table of examination results and gender

Level of attainment	Distinction	Pass	Fail
Results for males	40	33	5
Results for females	25	37	10

To perform the test suggested by Example 16.5, the first stage is to calculate what the expected frequencies would be if the null hypothesis were true. Under the null hypothesis, the probability of an individual student falling into any of the three score categories is assumed to be the same, whatever the student's gender. Thus, the probability of failure is assumed to be the same for both males and females. Using observed frequencies as estimates of probabilities, the probability of failing is estimated to be $15/150 = 0.1$. Since there are 78 males and 72 females, the expected frequencies, under H_0, are $78*0.1 = 7.8$ and $72*0.1 = 7.2$, respectively.

The expected frequencies for Example 16.5 are given in Table 16.4. The χ^2 statistic is calculated and under the assumption that the null hypothesis is true, this has a χ^2 distribution, with $(R - 1)(C - 1)$ degrees of freedom, where R and C refer to the number of rows and columns, respectively, in the contingency table.

For Example 16.5, $\chi^2 = 5.125$. The critical value for a 0.05 per cent test, using $(1)(2) = 2$ degrees of freedom is equal to 5.991. Thus, in this example, the null hypothesis is not rejected. We find no statistically significant difference in performance between males and females. When χ^2 is used to test for association between attributes, it is sometimes referred to as a test for independence. For Example 16.5, the null hypothesis could have been alternatively worded: 'Ability at

Table 16.4 Expected frequencies for examination results by gender

Level of attainment	Distinction	Pass	Fail
Expected results for males	33.8	36.4	7.8
$O_i - E_i$	6.2	−3.4	−2.8
$(O_i - E_i)^2$	38.44	11.56	7.84
$(O_i - E_i)^2/E_i$	1.137	0.318	1.005
Expected results for females	31.2	33.6	7.2
$O_i - E_i$	−6.2	3.4	2.8
$(O_i - E_i)^2$	38.44	11.56	7.84
$(O_i - E_i)^2/E_i$	1.232	0.344	1.089

using statistical packages is independent of gender'. Hence, if the null hypothesis is accepted, the evidence is consistent with the two attributes being independent of each other. The more powerful conclusion arises if the null hypothesis is rejected, since this means that one is fairly confident that there *is* an association.

An example referred to frequently throughout this book is the apparently high incidence of leukaemia in children near to nuclear installations. If geographical areas are categorised according to number of cases and proximity to nuclear installations then the reader might ponder how a χ^2 test could be used to contribute to this important debate.

SUMMARY

1 In formulating a hypothesis test one specifies a null hypothesis, H_0, and an alternative hypothesis, H_1, such that the alternative hypothesis must be true if the null hypothesis is false.

2 A Type I error is to reject the null hypothesis when it accurately describes a state of affairs in the world. A Type II error is to not reject the null hypothesis when it fails to accurately describe a state of affairs in the world.

3 The risk associated with making a Type I error is called the α risk. This is typically set at 5 per cent. The risk associated with making a Type II error is called the β risk.

4 Hypothesis tests are conducted by deriving a test statistic and specifying the sampling distribution of the test statistic under the assumption that the null hypothesis accurately describes a state of affairs in the world. The null hypothesis is accepted or rejected according to a statistical decision rule, which involves comparing

the value taken by the test statistic with critical values obtained from statistical tables.

5 If the null hypothesis is rejected with the α risk set at 5 per cent then the results are said to be statistically significant.

6 The 'power' of a test refers to the probability of committing a Type II error.

7 The p-value of a test is the probability of obtaining a test statistic equal to or more extreme than the result obtained, given that H_0 accurately describes the world.

8 Chi-square tests are commonly used to test whether a set of data conforms to a preconceived pattern, such as a normal distribution; or to test for association between attributes, such as whether heavy smokers tend to be heavy drinkers.

Appendix I
The sanctity of life

This argument is embedded in the text of Box 4.1. To appreciate the merits of an informal analysis of argument, compare the conventionally marked text with the displayed structure. Consider carefully how the unstated, intermediate conclusion and the assumed premise were arrived at to make the argument valid at both stages.

	$\boxed{\text{Because}}$, as stated,
R_{1s}	[A self-conscious being is aware of itself as a distinct entity, with a past and a future.]
&	$\boxed{\text{and}}$ $\boxed{\text{because}}$, as stated,
R_{2s}	[A being aware of itself in this way will be capable of having desires about its own future.]
$\Rightarrow$	$\boxed{\text{Therefore}}$, though unstated,
C_{ui}	[A self-conscious being will be capable of having desires
$= R_{a3}$	about its own future.]
&	$\boxed{\text{and}}$ $\boxed{\text{because}}$, as assumed,
R_{4a}	[A being capable of having desires about its own future has special value.]
$\Rightarrow$	$\boxed{\text{Therefore}}$, as stated,
C	There is special value in the life of a rational and self-conscious being.

Note: a) The conclusion underlined in Box 4.1 is presented as a rhetorical question. In the complete version of the argument, each claim is an assertion.

b) The subscript, 'ui', means 'undeclared' and 'intermediate'.

Appendix II
Valid arguments in predicate form

The chart maps out various ways to defend the four basic propositions. Each pair of premises is connected to a conclusion which it validly entails.

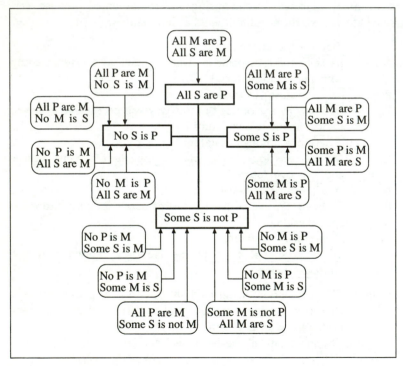

Figure A.1   Valid arguments in predicate form

Eight Venn diagrams represent fifteen patterns of valid argument. If you identify the predicate forms displayed by each diagram, you will get a check list for reference.

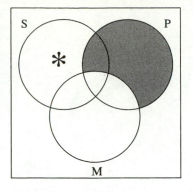

Figure A.2

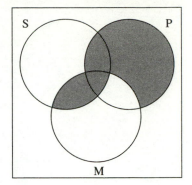

Figure A.3

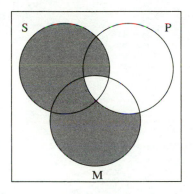

Figure A.4

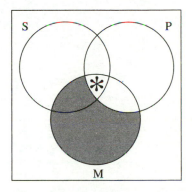

Figure A.5

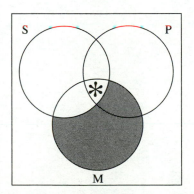

Figure A.6

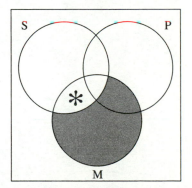

Figure A.7

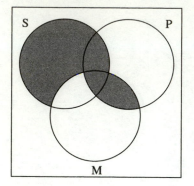

Figure A.8

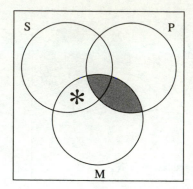

Figure A.9

Appendix III
Statistical tables

Table A.1 The normal distribution

z	.00	.01	.02	.03	.04	.05	.06	.07	.08	.09
0.0	.0000	.0040	.0080	.0120	.0160	.0199	.0239	.0279	.0319	.0359
0.1	.0398	.0438	.0478	.0517	.0557	.0596	.0636	.0675	.0714	.0753
0.2	.0793	.0832	.0871	.0910	.0948	.0987	.1026	.1064	.1103	.1141
0.3	.1179	.1217	.1255	.1293	.1331	.1368	.1406	.1443	.1480	.1517
0.4	.1554	.1591	.1628	.1664	.1700	.1736	.1772	.1808	.1844	.1879
0.5	.1915	.1950	.1985	.2019	.2054	.2088	.2123	.2157	.2190	.2224
0.6	.2257	.2291	.2324	.2357	.2389	.2422	.2454	.2486	.2517	.2549
0.7	.2580	.2611	.2642	.2673	.2704	.2734	.2764	.2794	.2823	.2852
0.8	.2881	.2910	.2939	.2967	.2995	.3023	.3051	.3078	.3106	.3133
0.9	.3159	.3186	.3212	.3238	.3264	.3289	.3315	.3340	.3365	.3389
1.0	.3413	.3438	.3461	.3485	.3508	.3531	.3554	.3577	.3599	.3621
1.1	.3643	.3665	.3686	.3708	.3729	.3749	.3770	.3790	.3810	.3830
1.2	.3849	.3869	.3888	.3907	.3925	.3944	.3962	.3980	.3997	.4015
1.3	.4032	.4049	.4066	.4082	.4099	.4115	.4131	.4147	.4162	.4177
1.4	.4192	.4207	.4222	.4236	.4251	.4265	.4279	.4292	.4306	.4319
1.5	.4332	.4345	.4357	.4370	.4382	.4394	.4406	.4418	.4429	.4441
1.6	.4452	.4463	.4474	.4484	.4495	.4505	.4515	.4525	.4535	.4545
1.7	.4554	.4564	.4573	.4582	.4591	.4599	.4608	.4616	.4625	.4633
1.8	.4641	.4649	.4656	.4664	.4671	.4678	.4686	.4693	.4699	.4706
1.9	.4713	.4719	.4726	.4732	.4738	.4744	.4750	.4756	.4761	.4767
2.0	.4772	.4778	.4783	.4788	.4793	.4798	.4803	.4808	.4812	.4817
2.1	.4821	.4826	.4830	.4834	.4838	.4842	.4846	.4850	.4854	.4857
2.2	.4861	.4864	.4868	.4871	.4875	.4878	.4881	.4884	.4887	.4890
2.3	.4893	.4896	.4898	.4901	.4904	.4906	.4909	.4911	.4913	.4916
2.4	.4918	.4920	.4922	.4925	.4927	.4929	.4931	.4932	.4934	.4936
2.5	.4938	.4940	.4941	.4943	.4945	.4946	.4948	.4949	.4951	.4952
2.6	.4953	.4955	.4956	.4957	.4959	.4960	.4961	.4962	.4963	.4964
2.7	.4965	.4966	.4967	.4968	.4969	.4970	.4971	.4972	.4973	.4974
2.8	.4974	.4975	.4976	.4977	.4977	.4978	.4979	.4979	.4980	.4981
2.9	.4981	.4982	.4982	.4983	.4984	.4984	.4985	.4985	.4986	.4986
3.0	.4987	.4987	.4987	.4988	.4988	.4989	.4989	.4989	.4990	.4990

Table A.2 The students' t-distribution

Degrees of freedom	10%	5%	1%
1	6.31	12.7	63.7
2	2.92	4.30	9.92
3	2.35	3.18	5.84
4	2.13	2.78	4.60
5	2.01	2.57	4.03
6	1.94	2.45	3.71
7	1.89	2.36	3.50
8	1.86	2.31	3.36
9	1.83	2.26	3.25
10	1.81	2.23	3.17
11	1.80	2.20	3.11
12	1.78	2.18	3.05
13	1.77	2.16	3.01
14	1.76	2.14	2.98
15	1.75	2.13	2.95
16	1.75	2.12	2.92
17	1.74	2.11	2.90
18	1.73	2.10	2.88
19	1.73	2.09	2.86
20	1.72	2.09	2.85
21	1.72	2.08	2.83
22	1.72	2.07	2.82
23	1.71	2.07	2.81
24	1.71	2.06	2.80
25	1.71	2.06	2.79
26	1.71	2.06	2.78
27	1.70	2.05	2.77
28	1.70	2.05	2.76
29	1.70	2.05	2.76
30	1.70	2.04	2.75
40	1.68	2.02	2.70
60	1.67	2.00	2.66
120	1.66	1.98	2.62
∞	1.64	1.96	2.58

Table A.3 The χ^2 distribution

Degrees of freedom	10%	5%	1%
1	2.71	3.84	6.63
2	4.61	5.99	9.21
3	6.25	7.81	11.3
4	7.78	9.49	13.3
5	9.24	11.1	15.1
6	10.6	12.6	16.8
7	12.0	14.1	18.5
8	13.4	15.5	20.1
9	14.7	16.9	21.7
10	16.0	18.3	23.0
11	17.3	19.7	24.7
12	18.5	21.0	26.2
13	19.8	22.4	27.7
14	21.1	23.7	29.1
15	22.3	25.0	30.6
16	23.5	26.3	32.0
17	24.8	27.6	33.4
18	26.0	28.9	34.8
19	27.2	30.1	36.2
20	28.4	31.4	37.6
21	29.6	32.7	38.9
22	30.8	33.9	40.3
23	32.0	35.2	41.6
24	33.2	36.4	43.0
25	34.4	37.7	44.3
26	35.6	38.9	45.6
27	36.7	40.1	47.0
28	37.9	41.3	48.3
29	39.1	42.6	49.6
30	40.3	43.8	50.9
40	51.8	55.8	63.7
50	63.2	67.5	76.2
60	74.4	79.1	88.4
70	85.5	90.5	100
80	96.6	102	112
90	108	113	124
100	118	124	135

Notes

1 INTRODUCTION

1 In situations where the right to silence no longer holds, the burden of proof is to some degree shared by the accused.
2 See *The Times*, 11 May 1993, p. 7.
3 There have been many newspaper references to BSE, especially during the period 1990–3. For example, James Erlichman wrote in 1991, 'John Gummer, the Agriculture Minister, has repeatedly said that beef is safe to eat . . .' (*The Guardian* 26 April 1991, p. 5). In fact, John Gummer was shown on television newscasts feeding a burger to his young daughter. In 1993, Michael Hornsby wrote, 'The Government's chief medical officer, Dr Kenneth Calman, last night issued a statement to calm fears that "mad cow disease" poses a threat to humans, after behind-the-scenes pressure from farmers' leaders' (*The Times*, 12 March 1993).
4 According to *The Times*, 'Helen Grant, a former consultant neuropathologist at Charing Cross Hospital, said, "It is wrong of the Government to give the impression that there is no risk at all, when the truth is that we simply do not yet know enough to be certain"' (*The Times*, 13 March 1993, p. 7).
5 Typical contributions include, from the USA, *Understanding Arguments: An Introduction to Informal Logic*, by R. J. Fogelin (1978) and from the UK, *The Logic of Real Arguments*, by Alec Fisher (1988).
6 See Macgill (1987: 10).
7 Leukaemia is a form of cancer which affects the white blood cells. It is quite rare, being responsible for approximately 1 in 40 of the deaths from cancer in Britain, though it is the main cancer among children. See Taylor and Wilkie (1988: 53–6).
8 Seascale lies within the vicinity of Sellafield and is approximately three miles from the site.
9 This point anticipates the work of Gardner and others (1990) which suggests the possibility that genital radiation of fathers employed by BNFL might be a factor linked with the incidence of cancer in their children. It is further discussed as appropriate later in the book.
10 For example, see Briggs (1982).
11 For example, see Barraclough (1957).

2 ARGUMENT AND EVIDENCE

1 There is one sense of argument, common in mathematics and computing, with which we are not concerned, namely, where the value of a mathematical function depends on the values of its arguments.
2 Fisher (1988b: 25) expresses this question in terms of truth and falsity. Our preferred formulation avoids some difficulties of interpretation and acknowledges the range of grounds available for accepting claims, as discussed in Chapter 9.
3 Sv. = Sievert. The Sievert, named after a Swedish scientist, is a unit of measurement for the effects of radiation. It represents a combination of the absorbed dose of radiation and the relative biological effectiveness of the radiation. According to NRPB, radiation doses to members of the public should be limited both by complying with a dose limit, which in the late 1980s was 5 mille-Sieverts (mSv.) per year, and by keeping all doses 'as low as reasonably achievable', the ALARA principle.

3 CONTEXT, CONVENTION AND COMMUNICATION

1 Lyons (1970) gives a short, clear and accurate introduction to Noam Chomsky's important contribution to linguistics.
2 Professor A. J. Ayer gives an account of the reasons in *Language, Truth and Logic* (1980).
3 Expressions of feeling, construed as performances, belong to a group of speech acts examined by Austin (1970).
4 For a helpful though longer discussion, see Dunleavy (1986).

5 PATTERNS OF REASONING

1 Haack (1978: 4) lists fourteen branches of logic, including 'extended' and 'deviant' logics.
2 On 29 July 1994 in a radio interview, Christopher Leslie claimed to have worked in the offices of the Labour Shadow Chancellor in London and those of the only independent socialist in the House of Representatives in the USA, while studying Politics and Parliamentary Studies at Leeds University. On 5 May 1994 he was elected to the Bradford City Council, being the youngest ever member at twenty-two.
3 On the basis that names are uniquely identifying descriptions, it is not a mistake to construe this claim as a universal proposition. If one were to interpret such claims as universals then, provided that one does so consistently, the outcomes of critical appraisals of arguments in which they occur would not be materially different.
4 Mathematicians and geographers also use Venn diagrams and stipulate conventions to suit their purposes. It is confusing when we suppose that the conventions with which we are familiar apply in all contexts.
5 For our purposes, we have adopted the style of Fogelin (1978).
6 In medieval times clerics were trained to follow and critically assess lines

of reasoning in public debates where the disputants spoke formally in such a fashion. The performances were called disputations. In those days, the abilities of students to reason syllogistically were so accomplished that Sir Francis Bacon was preoccupied with a mission to convince the governing bodies of universities that curricula should be changed to enable undergraduates to draw inferences from evidence with as much confidence.

6 ESTABLISHING VALIDITY

1 Copi (1965) and Lemmon (1971) are examples of formal approaches to logic.
2 Pratt (1978: 60–1) gives a useful account of the Nuer tribe project in the context of a wider discussion of the issues concerning the relativity of logic.
3 Haack (1978: 33) considers some of the implications involved.
4 The impact of 'only' on the positive universal proposition in predicate form has a similar effect. See Figure 5.6 on p. 52.
5 Lipsey (1967: 4) thinks that normative statements 'are inextricably bound up with our whole philosophical, cultural and religious position'. His discussion (1967: 4–7) facilitates appreciation of what this implies for the social sciences.

7 CRITICAL ANALYSIS IN PRACTICE

1 Notice that a negative universal premise rules out the possibility of those cases that the conclusion requires.
2 Enoch Powell's reasoning skills are outstanding in his political speeches, which are admired even by those who do not share his views.
3 Caroline Hough, from Heaton Moor, undergraduate student at Staffordshire University, 1989–92.
4 This kind of explanation is often called the 'covering law' thesis. Pratt (1978: Chapters 8, 9) offers a readable introduction in the context of the social sciences.

8 ASSUMPTIONS

1 For a relatively modern treatment of this model, see Briggs (1982: 176–80).
2 This consideration is comparable with A. J. Ayer's treatment of the verification principle as a demarcation criterion for distinguishing scientifically interesting claims from metaphysics, in *Language, Truth and Logic* (1980).
3 For further details see Patterson (1986).
4 The relationship between models and reality is discussed on p. 99.

9 EVIDENCE AS GROUND FOR BELIEF

1 See the fourth edition of the *Concise Oxford Dictionary* (1951). It is interesting to note that the eighth edition (1990) does not mention 'mammal' at all. The modern defining characteristics are '. . . having a streamlined body and horizontal tail, and breathing through a blowhole on the head'. The negation test applies equally well to any of the recent defining characteristics.
2 Ayer (1980) describes those claims which are not falsifiable as meaningless pseudo-assertions.
3 In July 1992, the Court of Appeal quashed Ahluwalia's murder conviction as 'unsafe and unsatisfactory'. At the retrial, the Crown accepted her plea of manslaughter on the grounds of diminished responsibility, based on new evidence that she had been suffering from 'battered wives syndrome'. On 25 September 1992, Mr Justice Hobhouse imposed a sentence of three years and four months – the period Ahluwalia had already served in prison. (Based on a report in the *Daily Mail*, 26 September 1992, p. 9.)
4 See Ayer (1980: 36).

10 WHAT COUNTS AS EVIDENCE?

1 The methodological tradition we have in mind is the hypothetico-deductive method (see p. 154).
2 Taylor and Wilkie (1988: 55–6).
3 *The Annual Abstract of Statistics* and *The Monthly Digest of Statistics* provide useful starting places for anyone seeking a flavour of the diversity of contemporary statistics from official sources in the UK.
4 For an introduction to the literature on this topic see Loomes (1989).
5 See for example Som (1973), Cochran (1963), Kish (1965).
6 Recording shopping patterns or traffic flows for town planning, arrival and departure times at railway stations or in banks and supermarkets, children's play activities and people's drinking habits might be examples.
7 Black (1984: para. 2.33).
8 Some statistics books use the term *universe* rather than population.
9 The importance of sampling is also indicated well by Leslie Kish: 'Sampling plays a vital role in research design involving human populations' (Kish 1965: v).
10 From foreword to Som (1973).
11 For a fuller discussion of these and other sampling methods see Som (1973), Cochran (1963), Kish (1965).
12 Kish (1965: 18–20) provides a brief review of some of these.

11 PRESENTING AND SUMMARISING EVIDENCE

1 This description is borrowed from Soper (1987).
2 Judge (1990), for example, is a book exclusively concerned with the potential uses of the spreadsheet, *Lotus 1–2–3*, for the teaching of various topics of interest to economists.

3 See Soper (1987) and Judge (1990) for a range of applications of spread-sheets, particularly in economics.

4 Sometimes the term 'observation' is used to refer to all of the information pertaining to – in this example – one particular family and sometimes it refers to a single item of information only, such as family income.

5 The use of the letter 'i' for a subscript is common when data are obtained from a *cross section* whereas 't' is common for *time series* data. Cross section data refer to a series of observations on different units, such as individuals or families, referring to the same time period. Time series data consist of a series of observations on the same unit, taken over a succession of time periods. Both subscripts might be needed together, for example, in a study involving the 'pooling' of cross section and time series data.

6 For the reader who is a little rusty in school mathematics, the expression X^3 reads 'X cubed' and is evaluated as X times X times X. For those who have difficulty understanding or remembering how to interpret such expressions, a very useful and sympathetic treatment of elementary mathematics is to be found in Graham and Sargent (1981).

7 Although in everyday usage the term 'average' is synonymous with 'arithmetic mean', the reason why the latter, more cumbersome, expression is preferred is that there is more than one type of average. Other measures include the geometric mean and harmonic mean, details of which can be found in most statistics textbooks.

8 There is a useful convention, which is followed throughout this book, to use an upper case N to refer to the total number in the population and a lower case n to refer to the total number in a sample.

9 When the data refer to the entire population, then the Greek letter μ – pronounced mu – is used in place of $\bar{X}$.

10 If the variance were being calculated using every single element in the population, the formula would be adjusted to use N in place of $n-1$ in the denominator and μ would replace $\bar{X}$ in the numerator. This is discussed in Chapter 15.

11 In fact, this result is just one example of a general relationship, known as *Chebyschev's inequality*: For any set of data, the fraction of observations lying beyond k standard deviations either side of the arithmetic mean cannot exceed $1/k^2$, where k can be any number.

12 FURTHERING KNOWLEDGE

1 Ricardo's best known work is probably *Principles of Economy and Taxation* (1971). This includes some of his best known examples.

2 See Schumpeter (1954).

3 A parody based on the account by Chalmers (1982: 14) where the bird is referred to as a turkey.

4 Skyrms uses this example in a discussion of 'The Goodman paradox, regularity and the principle of the uniformity of nature' (Skyrms 1975: 71–72).

5 Instrumentalism is sometimes called 'operationalism'.

6 See Pheby (1988) and Hodgson (1988).

7 See Weber (1949: 89 ff.).

8 See Hodgson (1988).
9 These ideas are based on Wittgenstein's notions of 'form of life' and 'language game', a useful introduction to which can be found in Grayling (1988, especially Chapter 3).
10 See Pratt (1978: 61–62), who reports on an account of the African Nuer tribe, considered by Evans-Pritchard (1940: Chapter V).
11 Plato (1958) argued that the philosophers' insights were privileged to the degree that they and they alone were entitled to hold power in society.
12 A useful introduction to hermeneutics can be found in Trigg (1985: 195–200). Habermas and Gadamer are mentioned as key contributors in the field.
13 H. G. Gadamer has contributed much to the understanding of hermeneutic methods, for example, *Truth and Method* (1993).
14 See Durkheim (1982).
15 Hearnshaw reviews aspects of Burt's work recommending a rigorous analysis of the argument and evidence, typical of the social sciences (Hearnshaw 1979: Chapter 12 'The posthumous controversies').

13 PROBABILITY AND UNCERTAINTY

1 In more advanced texts on statistics, the notation $P(A \cap B)$ frequently replaces $P(A \text{ and } B)$ and $P(A \cup B)$ replaces $P(A \text{ or } B)$. It should be noted that this corresponds to the *inclusive* use of the word 'or', as discussed in Chapter 6.
2 For mutually exclusive events, $P(A \text{ and } B)$ is equal to zero by definition, so that Equation 13.2 reduces to 13.1.
3 There are various ways in which the concept of probability can be interpreted. For example, the economist J.M. Keynes interpreted probabilities in terms of 'the degree of rational belief' (Keynes, 1921). Even the distinction between subjective and objective may become blurred. For a more detailed discussion of the various interpretations of probability, including detailed references, see Salmon (1967).
4 Venn 1962; Reichenbach 1949.
5 The reader is referred to any main statistics text, such as Berenson *et al.* (1988), Neter *et al.* (1988), Yamane (1973), Alder and Roessler (1977).
6 The distinction between discrete and continuous random variables is introduced in Chapter 14. All examples in this chapter refer to discrete random variables.

15 ESTIMATION AND RELIABILITY

1 For this chapter and Chapter 16, the terms 'probability distribution' and 'probability density function' will be used loosely. In many of the situations considered, there is a very large but finite set of data so that, strictly, the term 'probability distribution' is appropriate, though because of the very large number of values which the random variable can take, the continuous probability density function is a justifiable approximation.
2 In fact, it is more probable that incomes of one-parent families follow a 'log-normal' distribution. Under such circumstances, although the original

data do not follow a normal distribution, the logarithm of the data approximates to a normal distribution quite well. Deciding whether or not a particular set of data can usefully be approximated by a normal distribution and examining appropriate transformations under some other circumstances is considered in Chapter 16.

3 Strictly, if the sample is drawn from a finite population then Formula 15.2 should be multiplied by a *finite population correction factor*, as follows:

Finite population correction factor $= \sqrt{(N - n)/(N - 1)}$

The standard deviation of the sampling distribution for the mean is then given as:

$$\sigma_{\bar{x}} = \{\sigma/\sqrt{n}\}\sqrt{(N - n)/(N - 1)}$$

For relatively small samples, this correction factor makes only a tiny difference. A useful rule of thumb is that provided the sample is less than 5 per cent of the population, the correction can be ignored.

4 Most statistics textbooks refer to the efficiency of an estimator in terms of its variance rather than its standard deviation. However, since the standard deviation is the square root of the variance, if one estimator has a larger variance than another then it necessarily has a larger standard deviation.

5 As discussed in Chapter 12, there is no hard and fast rule as to what constitutes a large enough sample. If the original variable of interest has a normal distribution then the sampling distribution for the mean will be normally distributed anyway. The less the resemblance between the probability distribution (or density function) for the original variable and the normal distribution then the greater will be the sample size required before the approximation is sufficiently close that the theory of confidence intervals becomes appropriate. For sample sizes measured in hundreds there should rarely be case for concern. As already indicated, most statisticians tend to quote numbers of the order of 25–30 as being sufficient under many circumstances.

6 To be more precise, if we use tables of the normal distribution, there is a probability of 0.95 that the population mean lies within a range of 1.96 of its standard deviations either side of the sample mean. However, in situations where one is relying on the central limit theorem for an *approximation* to the normal distribution, it could be misleading to imply too great a degree of accuracy. For both the experienced researcher and the casual empiricist, it is a very useful rule of thumb that one can have 95 per cent confidence that a particular parameter is within 2 of its standard deviations either side of a particular estimate.

7 In fact, the use of $n - 1$ is precisely related to the use of $n - 1$ in the denominator of the formula for the sample standard deviation, though we omit an explanation.

8 For very small samples one would only be using this procedure if the original data were sufficiently close to having a normal distribution that one was confident that the central limit theorem applied. This is something that should not be taken too lightly!

9 Sometimes, instead of presenting the analysis in terms of a proportion, it is presented in terms of the total number of 'successes', i.e. in terms of X

= np. The formula for the standard deviation of X differs from that given for ρ below.

10 In fact, it can be shown that this is an unbiased estimator for infinite populations. For finite populations, Equation 15.9 may be multiplied by a correction factor equal to $\sqrt{(N-n)/(N-1)}$. Provided that the sample is only a small proportion of the total population, this makes such a small difference that it is generally ignored.

11 The reader is referred to a statistics text such as Neter *et al.* (1988) for an introductory discussion of confidence intervals for ρ based on small samples or to an advanced statistics textbook for a complete treatment.

12 *The Observer*, 25 February 1990.

15 TESTING HYPOTHESES

1 The precise wording of such a conclusion is important and is discussed at length below.

2 Fletcher and Lock (1991) is an excellent book on statistics for archaeologists.

3 Hammerton (1975:64).

4 The statistically literate historian would realise that accepting the hypothesis merely tells her that the data *could* have come from a normal distribution. It could also have come from a distribution which is similar to the normal distribution but not the same. However, if her purpose is just to find out whether or not a particular statistical procedure is justifiable, then this would probably be quite acceptable. What she should not do is to take acceptance of the null hypothesis as *confirmation* that the distribution is normal. This is discussed further below.

References

Alder, H. L. and Roessler, E. B. (1977) *Introduction to Probability and Statistics* (6th edn), San Francisco: W. H. Freeman and Co.

Allen, R. E. (ed.) (1990) *The Concise Oxford Dictionary of Current English*, Oxford: Clarendon.

Atkinson, A. B. (ed.) (1973) *Wealth, Income and Inequality*, Harmondsworth: Penguin.

Austin, J. L. (1970) 'Performative utterances', in J. O. Urmson and G. J. Warnock (eds) *Philosophical Papers* (2nd edn), Oxford: Clarendon.

Ayer, A. J. (1980) *Language, Truth and Logic*, Harmondsworth: Penguin.

Barraclough, G. (1957) *History in a Changing World*, Oxford: Basil Blackwell.

Berenson, M. L., Levine, D. M. and Rindskopf, D. (1988) *Applied Statistics: A First Course*, London: Prentice-Hall International.

Black, Sir D. (1984) *Investigation of the Possible Increased Incidence of Cancer in West Cumbria*, Report of the Independent Advisory Group, London: HMSO.

Breach, I. (1978) *Windscale Fallout: A Primer for the Age of Nuclear Controversy*, Harmondsworth: Penguin Books.

Briggs, K. (1982) *Human Geography: Concepts and Applications*, London: Hodder and Stoughton.

British Nuclear Fuels plc (1988) *Sellafield Visitors Centre*, Risley, Warrington: BNF Information Services.

British Nuclear Fuels plc (1989) *Nuclear Energy*, Risley, Warrington: BNF Information Services.

Chalmers, A. F. (1982) *What is this Thing called Science?*, Milton Keynes: Open University Press.

Cochran, W. G. (1963) *Sampling Techniques*, London: John Wiley.

Copi, I. M. (1965) *Symbolic Logic* (2nd edn), New York: Collier-Macmillan.

Craft, A. and Openshaw, S. (1987) 'A geographical analysis of cancer among children in the Northern Region', in A. Blowers and D. Pepper (eds) *Nuclear Power in Crisis: Politics and Planning for the Nuclear State*, Beckenham, Kent: Croom Helm.

Dunleavy, P. (1986) *Studying for a Degree in the Humanities and Social Sciences*, London: Macmillan.

Durkheim, E. (1952) *Suicide: A Study in Sociology*, ed. G. Simpson, London: Routledge and Kegan Paul.

Durkheim, E. (1982) *The Rules of Sociological Method*, ed. S. Lukes, London: Macmillan.

Evans-Pritchard, E. E. (1940) *Nuer Religion*, Oxford: Clarendon Press.

Fisher, A. (ed.) (1988, a) *Critical Thinking*, Proceedings of the First British Conference on Informal Logic and Critical Thinking, University of East Anglia.

Fisher, M. (1988, b) *The Logic of Real Arguments*, Cambridge: Cambridge University Press.

Fletcher, M. and Lock, G. R. (1991) *Digging Numbers: Elementary Statistics for Archaeologists*, Oxford: Oxford Committee for Archaeology.

Flew, A. (1975) *Thinking about Thinking (Or, Do I Sincerely Want to be Right?)*, London: Fontana/Collins.

Fogelin, R. J. (1978) *Understanding Arguments: An Introduction to Informal Logic*, New York: Harcourt Brace Jovanovich Inc.

Friedman, M. (1953) 'The methodology of positive economics' in *Essays in Positive Economics*, Chicago: University of Chicago Press.

Gadamer, H. G. (1993) *Truth and Method* (2nd revised edn), London: Sheed and Ward.

Gardner, M. J., Snee, M. P., Hall, A. J., Powell, C. A., Downes, S. and Terrell, J. D. (1990) 'Results of case-control study of leukaemia and lymphoma among young people near Sellafield nuclear plant in west Cumbria', *British Medical Journal*, vol. 300, pp. 423–34, 17 February 1990.

Geach, P. T. (1976) *Reason and Argument*, Oxford: Blackwell.

Graham, L. and Sargent, D. (1981) *Countdown to Mathematics*, Volumes 1 and 2, London: Addison-Wesley.

Grayling, A. C. (1988) *Wittgenstein*, Oxford: Oxford University Press.

Grice, H. P. (1975) 'Logic and conversation', in D. Davidson and G. Harman (eds) *The Logic of Grammar*, California: Dickinson, P.C.I.

Guardian (1977) *Windscale: A Summary of the Evidence and the Argument*, London: Guardian Newspapers Ltd.

Haack, S. (1978) *Philosophy of Logics*, Cambridge: Cambridge University Press.

Habakkuk, H. J. (1971) 'Economic history and economic theory' in *Daedalus*, vol. 100, pp. 305–22.

Habermas, J. (1983) 'Interpretive social science vs hermeneuticism', in N. Haan, *et al.* (eds) *Social Science as Moral Inquiry*, New York: Columbia Press.

Hammerton, M. (1975) *Statistics for the Human Sciences*, London: Longman.

Hearnshaw, L. S. (1979) *Cyril Burt, Psychologist*, London: Hodder and Stoughton.

Hodgson, G. (1988) *Economics and Institutions: A Manifesto for a Modern Institutional Economics*, Cambridge: Polity Press.

Hospers, J. (1970) *An Introduction to Philosophical Analysis* (2nd edn), London: Routledge and Kegan Paul.

Judge, G. (1990) *Quantitative Analysis for Economics and Business Using Lotus 1–2–3*, London: Harvester Wheatsheaf.

Kaldor, N. (1985) *Economics Without Equilibrium*, Cardiff: University College Cardiff Press.

Keynes, J. M. (1921) *A Treatise on Probability* (3rd edn published for the Royal Economic Society, 1973), *Collected Writings of John Maynard Keynes*, Volume VIII, London: Macmillan.

Kish, L. (1965) *Survey Sampling*, London: John Wiley.

Kuhn, T. S. (1971) *The Structure of Scientific Revolutions* (2nd edn), Chicago: Chicago University Press.

Lemmon, E. J. (1971) *Beginning Logic*, Wiltshire: Redwood Press.

Lévy-Bruhl, L. (1923) *Primitive Mentality*, trans. L. A. Clare, London: Allen and Unwin.

Lipsey, R. G. (1967) *Positive Economics* (2nd edn), London: Weidenfeld and Nicolson.

Loomes, G. (1989) 'Experimental economics', in J. D. Hey (ed.) *Current Issues in Microeconomics*, London: Macmillan.

Lyons, J. (1970) *Chomsky*, London: Fontana/Collins.

Macgill, S. M. (1987) *Sellafield's Cancer-link Controversy: the Politics of Anxiety*, London: Pion Books.

McIntosh, E. (ed.) (1951) *The Concise Oxford Dictionary*, Oxford: Oxford University Press.

McSorley, J. (1990) *Living in the Shadow: The Story of the People of Sellafield*, London: Pan Books.

Marwick, A. (1970) *The Nature of History*, London: Macmillan.

Neter, J., Wasserman, W. and Whitmore, G. A. (1988) *Applied Statistics* (3rd edn), Boston: Allyn and Bacon.

Patterson, W. C. (1986) *Nuclear Power* (2nd edn), Harmondsworth, Middlesex: Penguin Books.

Pheby, J. (1988) *Methodology and Economics*, London: Macmillan.

Plato (1958) *The Republic*, trans. A. D. Lindsay, London: J. M. Dent and Sons.

Popper, K. R. (1972a) *Conjectures and Refutations: the Growth of Scientific Knowledge*, London: Routledge and Kegan Paul.

Popper, K. R. (1972b) *The Logic of Scientific Discovery*, London: Hutchinson.

Popper, K. R. (1972c) *Objective Knowledge: An Evolutionary Approach*, Oxford: Clarendon.

Popper, K. R. (1983) *Realism and the Age of Science*, London: Hutchinson.

Pratt, V. (1978) *The Philosophy of the Social Sciences*, London: Methuen.

Reichenbach, H. (1949) *The Theory of Probability*, Berkeley: University of California Press.

Ricardo, D. (1971) *Principles of Political Economy and Taxation*, Harmondsworth: Penguin.

Russell, B. (1912) *Problems of Philosophy*, Oxford: Oxford University Press.

Ryan, A. (1970) *The Philosophy of the Social Sciences*, London: Macmillan.

Salmon, W. C. (1967) *The Foundations of Scientific Inference*, Pittsburgh: University of Pittsburgh Press.

Schumpeter, J. A. (1954) *History of Economic Analysis*, New York, Oxford University Press.

Singer, P. (1979) *Practical Ethics*, Cambridge: Cambridge University Press.

Skyrms, B. (1975) *Choice and Chance: an Introduction to Inductive Logic* (2nd edn), California: Dickenson P.C.I.

Som, R. K. (1973) *A Manual of Sampling Techniques*, London: Heinemann.

Soper, J. B. and Lee, M. P. (1987) *Statistics with Lotus 1–2–3*, Bromley: Chartwell-Bratt.

Stott, M. and Taylor, P. (1980) *The Nuclear Controversy: A Guide to the*

Issues of the Windscale Inquiry, London: The Town and Country Planning Association in conjunction with the Political Economy Research Group.

Taylor, D. and Wilkie, D. (1988) 'Drawing the line with leukaemia', *New Scientist*, 21 July.

Thomas, R. W. and Huggett, R. J. (1980) *Modelling in Geography: A Mathematical Approach*, London: Harper and Row.

Trigg, R. (1985) *Understanding Social Science*, Oxford: Blackwell.

Venn, J. (1962) *The Logic of Chance* (4th edn), New York: Chelsea.

Weber, M. (1949) *The Methodology of the Social Sciences*, Chicago: Free Press.

Winch, P. (1958) *The Idea of a Social Science*, London: Routledge and Kegan Paul.

Yamane, T. (1973) *Statistics: An Introductory Analysis* (3rd edn), New York: Harper International.

Index